The Positive Case for
Negative Campaigning

T0386099

The Positive Case for Negative Campaigning

KYLE MATTES AND
DAVID P. REDLAWSK

THE UNIVERSITY OF CHICAGO PRESS   CHICAGO AND LONDON

KYLE MATTES is assistant professor of political science at the University of Iowa. DAVID P. REDLAWSK is professor of political science at the Eagleton Institute's Center for Public Interest Polling at Rutgers University. He is coauthor of several books, including *Why Iowa?*, also published by the University of Chicago Press.

The University of Chicago Press, Chicago 60637
The University of Chicago Press, Ltd., London
© 2014 by The University of Chicago
All rights reserved. Published 2014.
Printed in the United States of America

23 22 21 20 19 18 17 16 15 14   1 2 3 4 5

ISBN-13: 978-0-226-20202-0 (cloth)
ISBN-13: 978-0-226-20216-7 (paper)
ISBN-13: 978-0-226-20233-4 (e-book)
DOI: 10.7208/chicago/9780226202334.001.0001

Library of Congress Cataloging-in-Publication Data

Mattes, Kyle, author.
  The positive case for negative campaigning / Kyle Mattes and David P. Redlawsk.
     pages cm
  Includes bibliographical references and index.
     ISBN 978-0-226-20202-0 (cloth : alk. paper)—ISBN 978-0-226-20216-7 (pbk. : alk. paper)—ISBN 978-0-226-20233-4 (e-book) 1. Political campaigns—United States. 2. Mass media—Political aspects—United States. 3. Campaign literature—United States. 4. Negativism. I. Redlawsk, David P., author. II. Title.
  JK2281.M388 2014
  324.70973—dc23
                              2014018277

♾ This paper meets the requirements of ANSI/NISO Z39.48-1992 (Permanence of Paper).

TO ALL THOSE WHO DISAPPROVE OF NEGATIVE CAMPAIGNING;
WHILE WE DON'T EXPECT TO CONVINCE THEM, WE HOPE THAT AT
LEAST OUR EFFORTS WILL CONTINUE AN IMPORTANT DISCUSSION
IN AMERICAN POLITICS.

Contents

Acknowledgments

Any project owes a lot to a lot of people; books like this are never a one- or two-person task. Thus, we are indebted to many who helped us along the way. Special thanks to Shannon Holmberg, research assistant at the University of Iowa, for invaluable help in building a database to keep track of all the negativity in the 2012 presidential campaign. Shannon's contributions are also evident in our pieces on the Brown vs. Warren and Dole vs. Hagan elections, the latter for which she receives a well-deserved coauthor credit. Many thanks to Sarah Miruzzi and Timm Krueger, research assistants at UI, for tirelessly searching through thousands of political ads to find (and, later, edit) many of the ads we used in study 4, and also for building and running a pilot experiment for this study. Thanks also to Mattes's UI research assistants Megan DeLanoit, Hannah Olson, Allie Panther, Allison Patch, and Joe Thorngren for their help early on—before we even knew we were writing a book.

A number of research assistants at Rutgers also provided very useful help. Undergraduates Ethan Glading and Max Van Zandt tracked down citations, wrote summaries of research, and helped with experimental work. Rutgers undergraduate Stefan Macevski did all this and more, working closely with Dave Redlawsk for more than a year. Stefan, in particular, helped run many of the laboratory sessions that generated the data for chapter 7. He was also instrumental in developing the background research on the role of the media and greatly deserves the coauthor credit he gets for chapter 2.

Special thanks to Silvia Russo, of the Università degli Studi di Torino, Italy, who spent a semester at Rutgers, during which she read over early versions of some chapters and provided useful comments and some key citations we had otherwise missed. Thanks to the many who provided help with chapter 5 and its earlier incarnation in the *Journal of Politics*, including Tom Palfrey, Mike Alvarez, Matt Jackson, Jonathan Katz, Rod Kiewiet, Andrea Mattozzi, Leeat Yariv, and Matias Iaryczower. Thanks also to APSA conference discussants John Barry Ryan and Johanna Dunaway for their helpful comments. John Geer, of course, earns our thanks for his insight into negative campaigning, upon which we drew quite extensively. Redlawsk's 2012 graduate Elections and Participation seminar also gave us very useful comments and critiques on the penultimate draft of the book. Finally, Dave Andersen, then a PhD student at Rutgers, now assistant professor at Iowa State, provided important guidance on the ZTree programming language we used to mount study 6 at Rutgers. Without Dave's help both in the initial programming of the study and in teaching Redlawsk what he needed to know to revise and extend the early version, the study would not have been completed as effectively as it was.

Our appreciation, also, to the Eagleton Institute of Politics at Rutgers University, directed by Ruth Mandel, and the Rutgers Center for the Study of Experimental Political Science, directed by Richard Lau. The lab facilities we used for study 6 are under their auspices. Study 5 was run through the Social Science Experimental Laboratory at Caltech. Thanks to Erin Hartman for her help running the experiments, and thanks to Chris Crabbe and Walter Yuan at the SSEL for their technical and programming help. We also thank the Eagleton Center for Public Interest Polling, the home of the Rutgers-Eagleton Poll, and the then–manager of the poll, Mona Kleinberg, for support for study 2, as well as the student callers who carried out the survey. Study 1 was administered through the University of Iowa Hawkeye Poll. Thanks to Caroline Tolbert, of Iowa, who worked with Redlawsk on that poll, providing great advice and energy, and thanks to the many undergraduates at Iowa who worked as callers for the Hawkeye Poll in 2008–9.

We also greatly appreciate the guidance of John Tryneski, our editor at the University of Chicago Press, as well as his enthusiasm in supporting this project as we navigated the process of turning ideas into a coherent manuscript. Rodney Powell, assistant editor at Chicago, was also tremendously helpful throughout the entire process. Both are great to work with, and we are really pleased to have been able to do so. We wish to also recognize the anonymous readers of this manuscript, who provided us with a wealth of positive (and some negative) feedback, all of which has made the book much better. Of course, in the end, any remaining errors remain our own.

Kyle Mattes would especially like to thank his wife, Melissa, for her love and support, for her interest and insight into politics, and for simply being extraordinary. Dave Redlawsk would like to give the obligatory, but incredibly heartfelt, thanks to his wife, Aletia Morgan, who continues to support him no matter how overwhelmed with deadlines he is at times. Her own interest and active involvement in politics makes Aletia a useful sounding board, a role she plays with good humor no matter how crazy the idea. I couldn't have done any of what I have over the years without her partnership.

CHAPTER ONE

Introduction

Finally, as regards the Roman masses, be sure to put on a good show.... It also wouldn't hurt to remind them of what scoundrels your opponents are and to smear these men at every opportunity with the crimes, sexual scandals, and corruption they have brought on themselves.
—Quintus Tullius Cicero

The psyche of the American voter is fragile. If we listen to many scholars and pundits discuss campaign conduct, this must be our inevitable conclusion. Apparently, voters' psyches have been (or will be) damaged irreparably by the onslaught of negativity in recent political campaigns, and so they must be protected from it. If so, voters have been slow to evolve since they have needed to defend themselves against negativity for most of America's electoral history, and probably for as long as there have been elections. The quotation that opens this chapter is from Quintus Tullius Cicero, in a letter to his brother Marcus on the occasion of the latter's campaign for consul of Rome in 64 BCE. While Quintus spends much of the letter talking about schmoozing the various interest groups that would decide the election, he also emphatically details the faults of Marcus's opponents and urges his brother to make sure all voters are aware of them.

Fast forward to one of America's earliest presidential elections. Running for re-election in 1800, John Adams was called a "hideous hermaphroditical character which has neither the force and firmness of a man, nor the gentleness and sensibility of a woman" by Thomas Jefferson's supporters (Cummins 2007).[1] Adams's camp attacked with similar furor. They suggested that if Jefferson won, "murder, robbery, rape, adultery, and incest will all be openly taught and practiced, the air will be rent with the cries of the distressed, the soil will be soaked with blood, and the nation black with crimes" (Scher 1997, 31). The simple fact is that when zero-sum elections result in winners and losers—as they always must—the candidates have a strong incentive to do whatever it takes to win the day. If this means tearing down the opponent while causing voters to become cynical about politics and about campaigns, so be it. Despite would-be reformers' well-intentioned attempts to protect voters through campaign pledges, clean election laws, and their general approbation of attack politics, candidates and their consultants continue to pummel each other as they have since the beginning. Perhaps political campaigns by their nature bring out the worst in candidates and their followers.

While negativity in campaigns is nothing new, there is some evidence that it has become more ubiquitous in recent years, with many scholars arguing the increasing volume of political attacks has deleterious consequences, blaming it for generating cynicism toward politics (e.g., Capella and Jamieson 1997; Dionne 1991), perpetuating a decline in campaign discourse (Jamieson 1992), and demobilization (Ansolabehere and Iyengar 1995b). Researchers generally agree that voters have an intense dislike of negativity in election campaigns, and the evidence of this disdain appears extensive. For instance, a 2004 survey by Pew found that "negative campaigning" bothered 61 percent of respondents "very much" and another 20 percent "somewhat."[2] In a July 2000 Gallup Poll, 60 percent of respondents agreed with the statement, "Negative advertisements make people feel less like voting on Election Day." And again in 2000, 61 percent of voters said negative ads are "usually full of lies and try to mislead people."[3] Results like these have led to a clear consensus that voters hate negative campaigning, to the point that researchers no longer routinely ask these questions.

As a result of these voter reactions, most discussions of campaign conduct begin with the assumption that negativity is inherently undesirable. Twenty years ago, West (1993) called negative television advertising "the electronic equivalent of the plague." More recently, Patterson (2002) noted that "negative politics appears to wear some people down to the point where they simply want less of politics. Our surveys," he argues, "indicate that a cumulative effect of negative politics, campaign after campaign, is reduced interest in [elections]." Even leaders of the Anglican Church have weighed in against negative campaigning (Watt 2001). Things have apparently not improved since, as Fowler and Ridout (2013) recently described in a paper entitled "Negative, Angry, and Ubiquitous." They write, "Advertising in 2012 was also extremely negative, especially at the presidential level, and frequently evoked the emotion of anger," adding that "whether the negativity will abate in the next presidential election" is an open question. This last point reinforces the idea that "negativity is bad" which is so prevalent in our discourse. But nobody seems to wonder if the *positivity* will abate.

Meanwhile, political candidates who are the perpetrators of negativity routinely state their opposition to it. Examples abound. Kathleen Brown, in the 1994 California gubernatorial race, ran an ad imploring all candidates to sign her proposal to "run a different kind of campaign. No negative ads bashing your opponent, but instead an election about the issues."[4] During the Senate debate on the Bipartisan Campaign Reform Act of 1997, Sen. John McCain argued that attack ads "do little to further beneficial debate and healthy political dialogue" and that "no one benefits from negative ads."[5] In the same debate, Sen. Dick Durbin said political advertising "has become so negative, so nasty, so dirty, that people are disgusted with it."[6] More recently, former Pennsylvania senator Rick Santorum, running for the 2012 Republican nomination for president, claimed that his opponent "Mitt Romney and his Super PAC have spent a staggering $20 million brutally attacking fellow Republicans" and that the "ugly attacks are going to backfire."[7] In the same campaign season, Newark, New Jersey, mayor Cory Booker, commenting on Barack Obama's attacks on Romney, called such ads "nauseating"—all the more ironic since he was on the show as an Obama surrogate.[8] Buchanan (2000) sums up this perspective by arguing that candidates "should emphasize their own plans and qualifications and strike tones much more likely to inspire than alienate." Moreover, at least some research suggests rebound effects, where the perpetrator of the negativity appears to lose ground rather than the intended target.

Of course most people pay little attention to scholars, and they probably assume candidates are not being entirely forthcoming in their condemnation of negativity. But pundits, especially televised ones, have a broad audience. And they, too, seem to simply assume negativity is bad.[9] David Brooks argued that for the Obama campaign "to start negative . . . seems to be self-destructive" because voters would no longer admire him.[10] Phillips's (2012) article in the *Huffington Post*, "How Negative Political Campaigning Is Crippling America," paints a grim picture of the 2012 campaign. "Mitt Romney has used personal appearances as opportunities to tear down the Obama administration," he laments. "When candidates use negative advertising, we see it as unfair. They are competing not by trumpeting their own merits but by undermining their competition." Other condemnations include Avlon (2012), who referred to the negative ads from the 2012 Florida Republican primary as a "tsunami of sleaze," and Karl (2012) of ABC News, who noted that "Mitt Romney and his allies spent more than $15 million on TV ads—only one was positive and it was in a foreign language," sardonically calling it "the statistic of the campaign."

Dangerous or not, negative campaigning has a long pedigree in politics. But what may be different in modern times is that claims about opponents are more easily spread (via electronic media and the Internet) and are thus more visible to the public. There is also good evidence that the amount of negativity in political advertising has increased over time (Fowler and Ridout 2013; Geer 2012a; Jamieson, Waldman, and Sherr 2000; Kaid and Johnston 2001). Whether it is to alert voters to negative attributes of the opponent, or simply an attempt to distract from one's own limitations, negativity is clearly an important part of the politician's campaign arsenal. Candidates no longer face the question of whether to "go negative" but, instead, how much negative advertising to use. For example, citing the University of Wisconsin Advertising Project, a *US News and World Report* article reported that during the final weeks of the 2008 presidential campaign, 100 percent of McCain's advertising was negative, as compared to 34 percent of Obama's (Halloran 2008). In 2012 Obama's early attacks on Romney were credited with (or accused of, depending on one's perspective) defining Romney as an out-of-touch, rich plutocrat, a definition from which Romney was supposedly unable to recover. Given the history of campaigning in America, and despite many efforts to put an end to it, candidates will almost certainly continue to run negative advertisements and paint nasty pictures of their opponents. And they will do this despite the apparent distaste of the public and the hue and cry of a wide range of observers.

Why? For one, psychology tells us that negativity is inherently attention getting (Pratto and John 1991) and often more memorable than positivity (Lau 1985); in general, impressions formed on the basis of negative information tend to be weighted more heavily (Cacioppo and Gardner 1999; Cobb and Kuklinski 1997; Fiske 1980; Hamilton and Zanna 1972). Negativity factors into voters' decisions (Fiorina and Shepsle 1989; Holbrook et al. 2001; Kernell 1977; Lau 1982) and impacts evaluations in important but complicated ways (Redlawsk, Civettini, and Emmerson 2010). Hence using negativity may not only assure more attention from voters in an otherwise crowded advertising environment, but also result in voters becoming more likely to incorporate the negative information into their evaluations.[11]

And yet, voters insist they are negative about negativity, suggesting a high likelihood they might punish candidates who resort to attack politics. Certainly voters themselves think negativity can create a backlash, as 70 percent of respondents in a 2000 survey agreed that "negative campaigning hurts a candidate's chance to win" an election.[12] Since politicians are driven to make campaign decisions on the basis of what they think will win the election, we would expect campaign consultants to take notice of voters' distaste and adjust their tactics to use less, not more, negativity. But, of course, they have not done so. While nearly every campaign features "positive" advertisements, as candidates introduce themselves and present the image they want the public to adopt, it seems evident that in most competitive campaigns politicians also decide that negative advertising is more likely than not to pay off.

To be fair, a number of scholars have advanced revisionist perspectives that do not paint so grim a picture. In particular, scholars who focus specifically on negativity seem less concerned than many of the observers we cited above. A pair of meta-analyses of over 100 negativity studies suggests that negative campaigns do not have the kind of antidemocratic effects many ascribe to them (Lau et al. 1999; Lau, Sigelman, and Rovner 2007) and that, in reality, their effects cannot be generalized across campaigns. Others, like Kahn and Kenney (1999), suggest that the negative effects are conditional and, in fact, some evidence suggests that negativity even mobilizes voters under certain conditions (Brooks and Geer 2007; Jackson and Carsey 2007). Among political scientists who study campaigns—especially those who specifically study negative campaigning—there is much skepticism about the apparent conventional wisdom that negative campaigning is destructive.

But for the most part these views are not widespread, leaving us somewhat puzzled about why campaigns would make ubiquitous use of a technique so roundly condemned. What is the reason for this discrepancy? Either the surveys that ask voters about negative campaigns are not really tapping their true feelings, or the political strategists are getting it wrong. Given the significant incentive for political campaigns to use strategies that work and to abandon those that do not, it seems worth investigating the extent to which our assumptions about voters and negativity are incorrect. There is little in the way of extant theory to explain the apparent paradox that candidates continue to rely on a strategy voters claim to dis-like and may punish. We know that when voters are asked about negative campaigning they react negatively; we do not know if they really mean it. When asked about something that is supposed to be condemned, voters are likely to condemn it. When asked about it differently, as we will show, they are less concerned and instead may even recognize the informational value of negative campaigning.

Negative Advertising and Information

What does it mean to "go negative"? The standard political science defi-nition uses "talking about the opponent" (Lau et al. 1999) as the key fea-ture that makes an ad negative. It is, of course, not really that simple, since many negative television ads are also identifiable by their typical use of ominous music, dark images, and scary language (Brader 2006) and those who study the question closely are usually somewhat more nuanced than this simple definition. Negative ads can certainly be delivered other than by television, including radio, mail, and, more recently, social media. But however they are delivered and whatever their ancillary content, at their core they are meant as a message about the opponent. Often, those mes-sages are informative in the sense that few if any candidates will offer up negative information about themselves, so negative ads have the potential to inject into the political environment information that otherwise would be unlikely to be part of the debate.

Geer (2006) develops both normative and empirical arguments for the informational benefits of negativity, showing that negative advertise-ments generally provide valuable data for voters, data that would other-wise never enter the political arena (see also Niven 2006).[13] After all, since the candidates are unlikely to criticize themselves, campaigns constrained to be only "positive" might well limit voter access to important diagnos-tic information. Moreover, Geer also shows that so-called positive ads are less useful and less scrutinized because they contain limited informational content. In perhaps an ironic twist, the elimination of negativity would not mean that positive ads would follow a straight and narrow path. In fact, positive ads could become more aggrandizing—in product advertising it is called "puffery"—and without the ability to attack an opponent, voters would have no contrasting information to challenge inevitably exagger-ated "positive" claims.

Even so, and in contrast to our argument, a July 2000 Gallup Poll found only 24 percent of voters agreed that "generally speaking, negative advertisements help me learn about the candidates." Perhaps voters are for the most part inured to negativity. But there is scant evidence for that here. Like these voters, many scholars and pundits tend to discount or ignore the positive informational effects of negative advertising, largely because of their assessments about the public's disdain for it. Those wishing to scrub campaigns clean of attack politics begin with negative assumptions about negativity. Given the nearly unanimous belief that negativity is inherently bad, dissenters have been compelled to react defensively. For instance, Mayer (1996) wrote a pro-negativity essay called "In Defense of Negative Campaigning," and ten years later Geer titled his book *In Defense of Negativity* (2006).

On the whole we are sympathetic toward attempts to defend the apparently indefensible and find the arguments and evidence quite persuasive. But we have one very significant disagreement: the limited efforts to place negative campaigning into a more acceptable light remain grounded in the idea that negativity is something to fear. Geer, a staunch defender, nonetheless admits that "there is little doubt from public survey data that the public does not like negative campaigning" (2006, 137). He consequently must defend negativity against concerns that politics may be at risk because if voters hate negativity, increasing and pervasive negativity might lead voters to distrust politics and government, to say a pox on all their houses, and to become cynical. But we are not so sure that voters are all that fragile, that they are led into a state of cynical withdrawal simply because candidates go negative. In fact, given the many other political factors that can drive the public's cynicism, such as the extensive role played by shadowy organizations pouring money into campaigns since the Supreme Court's *Citizens United* decision, or a completely deadlocked Congress that receives favorability ratings lower than used car salesmen, the idea that voters are uniquely damaged by negative campaigns seems unlikely.[14]

In this book we argue that we do not actually *need* to defend negative campaigning because voters are not turned off as much as many think they are. We challenge the conventional wisdom that voters hate negative campaigning, allowing us to breathe more easily as candidates pummel each other in the give-and-take of political campaigning. And if we can relax about negativity, then we can go beyond kneejerk reactions to negative campaigning to explore more in depth how voters really respond. At the core of our initial argument is the simple fact that the typical question wording used in voter surveys on negativity does not distinguish credible attacks from baseless attacks, or even relevant from irrelevant. Instead, it simply lumps all supposed "attack" campaigning into one category— negative. Yet, some research has shown that voters can be more receptive to specific types of negative messages—for example, those deemed more civil or more relevant (Brooks and Geer 2007; Fridkin and Kenney 2008)—an effect that cannot be captured without a more nuanced approach to negativity.

Rethinking Negativity

We develop a new perspective on negativity, building on and extending Geer (2006) in particular. Using multiple methods—surveys, experiments, and formal modeling—and making use of a wide range of research participants, we develop a more complete picture of the role of negative campaigning in elections.

We propose a formal model that describes how negativity is valuable to voters theoretically, and test it with experiments that show how voters use negative information (conditional on its accuracy). The model and corresponding laboratory experiments show that voters need more than just candidates' arguments for why they should be elected. They also need relevant and credible *negative* information.

But we need to show more than that. Even if negative campaigning provides valuable information, its value is quite limited if voters are in fact seriously repelled by it. We need to show that voters can actually accept negativity as a legitimate part of the political environment. So first, using survey and experimental data, we examine the extent of voter disdain for political attacks. Our surveys consistently show that, across many different samples and contexts, voters are not all that turned off by negative advertising. We show that not only does negative advertising have an important theoretical standing—following Geer and his arguments about the informational content of negativity—but that voters themselves are more accepting of so-called negative campaigns than many commentators seem willing to believe, though we must grant that voters are not exactly thrilled by negativity either.

Hence our conclusion that negative campaigning no longer needs to be defended. Americans might dislike a lot of things about politics, and may prefer to stay home rather than to get out to the polls, but in the end these supposed failures of democracy cannot really be laid at the feet of negative campaigns. Much of the supposed general voter sentiment against negative campaigning is not evidence that voters reject the information negative campaigning can provide them, but instead has more to do with the wording of the questions posed in the surveys, or the design of previous experiments. If we want to understand the dynamics of voter response to negativity, we need to measure public opinion more carefully. A good place to start is the standard definition of a negative ad. Because negativity may be a bit like pornography—"I know it when I see it"—the easiest approach to avoid that imbroglio has been to define it as a candidate talking about her opponent, with the quite reasonable assumption that few candidates will speak of their opponent in positive terms, other than perhaps in the insincere form of "my good friend across the aisle."

But not all negativity is the same, and so an improved understanding of how voters react to negativity will let us better differentiate the topics candidates use in negative advertising and how voters respond to them. An example of an unusual use of negativity might be helpful here. Missouri US Senate Democratic incumbent Claire McCaskill's 2012 campaign used negativity in a way that would only work if negative campaigning was integrated and accepted in the political system—she used it to praise her potential opponent. An underdog in the upcoming fall election, McCaskill faced a stiff challenge from one of three viable Republican candidates: Sarah Steelman, John Brunner, and Todd Akin.

Before the August 7 primary, the McCaskill campaign released negative TV ads about all three, each with a different theme. McCaskill presented Steelman as "just more politics as usual . . . taking thousands in gifts from lobbyists," and said that "hundreds of key documents from Steelman's office have gone missing."[15] She presented Brunner as unreliable, claiming that he "hasn't bothered to vote in 16 elections and that "as a CEO, Brunner nearly killed the family business, and ran up $245 million in debt. Around here," the ad says, "conservative means you don't spend more than you make."[16]

But, unlike the other two, McCaskill's ad against Todd Akin was noticeably upbeat. It started with a picture of Akin and the message "The most conservative congressman in Missouri" onscreen beside him. The next image showed Akin again, as a cheery voiceover proclaimed him "a crusader against bigger government," and onscreen text said the same. The ad went on to say that Akin has a "pro-family agenda," and that he would "completely eliminate the departments of Education and Energy" and "privatize Social Security." The final verdict on Akin: "Missouri's true conservative is just too conservative."[17] In a state where socially conservative candidate Rick Santorum had recently won the Republicans' presidential primary (55–25% over Mitt Romney), McCaskill's "criticism" was hardly an indictment.

If McCaskill was truly choosing her opponent, she did a masterful job. Akin won the primary and (unintentionally) returned the favor. Two weeks after the primary, in a local interview, Akin was asked whether he believed that abortion should be legal in the case of rape. Akin responded that pregnancies after rape were quite rare, saying, "if it's a legitimate rape, the female body has ways to try and shut that whole thing down."[18] Needless to say, the comment wasn't well received. The RNC quickly pulled Akin's funding while many in the party tried, unsuccessfully, to get Akin to drop out of the race. Meanwhile, McCaskill, as one might expect, made sure that voters didn't forget. For example, her ad "Real Words—Women" showed the Akin clip and featured testimonials from "real" women saying things like "Todd Akin is scary," and "He has no idea how it even works, and he wants to legislate about it?"[19]

This example compels us to go beyond a simple view of negativity. Other researchers have attempted this with some success. Kahn and Kenney (1999; see also Fridkin and Kenney 2008, 2011) in particular make the point that different kinds of negativity appear to have different effects on voter turnout. This suggests voters can and do recognize some negativity as useful (legitimate topics) while viewing "mudslinging" with abhorrence. But we know very little about how voters actually perceive the topics of negativity and the extent to which they agree with pundits and scholars who assert that talking about an opponent is negative and thus out of bounds. So here we take the novel approach of *not* simply devising our own replacement definition of negativity. Instead, we argue that as researchers we should focus more on letting voters define negativity for us rather than attempting to define it independently from them. And we find that when asked in principle how they feel about a candidate talking about an opponent, voters seem to be less concerned than we think they are. Though they tend to moderately dislike actual negative ads when they watch them, this affective response is highly conditioned by the topic of the ad and does not appear to interfere with the potential informational value of the ad. In this sense, voters are able to use these ads to extract useful content without being overly traumatized by their existence as so many seem to assume they are.

The Context of Negativity in American Campaigns

As endemic to the system as negativity seems to be, we should expect more in the years to come, as the political advertising industry in itself is still in a growth phase. For instance, in 2012, over 1 million television ad impressions were bought by just the presidential candidates and their supporting groups, by far the most of any election in history.[20] Obama had 215 distinct ads, with 142 of those produced directly by his campaign. Romney had 259 distinct ads, with 93 of those coming from his campaign (Haberman 2012). Total advertising expenditures in support of the two candidates surpassed $2 billion.[21] Of this, about $667 million came from "independent" sources, including the Super PACs, and 72 percent of that money went into efforts to defeat a particular candidate rather than supporting one. Though Super PACs technically could not coordinate with the candidates, they appeared to be well aligned with the candidates' campaign strategies, especially in regard to negative campaigning.

Across all levels of the US system, campaigns produced negative ads with astounding alacrity in 2012. A noteworthy example comes from Indiana on October 23, 2012. On this date in New Albany, the three main candidates for Indiana's US Senate seat (Republican Richard Mourdock, Democrat Joe Donnelly, and Libertarian Andrew Horning) participated in their second and final debate. One of the last questions asked the candidates, in a broad sense, to discuss their views on abortion. Mourdock was pro-life, more specifically believing that the only exception should be to save the life of the mother. About this belief, Mourdock said, "I struggled with it myself for a long time, but I came to realize life is that gift from God. And I think even when life begins in that horrible situation of rape, *that it is something that God intended to happen* [emphasis added]."[22]

Mourdock said this at about 7:45 p.m. By 10:30 p.m., a Super PAC supporting the Democratic Party (American Bridge 21st Century) released a negative ad featuring footage of Mourdock's answer from the debate, which had finished *fewer than three hours* prior. Their ad, called "The Romney-Mourdock Ticket," started with a clip of Mitt Romney, shown onscreen, endorsing Mourdock.[23]

ROMNEY: "This fall, I'm supporting Richard Mourdock for Senate."
[Onscreen text: "And what does Richard Mourdock support?"]
MOURDOCK (debate footage is shown): ". . . even when life begins in that horrible situation of rape, that it is something that God intended to happen." [A picture

of Romney, giving a thumbs-up sign, is shown in the bottom-right hand corner of the ad.]

MOURDOCK (from other footage): "We need more zealots in the Republican party ...";"I think the idea of man-induced global climate change is the biggest hoax that has ever been perpetuated on the species"; "I never took an economics class, an accounting class, a finance class ..."; "It's bipartisanship that's taken us to the brink of bankruptcy. We don't need bipartisanship ..."

ROMNEY: "I hope you'll join me in supporting Richard Mourdock ..."

[Onscreen text: "No thanks."]

The clip of Romney was from an ad that Mourdock's campaign had debuted the previous night, again showing the efficiency of the negative advertising machine. Mourdock took issue with the interpretation of his statement from the debate. "What I said was, in answering the question from my position of faith, I said I believe that God creates life. I believe that as wholly and as fully as I can believe it. That God creates life," he said at a press conference after the debate. "Are you trying to suggest that somehow I think that God pre-ordained rape? No, I don't think that. That's sick. Twisted. That's not even close to what I said. What I said is that God creates life." Prior to the debate, polls had Mourdock leading Donnelly by five points.[24] Donnelly won the election, 50 percent to 44 percent.

As these examples illustrate, negativity can be quite intense, but there is increasing evidence that, despite their protests, voters hardly even care. One final example from 2012 shows how a campaign can devolve into petty negativity and yet fail to irreparably damage voters' opinions about the candidates. In the Massachusetts US Senate race, Republican incumbent Scott Brown and his challenger, Democrat Elizabeth Warren, both vowed to stay positive.[25] In addition, in response to the *Citizens United* case, which allowed unlimited independent campaign spending by corporations, and *Speechnow.org v. FEC,* which led to the creation of Super PACs, Brown and Warren negotiated "The People's Pledge." Specifically, the pledge stated that if any outside group participated in any advertising during the race, the candidate who benefited from the ad would be required to donate 50 percent of the ad's cost to a charity of the opposing candidate's choice (Schoenberg 2012). According to Schoenberg, before the signing of the People's Pledge, both Warren and Brown had been the subjects of attack ads by outside groups, but in unequal proportions. The groups in support of Warren were outspending the pro-Brown groups 3 to 1. Warren and Brown claimed that they were setting a new standard of campaigning by limiting the influence of outside groups and the petty criticisms they often bring forth. Research has shown that attack ads from unknown third parties are more effective and less likely to redound upon the candidate(s) not being attacked (Brooks and Murov 2012), so many felt that independent groups could afford to be more reckless in their advertising. The People's Pledge held through Election Day in that the candidates largely used their own resources. The positivity did not.

Warren was the first to go negative in a campaign advertisement, claiming that Brown advocated tax cuts for the wealthy. Brown followed Warren's ad with one of his own, claiming that Warren was ignoring the important issues of the campaign and instead focusing on spreading lies about Brown (Bierman 2012). The more frivolous negativity centered upon Warren's claim of Cherokee heritage. Brown attacked Warren for this in a debate, concluding with "as you can see, she's not." One of Brown's ads questioned whether Warren "claimed to be a minority for professional gain."[26] After members of Brown's campaign staff were filmed at a rally doing tomahawk chops and whooping like "Indians," a Bloomberg article proclaimed that "it's getting ugly in Massachusetts" (Kolhatkar 2012).[27]

Both candidates were well liked before the campaigns started—Brown's net favorability rating in May 2012 was 55% favorable/30% unfavorable (+23%), and Warren's was 48/32 (+16%).[28] The negativity failed to change this. Eighty percent believed their vote was for, rather than against, a candidate.[29] Exit polls showed that Brown's favorability rating was at 60/38 (+22%) while Warren's was at 56/43 (+13%) (Schoenberg 2012). Another poll from November 2012 showed that in Massachusetts Brown had a higher job approval rating than Barack Obama.[30] Nonetheless Elizabeth Warren won the race in Massachusetts with 54 percent of the vote.

Kolhatkar (2012) argues that the candidates' disavowal of outside spending made voters view their interactions more positively: "In an odd way, the absence of outside spending may force a certain amount of honesty out of the candidates themselves—even if it doesn't prove to elevate the tone of their interactions—by eliminating some of the outside proxies who usually take on most of the truly dirty politics." In other words, given a promise of (relative) honesty, voters could tolerate the negativity. In essence, the candidates were policing each other and, in terms of public perception, it worked.

Plan of the Book

The nature of these attacks, and the many, many others that took place in the 2012 election cycle, returns us to our questions about why negativity is so pervasive and what, if anything, voters stand to gain from its pervasiveness. Our goal in this book is to bring multiple approaches—formal modeling, experimentation, and surveys—to the question of negativity in American campaigns. The idea of using multiple methods is that each of our approaches by itself has its limitations—as do all methodologies scholars employ in their studies—so by corroborating our findings across various methods, we are better able to leverage each methodology's strengths. Our telephone interviews have the advantage of drawing from random samples, thus allowing the results to be readily generalized to the populations from which they were drawn. Our Internet study, which uses a nonrandom sample, allowed us more time to present actual campaign ads to participants and to record their responses. While we cannot readily generalize our Internet sample, we do find that the responses these participants give to negativity in the real world are very similar to the ones our random sample survey participants give to the texted-based scenarios we provided them. Because we embedded experiments in both studies, we can use the strengths of the experimental method in helping us understand causality as well.

In what we believe is the most original contribution of this book to the existing literature on negativity, we employ formal modeling because it requires us to clearly delineate our assumptions, provides clearly testable propositions that arise from those assumptions, and allows us to simulate the interactive nature of a campaign—where candidates make choices and voters act on what they learn from the choices. Formal modeling allows us to take the complicated world of the campaign and simplify it in ways that illuminate our arguments. But the model without testing is theoretical; our interest here is empirical. So we test the model to determine what it is about voter information processing that seems to give negativity an important role in campaigns.

If we relied only on one of these methods, readers would certainly be right to argue that we are seeing only one view, much like the allegory of the blind men trying to describe an elephant after each man felt a different part. But we do not. Instead we use our multiple methods to triangulate on the question at hand. Of course, no study is perfect, and we are sure readers will identify questions we should have considered, but we do think that employing multiple methods to support our theory is clearly superior to relying on only one.

In the next chapter, we review key aspects of the literature on negative campaigning. We also provide the basis for our interest in the credibility of candidates' campaigns by discussing the watchdog role of the media in political campaigns and examining whether candidates or the media are the more credible sources of political information. We also use chapter 2 to set the stage for our empirical and modeling chapters that follow.

The first of these, chapter 3, describes the results of three survey experiments designed to measure voters' reactions toward negativity. Each of the three experiments was a population-based random sample survey. Study 1 was part of a national telephone survey fielded before and after the 2008 general election. This experiment examines our most basic question: are voters really negative about negativity? We did this by asking randomly assigned subsamples about negative campaigning, varying whether or not the question included the phrase "negative campaigning." We asked if voters accept or reject the idea of a candidate talking about his opponent, and we asked the extent to which truthfulness mitigates effects of negativity. Study 2 is a sample of New Jersey voters, collected in October 2009 just ahead of the New Jersey gubernatorial election that year. This is also a survey experiment, where we again manipulated the presence or absence of the "negative campaigning" cue but expanded the questions to include different topics and tested affective (anger) responses to negativity. Finally the third survey in this chapter was part of the 2010 Cooperative Congressional Election Study (CCES). Like the others, it presented respondents with text-based questions about different topics, asking voters to decide for themselves if the topics are negative, and giving them an opportunity to provide affect (anger), cognition (believability), and behavioral intent (vote).

While there are a number of negative affective responses we could have studied in addition to anger—for example, disgust and anxiety—we focus on anger because as a negative emotion it can generate a desire to respond and is generally triggered by a sense of being offended or being wronged. When we are angry, we are angry at something or someone, and we generally want to do something about it. Given that many suggest negativity has degraded our campaign environment, anger seems a potentially appropriate response. And while we made the choice to examine anger long before Fowler and Ridout's (2013) recent article showing three-quarters of 2012 presidential campaign ads made anger appeals, their work reinforces our belief that this is the appropriate focus for our studies. The ads may appeal to anger and in doing so may actually make voters angry at their very presence.

We find that large majorities of voters oppose the phrase "negative campaigning," but respond much more favorably when asked about the *activity* of negative campaigning—talking about an opponent. In essence, more of the reported voter opposition to negative campaigning appears to develop from a social desirability effect inherent in being asked about something that is "negative" than from disliking a candidate talking about his or her opponent. So, if voters do not particularly mind the idea of candidates "talking about the opponent," what is it about political campaigns that voters truly dislike? Their anger and frustration stem not so much from the idea of candidates talking about their opponents, but instead from candidates using irrelevant or false attacks. We find that voter reactions to negativity are quite clearly conditioned on the topic of the purported attack ad, but when *we* assert that the topics are negative, voters are *much* more angered by them. We find little evidence of a "backlash effect" where voters say they will punish a candidate for attacking the opponent by voting for the ad's target.

While the first three studies allowed us to get large samples and to test how voters respond to the typical survey questions public opinion studies ask, they do not really engage respondents as real ads would. So in chapter 4 we move to a study where we showed real ads to an Internet-based sample to test the extent to which "negative" ads—varying in content—generate the cognitive, affective, and behavioral responses that we see in the text-based survey data. As stimuli, we collected advertisements (positive and negative) from real-world campaigns that varied by topic as well as by intensity. We find that our participants do differentiate between ads that are "positive," those that are negative, and those that are not just negative but include clearly defamatory content. We also find significant variance in their responses to the "negative" ads, suggesting that the informational content of the ad affects the way it is judged. Again, we find backlash—defined as an ad that makes voters more likely to support the opponent—to be quite limited. Among the twenty-one ads we used— twelve of which were negative—only two ads created noticeable backlash. Both ads had a religious theme. One made the claim that the opponent was an atheist. The other claimed that the opponent had once promoted idol worship. In the same study we asked voters to tell us how helpful some types of ads were during the 2012 election season. Of respondents, 72 percent said that ads talking about a candidate's faith and religion were not at all helpful, even though we did not specify if these would be negative or positive ads. The overwhelming sense is that this topic is simply something that should be avoided, reinforcing the backlash findings for religion-themed attacks. But we do not find likely backlash for any of the other ads we use.

With our empirical base established using both random-sample telephone surveys and an online study that reinforces the survey findings, in chapter 5 we examine how voters use campaign information, including negativity. In this chapter we turn to a formal model of negative campaigning, since such a model yields specific behavioral predictions about voter decision-making when we control for the information sets given to the voters by the candidates. We use the model to structure a campaign experiment to test whether voters need negative information or whether they are able to infer it from a lack of positive information. We recognize that the formal model will be somewhat complicated for some readers, and probably not detailed enough for others. We see the formal model aspect of this project not as its ultimate purpose, but instead as another tool—along with surveys and experiments—to help us understand the role of negativity in political campaigns.

Formal models of negative campaigning are scarce. The two most relevant to our study are Harrington and Hess (1996) and Polborn and Yi (2006), as the informational aspect of negative campaigning is the central feature of both models. Polborn and Yi assigned candidates traits that are known to both candidates, while the voter only knows the probability distribution of the traits. The candidates are limited to two campaign options: either reveal the opponent's character trait (negative campaigning) or reveal one's own issue position (positive campaigning). They find that eliminating negative campaigning leads to information distribution inefficiencies that would be detrimental to voter welfare, since without the negative option candidates' choices are limited to revealing one's own issue position or not campaigning. In Harrington and Hess (1996), candidates inherit initial locations on both a valence and an issue dimension, and are restricted to campaigning on the issue dimension; negative campaigning relocates the opponent on that dimension.[31]

In our model two candidates, who have "positive" or "negative" traits on two dimensions, campaign by revealing to the voter either positive information about themselves, negative information about the opponent, or nothing at all. Voters, who are aware of the campaigns and the prior probabilities of candidates having positive traits, receive higher payouts for choosing candidates with positive (rather than negative) traits. Suppose that candidates did not engage in negative campaigning. Arguably, at least if candidates' statements were verifiable, voters could learn negative information simply by gauging which topics that candidates failed to positively campaign about. Our model provides different predictions depending upon whether voters can make such inferences.

We follow with an experiment in which subjects in a laboratory game take on the roles specified by the model (candidates and voters) and are incentivized to make optimal decisions (i.e., candidates to win, and voters to pick candidates with "positive" traits). This methodology in general has been successful in a wide array of political studies, including policy choice (Aragones and Palfrey 2004), retrospective voting strategies (Collier et al. 1987), committee bargaining (Diermeier and Morton 2005; Fréchette et al. 2005), and the Swing Voter's Curse (Battaglini et al. 2010). And as with any experiment, we are better able to minimize the impact of noise variables—real-world elections are both idiosyncratic and cluttered with confounding independent variables—to isolate our topic of interest, which in this chapter is how voters respond to informative positive and negative campaigns. As we show, voters tend to ignore topics that the candidates ignore, rather than attempt to make inferences about why the candidates ignored those topics. Thus, they fail to correctly attribute negative traits to candidates who do *not* engage in positive campaigning on a given dimension. A result of this voter decision-making approach is that it increases the effectiveness of candidates' negative campaigning. This provides a powerful explanation for why voters don't seem to mind negativity as much as has been assumed. It also explains why candidates must address many topics, regardless of whether they are providing "positive" or "negative" information.

One of the regularly expressed concerns about negative ads is that they may mislead voters by not only being negative, but by shading the truth, and perhaps outright lying about the opponent.[32] In chapter 6 we return to our survey-experiment data to examine questions of truth and credibility in negativity—including the extent to which potentially false content is a predictor of voter backlash. Voters, it turns out, seem to care more about whether ads are believable and relevant than whether they make a case against a candidate's opponent. In this chapter we develop a two-stage multivariate empirical model. In the first stage, we combine the effects of ad types (positive, negative, or defamatory), individual covariates (e.g., trust in media and candidates), and a range of demographic factors to predict affective response (anger) to a campaign ad as well as assessments of its believability and appropriateness. As noted above, we focus on anger, in particular, because, as Fowler and Ridout (2013) point out, many negative ads play on the emotion of anger in their very intent. In the second stage of the model, these three assessments then predict voter response in the form of potential for backlash. We find that contrary to many expectations, affective response to the ad is not the driving force that determines how voters respond, but instead response is based on the extent to which an ad can be believed and is judged appropriate. Thus, we find that assessments of ads are not driven by negativity itself.

In chapter 7 we return to our formal model, revising it to focus on the effects on the system from relaxing limitations on candidates' honesty.[33] We find that in the absence of any verification mechanism, voters are not especially skilled at determining the accuracy of candidates' statements, even when the information environment provides clues as to which (if any) of the candidates are telling the truth. On the other hand, our laboratory subjects—in the role of candidate—tended to avoid irrelevant (or potentially inflammatory) statements because of the concern that voters would assume candidates choosing such a statement were lying. The experiment provides compelling evidence for why we should think of negative campaigning as not simply being about attacking and defending, but also about credibility and relevance.

Finally, in chapter 8 we pull it all together, drawing the conclusion that while negativity in campaigns is not necessarily prized by voters, neither does it cause significant backlash. Voters learn important information when candidates (and their allies) go negative. Rather than the mere fact of negativity leading to negative responses by voters, as is widely presumed, the process is more subtle. Voters do get slightly perturbed by negativity and angrier still when the attacks are not particularly germane—specifically in our cases, attacks on religion or family. But rather than being driven by anger, in the end voter responses to negativity seem to be based more on cognitive assessments of negative ads: their believability and appropriateness, rather than affective response. This suggests that when voters say they are negative about negativity, they are more likely responding to the cues they are given—negativity is bad—than providing real insight into how they process negative campaign ads.

Conclusion

In this book we use multiple methodological approaches—formal modeling, experimentation, and surveys—to better understand the role of negativity in American campaigns. The first question we will address is from the beginning of this chapter—that of the fragile American voter. If voters are so turned off by negativity, why is it nearly inescapable? We find that voters are not all that angry about negative campaigning and in some cases fail to even connect campaigning against an opponent with negative campaigning.

One brief real-world example highlights this point: the 2006 Loebsack for Congress campaign (Iowa District 2). Democrat Dave Loebsack, challenging thirty-year-incumbent Republican Jim Leach, ran ads that included the announcer saying, "Jim Leach is a good man," but then subsequently attacking him as out of touch and too connected to George Bush and Dick Cheney. These ads were clearly within the working definition of "negative" employed by most research. But rather than voters and the media responding in horror, Loebsack got credit for calling Leach "a good man"; a *Los Angeles Times* story called this "the nicest campaign in the country" (Simon 2006). Maybe it was "nice" in the context of most congressional campaigns, but as a challenger Loebsack had two tasks. The first was to introduce himself to the voters and provide a compelling reason to vote for him after years of supporting Leach. The second—and the one all but requiring negativity—was to convince voters to stop supporting Leach, to give them reasons he should not be re-elected. Voters may express concerns about negativity, but we believe they also recognize the differences between negativity that simply tears down versus that providing necessary context for voter decision-making.

The same Jim Leach wrote an essay for *US News and World Report* in 2008 in which he condemned negativity. The essay was paired with one by political consultant Dick Morris who wrote a straightforward defense of negativity, arguing that Americans can "sift through a wide variety of claims and to determine for themselves which are specious and which are accurate" (Morris 2008). Morris credits American voters with the ability to differentiate between truth and falsehood, and says that in order to be effective "negative ads must be believable," going on to write that it is negativity that lets voters find the truth. Leach (2008), for his part, appears to be condemning negativity, arguing that "candidates who win by tearing down their opponents cannot govern." But, at the very same time, even Leach, known for his aversion to attacking his opponents, admits that "it is always appropriate to contrast approaches to government, to suggest an opponent is too big or tightfisted a spender, too heavy a taxer or too undisciplined a tax cutter, too quick to go to war or too slow to respond to a national challenge." In fact, what we learn is that Leach primarily objects to mudslinging, saying, "it is never appropriate to lie, to impugn patriotism, or feed or inspire prejudice." So it is not that Leach objects to negativity *per se*, but to certain types, just like the typical voter.

Morris's point is supported by some of our data on perceptions of the "helpfulness" of different types of ads. Voters are split on whether ads that "make broad claims about future plans for governing" are helpful. Thirty-nine percent of respondents in one of our studies thought such ads would be at least somewhat helpful, but 61 percent thought they'd be of little or no help. On the other hand, we find that ads that talk about an opponent's voting record, differences between candidates on issues, or why one candidate is better on the issues are thought to be helpful by 71 to 80 percent. But ads that "show the inconsistencies of an opponent's position on issues" are only thought to be helpful by half of respondents. What's the difference? The first three do not sound all that negative, but the last one does. Even so, voters clearly see value in ads that talk about an opponent.

Lest the reader think we come at this simply from our ivory tower, with little understanding of the real-world implications of negativity, we should point out that one of us—David Redlawsk—was not only a senior advisor and treasurer for the successful Loebsack campaign in 2006, but also has contested several local elections of his own. In both winning and losing campaigns Redlawsk has had experience with negative advertising, employed by him and against him. At a time when local governing body elections in suburban communities rarely made use of television, challenger Redlawsk's first campaign ran a cable TV ad suggesting the incumbents' policies were creating a "time bomb" for the community, complete with images of a bomb being disarmed. After losing this election, and the next one, Redlawsk won a third with a mix of negative and positive messages, mostly delivered by mail. Finally, as an incumbent running for reelection, Redlawsk and his opponent made extensive use of television spots, in what was (at the time) an incredibly expensive local campaign, with Redlawsk claiming "something smells" and his opponent arguing, "Redlawsk is lying."[34]

As a candidate, Redlawsk admits that it was never fun to be on the receiving end of negativity, but at the same time it seems all but required for challengers wishing to make a case against an incumbent, and voters seemed to take it in stride. And while we do not rely on this real-world experience in lieu of social science research, it does help inform our perspective. Where others have started a defense of campaigning almost apologetically, our data and analysis suggest that in the end there is little to fear about such campaigns. Voters may claim they do not like them, but often such campaigns are informative and voters appreciate information. At the same time, we should be careful about how far our claims go. We find no reason to support allowing candidates to lie with impunity about their opponents. Also, we are talking about voter reactions to negativity, not about the potential effects of negativity on the actions of the politicians themselves, once elected. Even though negative campaigns do not inevitably lead to the destruction of our political system by irreparably damaging the psyches of fragile voters, it is certainly possible—maybe even likely—that officeholders anticipate the attacks that might be made against them in future elections, leading them toward decisions in office that they otherwise might not take.

Ironically the same people who condemn negativity are usually quick to call for competitive elections, non-gerrymandered districts, and reduction of the role of money in politics. But these things may be mutually exclusive desires. The evidence is that as campaigns become competitive, money flows into them. As money flows into them, candidates use that money to get information to the voters. And by necessity some (if not most) of that information will be "negative," bringing to the attention of voters the failings of the opponent. The only sure way to limit negativity— short of a constitutional amendment overturning our First Amendment freedoms to say pretty much anything in the political arena—is to limit competitiveness. Noncompetitive campaigns are rarely negative, nor are they informative to the voters who find they have little choice anyway.

Competitive campaigns, however, bring on the rough and tumble of politics, something we believe can be embraced. Voters are not fragile; they do not hate it necessarily when candidates talk about each other negatively. They may say they do, but the evidence we have marshaled here suggests otherwise. Moaning about the quality of political campaigns is as old as campaigning itself. And while we are not arguing that things wouldn't be better if campaign discourse were somehow on a higher plane, we are arguing that there would be nothing particularly wrong if that discourse included legitimate attacks that provide accurate information. This may be the real problem: not that candidates increasingly go negative, but that sometimes they cross the line into the types of rhetoric that voters really do hate. Even so, we're pretty sure when this happens, voters can make up their own minds to reject such information. Embracing negativity does not mean embracing scurrilous, nonrelevant attacks, but it does mean recognizing the value in the full range of information that allows voters to make up their minds.

We opened this chapter with a quotation from Marcus Cicero's brother, urging him to at every opportunity remind voters of the failings of his opponent. While no doubt Quintas Cicero did not conceive of voter information processing in the way modern scholars do, it is just as clear that he thought voters should be well informed and, in this particular case, given the serious failures of his opponents, assumed his brother Marcus would benefit even though he would be the one perpetrating the attacks. We suspect modern political consultants feel very much the same way. If your opponent has weaknesses—and what opponent doesn't—it is incumbent on you to exploit them. After all, unless you win, you lose.

CHAPTER TWO

Voters and Negativity, and Why the Media Can't Help

with Stefan Mancevski

This has been the worst political year I've ever seen ... the ugliest, the nastiest, everything goes, no accountability.—President George H. W. Bush, in the heat of the 1992 campaign

President Bush may have thought 1992 was the nastiest election year ever, but more recent candidates might yearn for the good old days of 1992. Content analysis studies of campaign advertising have shown that campaigns have indeed become more negative since then (Geer 2012a), but the ramifications of this increase in negativity are not as clear. So before we develop our argument from surveys and experiments, we need to provide some context for our analyses. The goal of this chapter is to situate our work in the broader literature on negative campaigning, as well as to address a key question: why do *candidates* have to go negative? Accepting that voters need to know both the good and the bad of their choices does not mean that the bad has to come from candidates. It would be possible, or perhaps even preferable, for the media to take up the truth-monitoring role, to help voters recognize when candidates are (in their presumably positive ads) not being completely forthcoming about themselves. So we first consider the role of the media, and why it cannot be counted upon for this important task, before moving on to examining negativity itself.

We start by reviewing the broad contours of the existing literature on negative campaigning. There is a great deal of it and we do not want to get bogged down in every detail. Our purpose is not so much to challenge the existing research as to suggest a new perspective, informed by the idea that negativity provides important and valuable information to voters (as recently championed by Geer [2006]), and including the notions of truth and credibility and their importance across several campaign topics.

But valuable or not, if voters despise negative campaigning, whether it is informative may not matter. Our basic argument about negativity is thus threefold. First, voters are not as negative about negativity as much of the polling and many observers seem to suggest. Second, negativity carries valuable information about the candidates, information that voters otherwise would not have received. Important diagnostic data about an opponent's failures, or efforts to hold an opponent accountable for misleading voters, cannot be transmitted via positive campaigning.[1] Third, while candidates can make use of negativity to transmit information that benefits voters, the specific content of their attacks matter. Voters do not blithely accept that all topics are equally valid and useful. Taken together, these points suggest that not only is negativity here to stay but that it is not, in and of itself, something we should be particularly worried about. We should be more concerned with whether or not voters are getting accurate information—or in other words, whether or not the candidates are telling the truth. As Jamieson (1992) documents in *Dirty Politics*, both positive and negative ads can be designed to deceive.

So while we side with Geer and others who believe negative campaigns present information to voters, our argument goes further: negative ads serve another purpose—keeping candidates honest about themselves. Knowing that the opponent is free to attack may dissuade a candidate from making grandiose and unchecked claims about him- or herself. We take it as given that absent any policing at all, candidates have an incentive to lie, which is not the same as saying they have an incentive to attack. Dishonesty can (and probably would) be about one's own fitness for office if there was no chance that such lies would be countered (a point we will come back to when we test our formal model of negativity). In a world in which candidates are not allowed to talk about their opponents, a candidate has every reason to engage in puffery, not to mention downright lying, when persuading voters to choose him or her. As we will show in this chapter, we believe candidates themselves are in the best position to do this policing.

Of course, if negativity is about providing information that candidates would never provide about themselves or to incentivize more truthful claims, then we cannot ignore the possibility that such information can enter the campaign environment by other means. After all, one of the

hallmarks of the United States is a free and unfettered press, charged
with informing the public about important and relevant details about candidates through its reporting on the campaigns. Why should we care so
much about candidates policing each other? We have a free press, so why
not leave it to the media? If the media does its job, there should be no
need for candidate negativity to hold candidates accountable. The problem is the evidence suggests the press cannot or at least does not effectively police candidates. The incentive structure for it to do so is lacking,
as we shall explain shortly. But before we begin taking on the press, let us
take a quick trip down memory lane, examining some reactions to negativity in recent campaigns.

Negativity: It's Always Getting Worse

Many have written about the public cynicism toward politics that appears
to be fed by negativity. And, of course, it is all but accepted wisdom in
American politics that voters dislike negative campaigning. Yet as we all
know, intense negativity characterized the 2012 election season. *Washington Post* columnist Dan Balz was led to write, "it will take time and great
effort for the winner to drain the poison from the system" (2012). What
Balz reflects, more than some zenith in attacks, is the well-worn tendency
to think every campaign is a new ratcheting up of negativity, that every
campaign is worse than the last. A few examples should make the point.

The 1988 presidential election, according to the *New York Times*, was
"by all indications, the nastiest Presidential race in memory" (Applebome 1988). Every presidential campaign since then has been decried as
the "most negative ever." The campaign of 1992, during which President
George Bush made the comment that opens this chapter, was called "the
nastiest Presidential campaign in recent history" in the *Los Angeles Times*
(Bailey and Stewart 1992). By 1996, observers were predicting intense
negativity right at the outset. Larry Sabato predicted the "the nastiest
Presidential campaign ever"; CNN anchor Bernard Shaw concurred, saying 1996 would be "one of the nastiest, bare-knuckled, direct-to-the-gut
campaigns in America's political history."[2]

In November 2000 the *Seattle Post-Intelligencer* called that year's campaign "one of the scruffiest, nastiest, silliest and most devoid of responsible content in recent memory."[3] Four years later, a *Los Angeles Times*
article titled "Campaigns Accentuate the Negative" opined that "attacks

by both parties have taken incivility to a new level this year . . . the result is a divisive climate in and out of politics" (Hook 2004). In 2008, writing for CNN, scholar Darrell West was especially unhappy with ads in which John McCain and Barack Obama kept repeating knowingly false claims about each other. West thought those ads had "reached all-time lows in the use of misleading and inaccurate political appeals." But lest we think this is only about presidential campaigns, midterm elections have been similarly perceived. For example, as the *New York Times* wrote about the 2006 campaign, "academics, political operatives, and their client candidates say a number of factors have all converged to make 2006 the nastiest election in the modern era" (Horrigan 2006).

Voters readily agree with these sentiments. In 1996 the Pew Research Center asked voters to consider the following: "compared to past elections, would you say there has been more mudslinging or negative campaigning this year, or less mudslinging or negative campaigning this year?"[4] Forty-nine percent said more while 36 percent said less; two years later, in the 1998 midterm, "more mudslinging" jumped to 68 percent, with only 20 percent disagreeing.[5] After a brief respite in 2000, a majority of voters in every major election (the even-numbered years from 2002 to 2012) answering Pew's question have said the current election was worse than the last.

How does the public respond to all this negativity? One consistent theme about the "most negative ever" claims is that they are seldom made from a neutral perspective about negativity. "By all indications, the nastiest Presidential race in memory will leave in its wake a problematic residue for whoever wins," wrote columnist Peter Applebome in 1988. That's not exactly what happened, though. By March 1989, after less than two months in office, President Bush's approval rating had risen to 63 percent positive, 13 percent negative; after one year in office (January 1990) it was 80 percent positive, 11 percent negative.[6] The public hardly seemed devastated by the negativity of the presidential campaign.

Why not? In retrospect, we know that elections after 1988 have had much higher percentages of negativity. Does this suggest that the public in 1988 was able to overcome the onslaught of negativity simply because there had been no onslaught? Probably not. An important part of Bush campaign's strategy required negative campaigning to convince voters that Massachusetts governor Michael Dukakis's crime policy was far more lenient than Bush's. Their tactics were quite memorable, and for televised presidential campaign ads, unique as far as we can tell. The campaign introduced Americans to Willie Horton, a convicted murderer in

Massachusetts who, after being given a weekend pass out of prison, "fled, kidnapping a young couple, stabbing the man and repeatedly raping his girlfriend."[7] While doing the research for this book, we watched a lot of negative ads from the 2012 presidential candidates—and to be sure, there were a lot of negative ads. In none of them did a voiceover use the phrase "stabbing the man and repeatedly raping his girlfriend."

And yet, in a sense, both the media and the public have been correct about increasing negativity, at least in terms of volume. Geer's (2012a) content analysis finds that, indeed, the share of negative advertising in presidential campaigns has been on the rise. Only 10 percent of ads were negative in 1960. By 1984 it was 30 percent, and rising to over 60 percent in 2008, though there was a slight decline in 2000. But there is only so far the candidates can go. You cannot get more negative than 100 percent, and by some metrics we are getting close. For instance, in the Florida Republican presidential primary of 2012, 92 percent of the ads aired in the final week were negative (Liptak 2012). In July 2012 89 percent of Obama's and 94 percent of Romney's ads were negative (Giroux 2012). At a minimum this should suggest that the positive/negative dichotomy does not help much in studying the differences between ads when virtually all ads are placed in the same category.

This also leads to a bit of a puzzle: if voters hate negative ads so much, why are we not seeing more positive ads? They would noticeably stand out from the negative backdrop and might in fact, be more memorable for it, thus possibly having more impact. Yet, apart from Ross Perot's ads in 1992 in which he spent most of his time looking under the hood of the American economy and presenting his ideas to get it running again, this has yet to happen.

For this Geer (2012a) holds the media at least partly responsible. He notes that news stories about ads tripled from 1984 to 2008, with about 80 percent of the focus on negative ads, and argues that "news media now cover negative ads so extensively that they have given candidates and their consultants extra incentive to produce and air them." An August 2012 Pew Research Center Project for Excellence in Journalism (2012a) study found that 71 percent of Romney's media coverage was negative to that point, while 72 percent was negative for Obama.[8] Similarly, Ridout and Smith (2008) find that positive ads are less likely to receive media coverage. So, in a sense, by focusing on negativity the campaigns are getting free advertising and the media is complicit.

Geer uses the attack ads run by Swift Boat Veterans for Truth against

John Kerry in the 2004 presidential election to illustrate his point. In these ads, Vietnam veterans challenge Kerry's honesty regarding his war record, questioning whether he was loyal and whether he deserved his war medals. The ads were only shown to one million viewers in three states, yet 80 percent of Americans saw or heard them. This leads Geer to argue that the increase in negative ads might not be because campaign consultants believe negative ads work "better" than positive ads (Iyengar 2011), and he notes that recent research has also not supported that widely held assumption (Fridkin and Kenney 2011; Lau et al. 2007). Instead, given that media coverage of an ad can massively multiply its effects, the real value in negativity may have become the attention that gets paid to it by the media. A result of this negative media coverage seems to be the development of highly negative character narratives about the candidates.

In this description of negativity about negativity there still is something missing—something we cannot get from coding ads (or portions of ads) simply as "positive" or "negative." The negative ads we remember are different from the ones we forget—perhaps more vicious, more sensationalistic, or more false. In 1988 there were plenty of other negative ads besides the Willie Horton ad. The Bush ad "Harbor" showed pictures of a polluted Boston Harbor, accusing Dukakis of lax environmental policy as Massachusetts governor. Dukakis's "Bay" ad criticized Bush's administration for cutting clean water spending. The Dukakis ad "Counterpunch" was negative about the negativity—it showed Dukakis turning off a television set that was showing a Bush negative ad.

Similarly, the Swift Boat Veterans ads were not the only attacks in 2004. Bush's entertaining "Windsurfing" ad is comparatively light-hearted. In the ad, John Kerry is shown windsurfing as Strauss's "The Blue Danube" waltz plays. The image flips directions as the voiceover lists Kerry's policy stances, such as "John Kerry voted for the Iraq War, opposed it, supported it, and now opposes it again . . . John Kerry—whichever way the wind blows."[9] Before drawing conclusions about negative campaigning as a whole, shouldn't we first consider why some of them tend to be viewed as more negative than others?

The Effects of Negativity: A Scholarly Perspective

In the early days of negativity research, Ansolabehere and Iyengar's book *Going Negative* (1995b) set the tone, as their experiments appeared to show that negative advertising is a dangerous tool—making voters upset and leading to decreased turnout. This finding was echoed by most commentators and set the research agenda. Studies of negative campaigning, for a time, focused heavily on the extent to which it depressed voter turnout, which, if true, would make the prospect of greater negativity in campaigns to be especially disconcerting.

But the results of later studies have been mixed. While Ansolabehere and Iyengar (1995a; see also Ansolabehere et al. 1994) concluded that negative campaigning decreases turnout, Wattenberg and Brians (1999) and Freedman and Goldstein (1999) determined that it increases turnout, and Finkel and Geer (1998) identified no consistent relationship between negative campaigning and turnout. Using Ansolabehere and Iyengar's data, Brooks (2006) found voters were resilient toward negativity, seeing no conclusive evidence that negative campaigning decreases turnout. Kahn and Kenney (1999) argued that "useful negative information" increases turnout, while "unsubstantiated and shrill attacks" decrease turnout. But Niven (2006) claimed that more informed voters are more likely to vote regardless of information tone. Mixed results indeed.

At one time, negative campaigning appeared to be a strategy used primarily by challengers facing advantaged incumbents or by candidates trailing badly in the polls—the implication in both cases being that negativity was caused by the lack of competition. Theilmann and Wilhite (1998) found that a candidate tends to go negative if behind or in a dead heat. Sigelman and Buell (2003) saw that in US presidential races, major-party tickets were far more attack-oriented if their election prospects looked bleak. In close elections, according to this theory, candidates would not take the risk of going negative. The perceived risk was voter backlash against the negative campaigner—voters siding with the attacked candidate over the attacker. Lau and Pomper (2004), however, showed that position in the polls does not affect a candidate's usage of negative strategies. And conventional wisdom about this has shifted more recently; the more common belief now is that in competitive elections, candidates who fail to "go negative" often lose. While it is true that candidates who are far ahead in the polls have little to gain from negative campaigning because the opponent is already poorly regarded, in competitive elections negative campaigning is more often viewed as a necessary strategy than as a last-ditch resort. This is not to say that backlash is nonexistent. Several studies have found instances of such backlash effects (Haddock and Zanna 1997; Houston, Doan, and Roskos-Ewoldsen 1999;

Kaid 1997; Pinkleton 1997) and others have shown that personal (defamatory) negative campaigns are more likely to backfire (Carraro and Castelli 2010; Fridkin and Kenney 2004).

Though the general view among scholars is that negativity is a serious problem, there has been dissent among those who focus specifically on campaign negativity, represented most notably by John Geer's 2006 book *In Defense of Negativity*. The main reason for defending negativity, he argues, it that negative campaigns provide meaningful information to voters. This viewpoint has slowly but steadily gained support. Rose (2012, 150) explains that negative ads "can improve the quality of our political conversation," and that the most effective negative ads are those that give information that differs the most from prior expectations, adding that "communication scholars note that entropic messages—ones that have a high amount of novel information and are unexpected—are more likely to be remembered than redundant messages that reinforce existing knowledge and are routine in their delivery. Negative ads exemplify entropic communication."

A third view on negative campaigning is that we lack proof that negativity has any impact at all. Most notably, a pair of meta-analyses of empirical studies of negative campaigning (Lau et al. 1999; Lau, Sigelman, and Rovner 2007) found no reliable statistical basis for concluding that negative ads are liked less than positive ones, or that negative political ads are more effective than positive political ads, or that negative campaigning affects voter turnout. The inconclusive results of these meta-studies should not be that surprising. As noted earlier, the definition of negative campaigning often used by political scientists has been "talking about an opponent." Even though negative ads vary greatly in content and tone, many researchers, when examining their effects, had tended to treat all negative ads as equal under this definition. To avoid this, Brader (2006) suggests that multiple aspects of negative advertisements may influence citizens, and thus every possible dimension of an ad must be studied. Several different means of distinction have been studied, such as separating ads that only discuss the opponent (negative ads) from those that talk about both candidates (contrast ads).

Another approach has been to separate ads into campaigning on political issues and campaigning on character traits (e.g., Brooks and Geer 2007; Min 2004). This difference is theoretically compelling since political issues, such as gun control and abortion, are generally represented by a left-right continuum (Poole and Rosenthal 1985), while character issues, such as honesty, competence, and leadership ability, are more typically represented by a valence dimension. A valence dimension measures an attribute on which all voters have the same preferences, generally preferring more to less (or vice versa). Adding a valence dimension to definitions of campaign discourse provides a simple means of separating political issues, on which voters have varied opinions, from character traits, about which voters' preferences essentially agree. Stokes (1992) shows that both left-right and valence dimensions are needed to accurately represent voters' preferences. Surveys suggest that voters can differentiate between attacks on an opponent's personal life and attacks on policy issues, and perceive attacks on a candidate's personal qualities as more negative than issue attacks (Jamieson 2000). Popkin (1991) argues that voters use personal information about a candidate as a proxy for information that is otherwise difficult to obtain—specifically, evidence regarding how that candidate might behave in office.

Fridkin and Kenney (2008, 2011) focus on another means to classify negative ads—by civility and relevance. They find that relevant, uncivil messages are the most effective (i.e., lead to the most negative views of the target), and especially effective with people with a low tolerance for negativity. Irrelevant messages, however, have no effect on evaluations of the targeted candidate, though they could possibly produce backlash for incumbents when both irrelevant and uncivil. Brooks and Geer (2007) tested negative ads using an experiment focusing on three dimensions: positive/negative, issue/personal, and civil/uncivil. Subjects were asked if the ads were informative and/or important. They found that people preferred issue-based ads to trait-based ads, whether they were positive, negative, civil, or uncivil. Uncivil negative ads about personal traits were received very poorly and accounted for much of that difference. At the same time, they found that incivility generally increased political interest without deleterious effects on political trust or efficacy. The authors, however, noted a study by Mutz and Reeves (2005) with a different result, that negativity lowers trust and efficacy.

While voters claim to dislike negative advertising, they may see value in the informational content of those ads and find positive ads to be less useful. In a recent blog posting drawing on data from an early 2012 Economist/Yougov poll, John Geer agrees—in keeping with the thesis reflected in this book and which we have been expressing in our own papers for some time—that voters key on the word "negative" rather than on negativity per se. He finds that ads that "show the differences between candidates on the issues" were judged by a majority (69%) as helpful. On the other hand, a majority deemed positive ads about a candidate's personality (69%) or "making broad claims about a candidates' future plans for governing" (71%) as not all that helpful, something we confirm in our own data (Geer 2012b). Sides, Lipsitz, and Grossmann (2010) also focuses on voters' responses to campaigns, rather than how the campaigns affect turnout or candidate evaluations. They asked people to rate the negativity and the usefulness of ads from the 2000 US presidential election and two 1998 gubernatorial races, and found that voters judge the tone of a campaign separately from the quality of the information it provides.[10] This is a key point for us: we will build on it by looking at how differences across campaign ad topics—rather than differences in tone—condition responses to negative ads.

Freedman, Wood, and Lawton (1999) along with Kahn and Kenney (1999) establish that what counts as negative may be more a matter of the topic of the attack than the existence of an attack itself. Some attacks are mudslinging (Kahn and Kenney 1999) and may turn voters off. These potentially include topics like a candidate's family (Freedman and Lawton 1999) or, more generally, are related to the relevance voters apply to the topic of the attack. Voters will accept topics they think will help them to diagnose the candidates' issue positions, effectiveness and potential behavior in office.

Daniel Stevens and his colleagues (Stevens et al. 2013) effectively reinforce these points, showing that voters' perceptions of the "fairness" of an attack plays an important role in whether the attack is considered to be legitimate. At the same time, Stevens et al. caution that the content of an ad is not the only factor voters take into account, and in fact partisan cues condition how voters perceive negativity, something we have consistently found in our own data. Maisel (2012) shows the difficulty in defining the line between civility and incivility—polarization, and viewing opponents as the enemy, makes it so supporters appreciate their own candidates' brand of incivility. In another paper, Stevens et al. (2008) argue that while negative campaigning mobilizes partisans, that if criticism of one's favored candidate is perceived as fair, or if one's own candidate uses an unfair attack, negative campaigns can be demobilizing.

One important topic in this litany of research that seems to be missing, however, is the extent to which voters perceive negative advertising to be accurate, to be telling the truth. As Geer (2006) shows, negative ads are on average much better documented than are ads that do not talk about an opponent. This rises from the belief that voters will discount negative ads unless they are convinced that they are accurate. Thus, citing sources for the claims in the ads is meant to get past this potential problem. But there seems to be little if any research on the degree to which voters find negative ad topics and the actual ads believable, and the extent to which perceptions of believability condition voters' responses to the ads. We hope to rectify that here.

An underlying assumption of much research in negativity is that candidates constrained to be only positive would have to focus on telling voters about what they would do in office, rather than attacking an opponent for what he or she did (or did not). Thus, the argument goes, voters would have better information on what to expect if any given candidate wins election. But of course, for that to actually work it would require that candidates who stay positive also stay truthful. This seems a pretty unlikely assumption to us, given what we know about human nature, and about the stakes in an election. The incentive to lie about oneself—to promise everything to everyone as Quintus Tullius Cicero urged his brother Marcus as he ran for Consul of Rome—would be rather overwhelming if there were no chance the lie would be exposed. But maybe even if candidates cannot attack, the media can, after a sort. That is, we should be able to count on a free media to do its part in ensuring that candidates stay on the straight and narrow by pointing out when they do not. Perhaps we should, but reality suggests otherwise.

The Media Watchdog: Why We Cannot Count on the Dog That Cannot Bark

In our view, negativity used by a candidate is a primary means by which opponents are held accountable for what they say and do. But, this need not be the only option for keeping candidates honest. Another force that might act as the arbitrator of candidate statements, by informing us when candidates lie, is of course the media. We refer here to the traditional "mainstream" media—those employing professional journalists trained in the traditions of reporting that seek to provide information to the public—as opposed to what we might call the "talking head media" which is more about opinion and persuasion.

Perhaps if the media would simply do their job we would have no need for candidates themselves to go negative. The media certainly play the role of voters' eyes and ears and, by choosing what news to present, interpret the campaign for the masses. With the exception of televised debates, and the occasional political rally, voters do not hear the candidates directly, but instead see and hear media reports discussing what the candidates said and did. Since the media's role is to monitor and report on the campaign, perhaps we should also expect the media to arbitrate, to tell us when candidates are telling the truth, when they are lying, and when they are simply failing to inform us at all.

Unfortunately, the weight of the evidence suggests the media are not terribly effective in this role of arbitrator of truth or as an information source for everything voters might need to learn. Rose (2012) illustrates this with an example from Canada in 2008 when Stephen Harper claimed an election was required to become prime minister rather than simply taking office upon being named leader of the majority party. This claim is actually false, but as Rose notes the media "were mostly silent" in correcting Harper, while a majority of voters believed his statement was true. As this was a question of fact about the Canadian electoral system, it seems to be an easy correction. But the media had failed to make the point. Rose suggests the problem is that because of the intense competition and the twenty-four-hour news cycle, the media emphasize events rather than substance. Campaigns, of course, spend a great deal of time on public relations; as a result the media spends much of its time covering these PR events rather than ferreting out new information or correcting errors.

Amber Boydstun's recent book tells a similar story, although she focuses on media coverage of issues (2013). While the media play a "watchdog" role, as she conceives it, this role entails informing the public on implications of policy that could be much like informing the public about candidates. However, and this is the key point, this watchdog role is easily interrupted when the media move into "alarm mode" in a scramble to cover breaking news stories, which then push other coverage out of the way, and shift the attention of the media as well as viewers. A media focused on alarms would have difficulty staying focused long enough to help voters disentangle truth from fiction.

We see four key reasons for this kind of media behavior. First, the political media are given other responsibilities besides correcting the record—such as reporting on the polls or speculating on the effectiveness of the candidates' campaigns. These competing tasks seem to shade campaign coverage so that it is not as unbiased as one might assume. Moreover, incentives for speed in media coverage may work against accuracy.

Second, it is difficult to call out a candidate for not telling the truth with-out, in some way, helping to disseminate the candidate's message. Third, as was evident in the 2012 presidential campaign, campaigns can and do ignore the media's attempts to fact-check them. Fourth, while voters say they are dubious about politicians, it turns out they may be more dubi-ous about the media. Public opinion polling has shown that media sources are not necessarily viewed by the public as especially trustworthy. We will take a look at each of these points in turn.

Does the Media Effectively Cover the Campaigns?

Our first point is that the media cast such a wide net that time spent fact-checking and filling information gaps can interfere with other goals. Even when covering political ads specifically, the media have a dual mandate—to report on both their effectiveness and accuracy. Pointing out an ad's in-consistencies while acknowledging its political appeal lessens the effect of the former (Min 2002). Part of the problem may be because media coverage of campaigns does not represent their nature particularly faith-fully. Rather than reporting on campaigns as they happen, many news-papers, television networks, and websites seem driven to sensationalize small things and to emphasize process over policy. Voters then get a dis-torted view of the candidates and the campaign.

A study of media coverage of the 1996 Republican presidential pri-mary campaign by Lichter and Noyes (2000) demonstrates this point quite effectively. They found that most of the information voters learned from the media came from media "talking heads" rather than the actual candidates, who got only one-sixth as much speaking time as the TV re-porters covering them. Maybe even more important is that the messages conveyed by news outlets emphasized candidate viability rather than sub-stantive issues and candidate traits. The media picked an early primary front-runner (Sen. Robert Dole) and then focused on controversies re-lated to the candidate or his staff, how his campaign was being run, and his personal behavior. Dole's news coverage became mostly negative, with only 32 percent of stories portraying him and his campaign positively. Typical criticisms of Dole were *not* that he would make a bad president, but instead that he was an unviable candidate and a poor campaigner.

Lichter and Noyes (2000) further argue that media incentives lead to campaign coverage that is an "exaggerated caricature of politics American-style." Their detailed analysis of candidate communications in the 1996 primary suggests that reality was quite different from what was presented. Unlike the news coverage, candidates' messages in the primary were not dominated by negativity, with candidates rarely mentioning opponents in speeches, and even more rarely making direct attacks. Instead, their typical messages—encompassing 80 percent of their speeches and ads—concerned policy issues, while media stories focused elsewhere. The point to be made here is that news media coverage tends toward overstatement, oversensationalism, and self-serving behavior with coverage of the campaigns.

In misrepresenting campaign reality, news outlets not only make candidates and campaigns seem more negative than they actually are, but they also distort their own ability to act as campaign watchdogs. Talking about the same 1996 primary campaign, Kann (1996) wrote in the *Wall Street Journal*, "As the public's umbilical cord to the political process, the mass media thrive on filtering out the all too rare nutrients in favor of the all too abundant junk food." Gresham's law, as reformulated by Popkin (1991), may be at work: new personal information (no matter whether truthful or not) drives out old impersonal information (including "facts"). Analyzing newsworthiness allows for sensationalized news, thus bringing in more viewers and readers. After all, conflicts, mistakes, drama, and surprise are more exciting and interesting for news consumers than speeches and the substance of issues. Moreover, media coverage of campaigns is often not focused on issues so much as on the horserace. As Wayne (2007) notes, campaign coverage from 1988–96 shows that "the only time when policy issues rise to public attention is when the race isn't close."

Perhaps even more problematic for accurate campaign coverage is that even the "traditional" media seem to be more interested in getting stories out first rather than getting them right. Three recent examples might suffice to explain why we are dubious about the media's ability to set the record straight. First, after a school shooting in Colorado, ABC News linked the killer to the Tea Party, based solely on finding someone with the same name on a Colorado Tea Party website (Wemple 2012). Their information was simply wrong. Second, both CNN and Fox News, in their rush to get the scoop on the Supreme Court's 2012 Obamacare ruling, got it very wrong despite having copies of the decision available to them. They both announced that the law had been declared unconstitutional and overturned; apparently they read the first sections of the ruling and extrapolated, but then later read the complete ruling and realized that they were incorrect (Blake 2012).

Third is an example of a much more common occurrence—the reporting of political rumors as newsworthy events not because the rumors
might be true, but because the rumors exist. This approach nicely skirts
the line between fact and fiction. On one hand, the media are reporting
truth, because it is true that the rumors exist. On the other hand, many
of the rumors turn out to be false, or cannot be proven one way or the
other. For instance, in the run-up to Republican challenger Mitt Romney's announcement of his vice-presidential pick, a number of sources
began reporting that former secretary of state Condoleezza Rice was
the leading candidate. Even reputable news sources took up this rumor,
dedicating to it significant amounts of air time in which Rice's creden-
tials were interspersed with speculation as to whether the rumor was true
(Hughes 2012). Such an approach has become commonplace—reporting
on a story and immediately afterword casting doubt upon the accuracy of
one's own report or the honesty of one's sources. In this particular case,
the story didn't come from multiple sources. It came from a single web-
page released by a single source (the Drudge Report) that vaguely cited
"sources." The mainstream media's online articles helpfully offered links
to Mr. Drudge's report but offered no corroboration of its accuracy.[11] In
fact, showing they did not really trust the Drudge Report, most generally
reported some level of skepticism (O'Connor and Murray 2012). A *New
York Times* article suggested that the rumor was a "trial balloon" released
to divert attention from Mitt Romney's history at Bain Capital (Shear
2012a). But this suggests the media were covering a rumor they thought
was probably false, mainly because they believed the Romney campaign
had released false information purposely in order to get the media to
cover it, and then, ironically, they spent more time covering it by covering their own coverage of it. Things can get confusing, and do so quickly.

While there is an ethic in journalism about playing it down the middle,
balancing coverage so that both sides are always represented in news stories, there is also evidence that editorial bias can creep into news coverage. While traditional television news has typically shied away from editorials expressing the outlet's opinion, newspapers virtually always provide
two types of information about candidates and campaigns: news stories
and editorials. For some voters it may be unclear what the difference is,
and others may simply assume that the editorial judgment of the newspaper drives news decisions and the ways in which news is written. While
newspapers deny that the editorial page influences the news pages, it is
not clear that this is the case. The last months of an electoral cycle see

editorial boards of newspapers, magazines, and other journalistic sources handing down endorsements. Once an editorial board has openly declared its support of a candidate, the coverage of that candidate and the opponent can shift markedly.

In a comprehensive study of two competing newspapers in the Minneapolis–St. Paul metropolitan area, Druckman and Parkin (2005) found that editorial slant—defined as "the quantity and tone of a newspaper's candidate coverage as influenced by its editorial position"—was a significant factor in the formation of and shaping of voter opinion. In the 2000 Minnesota Senate campaign, once the *Star Tribune* and the *Pioneer Press* decided on their editorial stance on the race, editorial bias began to show in noneditorial news pieces. The *Star Tribune* not only became more positive in its news coverage of its endorsed candidate, but also much less negative in its news coverage of him compared to his opponent. In the *Star Tribune*, the unendorsed Republican candidate Rod Grams received only 14 percent positive coverage while incumbent Democrat Mark Dayton, whom the newspaper endorsed, received 47 percent positive coverage. But, in the *Pioneer Press*, which endorsed Grams, 26 percent of coverage was positive toward Grams while 33 percent of coverage was positive toward Dayton. Druckman and Parkin found evidence that this shift influenced voters. Those who read the *Star Tribune* gave Dayton significantly higher evaluations than those who read the *Pioneer Press*.

This impact of media editorial bias on the electorate does not stop at newspaper coverage. In a study on the impact of Fox News on voting behavior, DellaVigna and Kaplan (2007) found that viewing Fox News significantly affected presidential vote share in 1996 and 2000, with the Republican Party gaining a 0.4–0.7 percent increase in votes in areas that broadcast the channel. They estimate this resulted in an additional 200,000 votes for Republicans nationwide. They further estimated that 3–8 percent of viewers were convinced by Fox News to vote Republican. The source of editorial slant in Fox News is their primetime programming. Much like the editorial staff of a newspaper, pundits like Bill O'Reilly and Sean Hannity disseminate not only news but also their interpretation of and their analysis of said news. Just as with newspapers, pundits' editorial slant sneaks into regular news coverage, giving Fox News a conservative tilt.

Whether or not editorial slant in newspapers and television media is a conscious effort on the part of networks or a subconscious manifestation of the editorial process is often unclear. Kahn and Kenney (2002) speculate that the way that newspapers are organized could be the cause of editorial bias. They describe reporters as "employees of complex organizations who see their [articles] go through layers of editors" and deem it "inevitable that the views of the editors will shape the content of the news." They also posit that news outlets hire reporters who share the political views of the editors that work for their organization. These reporters are more likely to be satisfied with their jobs and more successful than they would be at outlets where they do not share the same views as the editors and, as a result, a majority of their coworkers.

While there are many reasons to be concerned about the accuracy and quality of campaign coverage, voters may also get a less-than-complete understanding of the campaign no matter how careful the coverage. Voters cannot really rely on the media to discuss the things the candidates are *not* saying. Candidates know more about their opponents than does anyone else, even the denizens of the press. This suggests it is candidates who can present a better case as to why the opponent should not be elected, bringing to light information that might otherwise not be part of the media's campaign coverage.

An example comes from the 2012 Republican primaries. In December 2011 Newt Gingrich was ahead in the national polls and was emerging as the primary challenger to Mitt Romney, the favorite to win the nomination. Due to his rapid ascent in the polls and well-received debate performances, the coverage of Gingrich was very positive.[12] After a strong debate in Iowa, an ABC pundit went so far as to call him "the inevitable nominee" (Ward 2011).

Meanwhile, the Romney campaign was attempting to give people a different take on the story, running an ad called "Smiling." The ad started with a picture of Obama grinning. "Why is this man smiling?" asks the voiceover. "Because his plan is working," it says. "Brutally attack Mitt Romney and hope Newt Gingrich is his opponent." "Newt has a lot of baggage," the ad goes on, and then proceeds to attack Gingrich for the rest of the ad, noting "the fact that Gingrich was fined $350,000 for ethics violations," and "that he took at least $1.6 million from Freddie Mac just before it helped cause the economic meltdown" (Friedman 2012).

While Romney ran the "Smiling" ad—and later, a similar ad for the Florida primary entitled "Happy"—the media's main "criticism" of Gingrich was an allegation by Gingrich's ex-wife that he had wanted an open marriage. In a South Carolina debate, the moderator's first question asked Gingrich about this. "I am appalled that you would begin a presidential debate on a topic like that," said Gingrich.[13] "Every person in here has had someone close to them go through painful things. To take an ex-wife and make it two days before a primary a significant question in a presidential campaign is as close to despicable as anything I can imagine." We agree, and would add that the chance of the first question in that debate being about ethics violations was virtually zero.

Many of Romney's arguments in the ads against Gingrich—accurate or not—were old news and probably less interesting fodder for a media report. But from Romney's perspective, why would he just sit back and allow the media to shower his opponent with accolades? Shouldn't voters be able to hear the other side—why they might not like Gingrich—and then decide for themselves? Who else was going to bring it up? If voters can rely only on media to report campaigns and to provide information, they are likely to get a biased view of the campaign, focused on much more on trivia than important issues, and potentially even biased coverage in favor of one candidate or the other. Overall, media limits on campaign coverage suggest a first reason why we cannot rely on political media to solve problems of campaign information and candidate accountability.

Do Fact-checks Effectively Counter Candidate Claims?

This is not to say that the media make no attempt to hold candidates accountable. Some outlets are quite focused on candidate accountability and provide fact-checking of both candidates' statements and advertisements. Broadly speaking, fact-checking is the attempt to assess the veracity of statements made by politicians, campaigns, and other public individuals and includes pointing out factual errors, lies, misconceptions, and misstatements, with a goal of holding them accountable. One of the first broad, consistent national efforts was Factcheck.org, from the Annenberg School at the University of Pennsylvania. During the 2012 presidential campaign many media operations such as CNN and the *New York Times* ran their own extensive fact-checks. The most prominent of these were the *Washington Post* and PolitiFact, which is run by the *St. Petersburg Times*.

PolitiFact, whose slogan is "sorting out the truth in politics," won a Pulitzer Prize for national reporting in 2009.[14] They label politicians' statements and campaign ads on a five-point scale from "true" and "mostly true" to "mostly false," "false," and "pants on fire." For 2012 PolitiFact

teamed up with National Public Radio to create "The Message Machine."[15] Their goal was to fact-check as many statements and ads as possible from the campaigns, both nationally and for states where they had
newspaper affiliates. By the end of the campaign season, the resulting
website had seventeen pages of fact-checks, representing about 340 specific examinations. These were not only featured on the web but printed
in newspaper affiliates and the subject of many stories on NPR radio
programs.

The *Washington Post*, similarly, used a system of "Pinocchios" rating
the 2012 presidential candidates' statements and advertisements, and
awarding them from one to four Pinocchios, with four being the worst.
Their "Pinocchio tracker" web application provided average scores for
each candidate over a combined 250 examinations. The *Post*'s rating system was prominently featured in a December 2011 Republican presidential primary debate in New Hampshire. Newt Gingrich, commenting on
the *Post*'s rating of one of Mitt Romney's negative ads, said, "One of the
ads got four Pinocchios from the *Washington Post*. Now, to get four Pinocchios in a 30-second ad means there's virtually nothing accurate."[16]
The less you know about politics, the more bizarre the quote sounds. Gingrich's lines at once combine the boldness of addressing an opponent's
lies with the absurdity of men arguing about Pinocchios.

Are Pinocchios and flaming pants convincing to voters? Newt Gingrich's statement actually provides anecdotal evidence that they are—he
is a veteran politician and presumably would not have brought it up if
he did not believe voters would find it convincing. However, there is no
general consensus among researchers as to whether fact-checks can successfully change voters' opinions. One problem is that "false facts" are resilient. As Nyhan (2010) discusses, misinformation is difficult to correct,
even with new information that is based on fact. Simply put, partisans
have a tendency to reject inconvenient truths (Redlawsk 2002; Redlawsk,
Civettini, and Emmerson 2010; Taber and Lodge 2006). So fact-checks
have one strike against them right from the beginning. Moreover, effectiveness varies depending upon the competence of the fact-checker.
Strong, critical commentary can help undermine an ad's justification (Jamieson and Capella 1997). However, the dubious practice of replaying
an advertisement in full prior to critiquing it tends to amplify rather than
counteract its effect (Ansolabehere and Iyengar 1995b). And, perhaps
ironically, fact-checking means the media focus almost exclusively on
negative ads, which are, first, more interesting, and, second, more likely to

carry actual information that can be checked (Geer 2006). And so, it may be that fact-checking encourages negativity in an odd way.

Can Fact-checks Censor Candidate Claims?

In any case, we might think that given the substantial effort undertaken by numerous fact-checking organizations and the popularity they seem to be enjoying, that lies and misstatements in politics and campaigning would be less prevalent. The reality is that candidates still consider such tactics to be viable, and it is a rarity for candidates to retract ads in response to fact-checks. Some examples from the 2012 presidential campaign—probably the most "fact-checked" in history—should drive home the point.

In August 2012 Mitt Romney's presidential campaign released an advertisement containing a clip of President Barack Obama saying, "If we keep talking about the economy, we're going to lose." This quotation was taken out of context; the full statement was in fact a charge made by Obama against the *McCain* campaign in 2008, and had nothing to do with 2012. The full Obama quote read: "Senator McCain's campaign actually said, and I quote, 'If we keep talking about the economy, we're going to lose.'" Fact-checkers went wild over the advertisement, calling it a lie (e.g., a "pants-on-fire" rating from PolitiFact), showing exactly why it was factually inaccurate, and telling the public that the Romney campaign had taken great liberties with video and sound editing. And yet the effect of such efforts was that the media brought massive attention to the ad and got the public talking about the economy (Cooper 2012). Romney pollster Neil Newhouse commented in a discussion before the Republican National Convention that the Romney campaign was "not going to let our campaign be dictated by fact-checkers," charging that fact-checkers were biased and brought their own worldviews into their business, and as such could not be trusted (Smith 2012).

Both the Romney and Obama campaigns generally ignored fact-checkers, putting out messages and sticking with them no matter how factually accurate or inaccurate they were deemed. And the public responded predictably. No real measure of outrage was seen over the candidates' blatant lies, not when the Romney campaign released the above-mentioned advertisement, nor when vice presidential candidate Paul Ryan's Republican National Convention speech was fact-checked and found to have been "an apparent attempt to set the world record for the greatest number of blatant lies and misperceptions slipped into a single political speech" (Blow 2012), nor when president Obama was blasted for his claim that Governor Romney had called Arizona's immigration law a model for the entire nation.[17]

After it was all over, PolitiFact designated a late-campaign Romney commercial the "Lie of the Year." This ad, running in Ohio in the closing days of the campaign, claimed Obama had "sold Chrysler to the Italians" and that the company was moving its Jeep production to China (Holan 2012). PolitiFact called it "brazenly false." PolitiFact also in effect took credit for challenging it, arguing that Romney paid a price for the ad as "a flood of negative press coverage rained down on the Romney campaign, and he failed to turn the tide in Ohio, the most important state in the Presidential election." True enough, but the most persuasive challenger was the actual target of the attack—not Barack Obama, but Chrysler Chairman and CEO Sergio Marchionne, in sharp refutation, wrote, "I feel obliged to unambiguously restate our position: Jeep production will not be moved from the United States to China. . . . We also are investing to improve and expand our entire U.S. operations, including our Jeep facilities. . . . It is inaccurate to suggest anything different."[18]

The Chrysler ad is more of a unique success story rather than a prevailing trend of the truth winning out. Most often, campaigns stick with demonstrably false attacks in part because the attacks might work and because the fact-checking only serves to spread the message they want to spread. Even in Ohio—where perhaps fact-checking played a role— there is actually little evidence that Romney was making gains before the ad aired. More likely, the ad just failed to be effective. This point of view was in fact supported by Romney campaign aides, who generally stood behind their ads as powerful types of "new" information, and seemed pleased that the fact-checking meant more people would hear the claims (Smith 2012).[19] On the other hand, if making Jeeps in China was the worst lie of the entire presidential campaign, American society is hardly threatened by the scourge of negative campaigning. Evidently, candidates' lies are kept *somewhat* in check; it certainly would be worse without the candidates monitoring each other via negative campaigning, but better if we had a reliable and trusted independent monitor.

Extensive fact-checking, rather than setting the record straight in the minds of voters, often seems instead to introduce another area for partisan disagreement. For a partisan, fact-checkers are to be cited when they agree with your candidate and debunked when they do not. Fact-checking the fact-checkers has become a new trend, where ideologically partisan groups defend their own candidates by questioning the accuracy of the original fact-check (Cooper 2012). For example, Senate Majority Leader Harry Reid claimed at one point that Romney paid no income taxes for ten years, but offered no proof. Understandably, PolitiFact rated this as a "pants-on-fire" lie. For this supposed slight, liberal-leaning website Daily Kos took them to task in a post entitled "Proving the Incompetence of PolitiFact." The author declared that PolitiFact's assessment was made rashly, and that they failed to consider what he claims were key pieces of information.[20]

As Cooper (2012) notes in the *New York Times*, the advent of partisan fact-checkers has turned the fact-checking endeavor into a mere opinion statement, where partisans on both sides view claims against their own campaigns to be opinions of the fact-checkers while they actively embrace criticisms of opposing campaigns. The effectiveness of fact-checking appears to have become so diluted that nonpartisan media sources and campaigns accord them little respect. Fact-checking has sadly failed to provide for Americans a legitimate source of truth in politics and campaigning, and has instead served to give the appearance that truth is subjective. No watchdog can be effective when it is so easily and readily dismissed by the public. And one reason it may be so easily dismissed is that the public does not necessarily trust the "media" to be unbiased any more than it trusts the candidates themselves, as we will discuss below.

One final example serves here, that of Republican vice-presidential candidate Paul Ryan's national convention speech. The fact-checking of his speech was intense, yet the impact appeared negligible outside of the media doing the fact-checking. Reading the fact-checks (and the stories about the fact-checks) leaves one with a sense that the writers were busy patting themselves on the back for taking on Ryan's speech. Apparently the general feeling was that since Ryan's lies were particularly egregious, and that on the previous day the Republicans dedicated an entire day to an out-of-context Obama quote, the media was to be congratulated for pointing out all of this. But of course, that simply leads to the question of why then? That is, why did the media suddenly become so fact-oriented? As they appeared to single out Ryan, one could understand why it appeared to Republicans as a coordinated mainstream media attack.[21] So if candidates ignore fact-checks, and voters seem immune to them, how can we expect them to serve the purpose of holding candidates accountable? The answer (that suggests itself) is that we simply cannot expect media fact-checks to effectively alert voters to the mendaciousness of candidates, at least not without simply further spreading the lies.

Public Perceptions Limit Effectiveness of the News Media

Even as it engages in fact-checking, the media cannot act as a legitimate watchdog if those whom it serves do not trust it or perceive it as biased. The rise of "talking-head" media, which is the television equivalent of the newspaper editorial page magnified a thousand times over, has left people unsure of the intent of news media generally. When an organization like Fox News, which has clearly become a part of the Republican political effort, has as its slogan "Fair and Balanced," and once ran a promotion entitled "We Report, You Decide," what are citizens to think about the media as a whole? Likewise, on the left, MSNBC—clearly aligned with Democratic political efforts—even includes "NBC" as part of its name, suggesting that NBC News—a traditional mainstream news operation— may also be subject to bias. A recent Gallup poll found that a vast majority of Americans see the media as ideologically biased, with only 36 percent of respondents saying that the media are neither too conservative nor too liberal.[22]

Thus it may not be surprising that public opinion of news media has steadily declined over the last decade. In a September 2012 Gallup poll, 60 percent of Americans answered "not very much/none at all" when asked how much trust and confidence they have in mass media.[23] Averaging across thirteen news outlets, a Pew survey found that the percentage of people who believe "all or most" of what the organizations say fell fifteen points from 2002 (71%) to 2012 (56%).[24] Some of the most watched and most circulated news outlets—MSNBC, the *New York Times*, Fox News, and *USA Today*—rank the lowest in believability ratings.

That the mass media are losing the trust of the American people heavily impedes any ability to act as a watchdog in political campaigns. An effective watchdog is one that provides a fair and unbiased evaluation of a candidate, accurately reports on campaigns, and is not beholden to outside influences. And yet a 2011 Pew Research Center poll evaluating public criticism of the press found the public's perception of the media is that their stories are inaccurate (66% of respondents), tend to favor one side (77% of respondents), and are often influenced by powerful people or organizations (80% of respondents).[25] Compared to 1985, these numbers have jumped dramatically from 34 percent, 53 percent, and 53 percent, respectively. While a vast majority of online news consumers (74%) say that they would rather visit party-neutral Internet sources than ones that have a partisan tilt, the evidence shows that many believe neutral sources are increasingly difficult to find. Even more damning is sentiment that the press actually *hurts* (42%) rather than protects (42%) democracy, which has steadily risen since 1985.[26] These polls paint the picture of a general public that is confused over what the media do or are trying to do, which is especially difficult to ascertain when a news anchor opines about the lack of honesty, and then kicks it over to a colleague in the "spin room."

In sum, attempts to fact-check often seem to backfire—or at least to be ignored by candidates—perhaps in part because of the public's view that the media is not an independent force striving for a strong democracy, but is instead a haven of biased talking heads and reporters who express their point of view regardless of the facts. There is little doubt that talking heads, whose job is commentary rather than news, have become the literal face of television media.

Yet traditional news-gathering organizations still adhere to a basic tenet of ethical reporting that requires them to attempt to fairly report the facts allowing readers to decide on their own. This ethic of balance, ironically, is what historically limited fact-checking efforts, and even now leads reporters to create potentially false equivalencies. If one side says the same thing 800 times but it is clearly false, the traditional media will report it but will "balance" that report with at least one example of dishonesty from the other side, no matter how much they must stretch to do so. James Bennet notes this in his *Atlantic* column of August 28, 2012, when he writes, "Critics have for many years inveighed against 'false equivalence' or 'false balance' in the mainstream press." And for many years, he says, the media have resisted change to this ethic, generally for good reason, since belief in the media requires that people trust it to be telling things "the way they are." Bennet points out that 2012 may represent a sea change, with the fact-check no longer being relegated to the editorial pages.

But given that fact-checks themselves are being contested, this may simply add to the public concern about an even-handed media. We cannot expect the public to view the news stories as unbiased if the stories seem to take a position. And this is the rub, since at the same time the old ethic of balance seems to suggest that each side is equally bad, when in fact that may not be the case. The media are damned if they do and damned if they don't.

Conclusion

The preceding litany of complaints is not simply an opportunity for us to express frustration with the media. Indeed, we would argue that for the most part the news media do a pretty good job of informing Americans about their choices in high-profile elections. That information may be intentionally or unintentionally biased, but most *journalists* take their role seriously and strive to do the right thing. Our point is simply that there are practical and structural reasons that we cannot simply assume that the media can effectively play the role of watchdog alone, alerting us any time a candidate fails to tell the truth. In a world where candidates are unable to go negative, and hence police each other, we would be left with either a hobbled media voters do not trust or, more likely, no one policing the large majority of what candidates would say about themselves. Instead, we argue, limitations of the media mean that in the world in which we operate, candidates themselves must be allowed to play the watchdog role by going negative, by telling voters the things their opponents won't say about themselves and further acting as a potential check on any mendacity by the opponent in presenting his or her own resume to voters.

The point we make here is not that the media cannot help in holding candidates accountable, but that structure and incentives make it less likely than we might expect that they will do so effectively. So if we ban candidates from going negative, voters will have to count on a media that may not be a reliable source. Traditional media are challenged by an ethic of fairness, that they must play things down the middle rather than take one side or the other. Clearly stated criticism of candidates presents the difficulty of appearing to choose sides. Given the limitations of the media, candidates themselves may be the best source of information about each other. Sometimes the information they possess is passed along to friendly media sources that then help spread it. However, much of the time it is best done directly through advertising. Whichever the case, candidates are usually the impetus and are probably best suited to draw comparisons with their opponents, so it makes sense for voters to look to them for information. After all, voters know more or less for certain the biases inherent in candidates' communications, and they can make appropriate assessments of the information they receive. This is simply not true for media sources, where biases may be less obvious. And even where media biases are obvious, their incentives may be less so. There is nothing clearer than the incentive of a political candidate.

But of course, this means candidates must be able to talk about each other. When they do, however, it is unlikely they will say "my opponent is a good man" very often. We are left with a trade-off related to Geer's (2006) argument—negative ads provide information that otherwise would not be in the environment, information that is important and even diagnostic for voters. But if voters really hate negativity, if they tune it out, and simply refuse to consider it, what are we left with? To get that important information, voters must endure negative campaigns. And if more information—at least more *relevant* information—is to be preferred to less, then negativity is the price of that additional information. But it is only a price if voters truly are negative about negativity. The more accepting the general public, the more effective negative campaigning can be in both its informational value and its ability to keep politicians "honest" about themselves. We begin to explore this point in depth in the next chapter.

CHAPTER THREE

What Do Voters Think?

Social Desirability and Attitudes about Negativity

I love negative ads. When I see a positive ad, even one from a candidate I support, my re-action often ranges from bored to annoyed.—Paul Begala, "Why We Need Negative Political Ads" (2012)

As we described in chapter 2, the literature on negative campaign-ing is as voluminous as it is inconclusive. At the same time there seems to be no avoiding the accumulation of evidence that voters do not like negative campaigning, given the consistent opposition they express in surveys. In this chapter we begin to challenge that evidence as part of our larger argument that negativity plays an important and valuable role in political campaigns. Maybe one of the reasons politicians stick with nega-tivity is that they understand voters are not as turned off by it as the polls appear to show and pundits seem to assume. Either surveys asking vot-ers about negative campaigns are not really tapping their true feelings, or political strategists are getting it wrong. Given the incentive for political campaigns to use strategies that work and to abandon those that do not, it seems worth investigating the extent to which our assumptions about vot-ers and negativity are incorrect.

We think a great deal of the public's apparent distaste is an artifact of the survey questions they are asked. It may be that negativity persists at least in part because voters are not really all that bothered by it and do not really care if it continues. Or maybe they do care when asked in sur-veys, but at the same time incorporate the information into their decision-making. The typical survey questions about negative advertising—asking voters if they approve of "personal attacks," "negative campaigning," or "negative advertising"—are unlikely to properly tap attitudes towards both the *content* and *effect* of negativity. Instead, we argue these questions tap a reaction to the very words "negative" and "attack." Including these words in survey questions makes supporting such tactics inherently unappealing—how many people are eager to say that they approve of something that seems so socially unacceptable?

The studies we present in this chapter show that while large majorities of voters appear to oppose "negative campaigning," voters respond much more favorably when asked in a neutral way about the basic *activity* of negative campaigning as generally operationalized by political scientists—talking about an opponent. Voters not cued with the term "negative" are far less likely to be angered by the idea of advertisements about an opponent. When given the opportunity to define the tactic of talking about an opponent as negative, voters' opinions are more nuanced than most research suggests—they consistently rate some topics as more negative than others. There is little strong opposition to a candidate talking about an opponent on "legitimate" topics such as issues, prior record, or experience. But, voters are in fact negative about negativity when they believe it goes too far, such as commenting about an opponent's family or religion.

Negative Responses to Negative Questions

A great deal of evidence has accumulated in the survey research literature that respondents can be subject to *social desirability biases* under certain circumstances. When confronted with questions that have a clear socially "correct" answer, respondents may give an interviewer that answer rather than one that represents the respondent's actual belief. This phenomenon results in data that are systematically biased toward respondents' perceptions of what attitudes are socially acceptable (Maccoby and Maccoby 1954). Berinsky (1999, 2002) cogently argues that individuals are often not willing to give answers that appear to violate social norms, pointing out that "it is plausible that under circumstances where respondents fear they might be 'censured' or socially shunned for their attitudes . . . they might shade those attitudes when reporting them to the interviewer" (1999). In political science research, social desirability bias has been shown not only in reference to racial attitudes (Kuklinski, Cobb, and Gilens 1997; Redlawsk, Tolbert, and Franko 2010; Sniderman, Crosby, and Howell 2000), where most work has been focused, but also concern-

ing attitudes toward the possibility of a female president (Heerwig and
McCabe 2009; Streb et al. 2008), as well as over reporting of voter turnout (Karp and Brockington 2005). Other research has shown that respondents may adjust their answers based upon perceived characteristics of a
telephone interviewer, such as responding differently to male and female
interviewers when asked about gender-related issues (Durrant et al. 2010;
Kane and Macauley 1993).

In a similar vein, it may be that voters have been cued to say they dislike negative campaigning in an almost knee-jerk way, especially considering that the terms "negative campaigning" and "positive campaigning"
use adjectives that sound like value judgments. As we noted earlier, there
are few voices that speak up in favor of negativity. Certainly, pundits and
scholars have been more likely than not to tell us, repeatedly, that negative campaigning is bad. Thus the use of the very phrase "negative campaigning" or its variants may trigger something like a social desirability
effect because respondents know negative campaigning is something they
simply should not like. Most attempts to tap public opinion about negativity in campaigns do so using questions that appear on their face to be
biased—and thus very likely to elicit exactly the kind of disdain prevalent
in the political environment. Given this, it is no surprise that voters say
they dislike negative campaigning.

We also know that small changes in question wording can produce big
changes in supposed public opinion. For many years one of the most intense debates in voter decision-making was the extent to which voters had
become ideological. *The American Voter* (Campbell et al. 1960) found that
very few voters were making voting decisions on the critical issues of the
day, while Nie, Verba, and Petrocik (1976) reported evidence to the contrary. For our purposes the debate itself is not the important point. What
is important is that the American National Election Study, the underlying data from which these conclusions were drawn, made a significant
change in how issue questions were worded in 1964 and subsequent surveys. Bishop, Tuchfarber, and Oldendick (1978) show that much—if not
all—of the increase in voter ideological constraint was due to the changes
in question wording and response options. Weissman and Hassan (2005)
examined a range of public opinion polls on campaign finance and found
that changes in question wording created very different responses; many
other studies show similar effects (e.g., Rasinski 1989). The key problem
they identify is the challenge of asking neutral questions so that respondents are not pushed in one direction or another. It seems quite clear to

us that questions in which the word "negative" is used to assess attitudes toward campaigning against an opponent do exactly this, activating something akin to a social desirability effect, resulting in the near-universal dislike expressed in polls.

In this chapter we work to disentangle the rhetoric of negativity from the actual nature of negative campaigning. We measure response to negative advertising by altering the question wording typically used in assessing the public's tolerance of negativity. Our goal is to identify actual voter attitudes toward the *activity* of negative campaigning, as opposed to attitudes toward the *phrase* "negative campaigning." We employ three survey experiments to test our argument about how citizens view negativity.[1]

For these experiments, we adopt the well-established idea that negative campaigning is providing information about an opponent. While there have been many attempts to define "negative campaigning" and "negative advertising" (see Geer and Lipsitz 2013; Lau et al. 1999) the most often used definition of negative campaigning is "campaigning against an opponent," usually operationalized as *any* mention of an opponent in a candidate's ads, literature, or speeches—in other words, talking about an opponent. It seems obvious that no candidate will speak positively about an opponent, at least in paid advertising. In an exception that proves the rule, one report of the 2006 David Loebsack congressional campaign (IA-2) described in chapter 1 (Simon 2006) found the statement "[Loebsack's opponent] Jim Leach is a good man" unusual enough to overlook the remainder of the ad, even though what follows the statement are dark and grainy images of Leach while the announcer says, "we cannot afford to support him anymore."

Our expectation in these survey experiments is that we will find a significant increase in support for talking about an opponent when the concept is presented without socially undesirable phrases like "negative campaigning" embedded in the question. We do not expect people to reject a candidate providing information about an opponent in the same way they do "negative campaigning." After the initial study, where we test this basic premise, in study 2 we expand our assessment of negativity to address specific topics. Here we expect to find that the topics covered in campaign ads matter. Voters should recognize that some topics are fair game for attacking an opponent, but that others are much less so.

Finally, in study 3 we expand on the question of appropriate topics with another survey experiment examining in more detail the *types* of topics voters find acceptable. If citizens are not all that concerned about negativity *per se*, despite the seemingly national obsession with it in every election cycle, maybe it's because they simply expect it in many cases and are fine with that. But as Kahn and Kenney (1999) have pointed out, certain topics may go beyond the pale and into what they call mudslinging, in which cases voters may in fact be turned off.[2]

Data Sources

All three of the survey experiments discussed in this chapter were embedded in larger surveys. Study 1 was part of a national election survey fielded during October and early November 2008 by the University of Iowa Hawkeye Poll. This survey included both a pre-election random sample of 1,666 registered voters and a post-election panel back to a subset of these respondents. All of the questions we use in this analysis were part of the pre-election data collection. The full survey asked the usual range of questions about the upcoming election, including vote preference, awareness of and interest in the campaign, and political issues. The negative campaigning questions were asked around the middle of the survey, after vote intention and issue questions, and before awareness and information sources. The survey included an average of just over fifty respondents per day and was in the field for thirty-three days to examine the dynamics of the election campaign in its last month. Date of data collection does not interact with any of the variables in which we are interested here.

The second survey experiment, study 2, was fielded in October 2009, just ahead of the New Jersey gubernatorial election, with a random telephone sample of 903 registered voters from the state of New Jersey. The study was fielded by the Eagleton Center for Public Interest Polling, as part of a regular Rutgers-Eagleton Poll from October 10–15, and was primarily designed to capture vote intentions in the election for governor. Our questions came in the last third of the survey, immediately after a series on attitudes toward political corruption. While not a national survey, the New Jersey study was our first effort to examine how specific topics affect the way voters respond to negativity. A second key difference between study 1 and study 2 is that the first survey assumed a definition of negativity drawn from the literature—the idea that it is inherently negative to talk about one's opponent—while the second allowed a random subset of respondents to decide for themselves whether some types of advertisements would in fact be considered "negative."

As an extension to the previous two studies, we placed a third series of questions on a national Internet survey through the 2010 Cooperative Congressional Election Study (CCES). As with the second telephone survey, study 3 allowed voters to determine negative topics themselves. The survey questions capture three stages of decision-making: cognition (whether the ads are believable), affect (whether the ads anger them), and behavior (whether the ads would impact their voting decision). The sections of the three surveys that are relevant to these analyses are provided in an online appendix accessible at http://www.press.uchicago.edu/sites/mattes/.[3]

Study 1: Negative about Negativity

The Survey

The 2008 national pre-election survey (study 1) included two key questions of interest. The first asked respondents to indicate how angry they would be if a candidate began to use negative campaigning. For a random half of respondents, the question contained the phrase "negative campaigning," while for the other half the phrase was not included. The first question read (with the words in italics removed for half of the sample):

> How would you feel if a political candidate *began to use negative campaigning, that is,* began to run ads to give you information about what his opponent had done in office? Would you feel very angry, somewhat angry, not very angry, or not at all angry?

This question format provides us with a simple yet clear test of the power of the phrase "negative campaigning" to condition affective responses to the issue.

The second question then asked both groups (again, the italicized words were removed for the group not primed to think of negative campaigning):

> What if these ads, *while negative,* told the truth about the opponent? Would these ads be much more acceptable, somewhat more acceptable, or no more acceptable than other *negative* ads about an opponent?

We postpone discussion of this second question until chapter 6 when we consider the issue of truth and falsehood in depth and the impact of mendacity on how voters perceive ads.

Let us reinforce the very simple idea behind study 1. Both forms of the first question make clear that we are talking about giving information about an opponent's performance in office. But only one version labels this as "negative campaigning." The same is true about the second question probing support for truthful information about an opponent. Only one version of the question explicitly uses the phrase "negative campaigning." We are interested in whether this simple wording change has the effects we expect by removing the cue that respondents are supposed to think of this activity as negative.

As we noted briefly in chapter 1, we chose to ask about "anger" as the affective response to negativity. There are many other emotions we could have chosen, both positive and negative, but space and time (of course) precluded us from doing so. Moreover, we were not particularly interested in finding out if people had positive responses to negativity; given the prevailing wisdom of pundits and scholars it seemed more important to investigate negative responses. Alternative negative emotions we might have examined include anxiety, a response to negative stimuli over which one feels little control and which appears to motivate the anxious person to learn more (Marcus, Neuman, and MacKuen 2000), or fear, a negative emotion that usually has a specific referent and can generate a fight-or-flight response.[4] Specific negative messages could attempt to instill anxiety or fear in voters, but it seems less likely that either would be the dominant generalized response to negative campaigning. Anger, according to Ortony, Clore, and Collins (1988), focuses on others' actions and violations of expectations and norms. The rhetoric surrounding negativity seems very much about violating some "clean campaigning" norm and, as such, suggests anger as a likely response on the part of voters subjected to it. Thus, we use anger throughout our studies as the emotional response we attempt to assess.

Results

As figure 3.1 shows, voters explicitly asked about "negative campaigning" respond as expected, with nearly 64 percent at least somewhat angry with a candidate employing negativity. Using this form of the question— which represents the typical question format in most research—voters are in fact quite negative about negativity even though we do not provide them with much context or detail about the nature of the negativity. We simply suggest that giving "information about what his opponent had

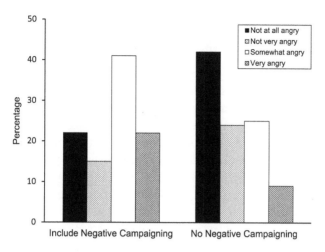

Figure 3.1. Anger toward negative campaigning by explicit use of "negative campaigning," Study 1

done in office" is inherently negative through the wording of the question. And for the most part voters agree, reacting negatively toward such campaigning.

However, these attitudes change markedly when the phrase "negative campaigning" is excised from the question. Among those asked the neutral version, only about one-third said they would be at least somewhat angry. Thus only *half* as many voters express anger at the idea of negative campaigning when the actual phrase "negative campaigning" is removed, a statistically significant and substantively important difference ($\chi^2 = 135.3, p < .001$). When specifically directed to think of providing information about an opponent as "negative campaigning," a large majority of voters express anger at such behavior. Yet when not cued to think of this same activity as negative, just as large of a majority is not especially angered by the idea. We take this as clear evidence that the wording of this question matters, and that in fact most voters are reasonably comfortable with the idea that candidates might provide information about their opponents—what political scientists typically consider the essence of negative campaigning. Only when we actually tell voters that this behavior is in fact negative campaigning do respondents recoil against it. This finding alone, simple as it is, should give some pause to those who argue that the public is automatically repelled by the underlying activity of "negative campaigning," discussing one's opponent.

Perhaps this is too simplistic. Maybe voters do not connect the idea of providing information about an opponent with negativity the way political scientists do. Or perhaps they think of our phrase "giving information" as a good thing. Of course, it should be obvious that few if any candidates are going to say *nice* things about the competition within a campaign context. Still, maybe what we are really finding is that voters are fine with providing information as long as it is positive. However, the logic of our experiment suggests otherwise. Recall that the only difference in the questions is the removal of the phrase "negative campaigning" for half of the respondents. In such an experimental design, where the groups who are randomly assigned to one or the other treatment are otherwise the same, the removal of the phrase almost certainly causes the change in response; other observed and unobserved variables are washed out by the random assignment.

Further examination of our data confirms our assessment. Since these data were collected in the context of the 2008 presidential election campaign, we can look at how partisans and nonpartisans respond to the experiment. Not surprisingly, there are clear differences. However, in contrast to Ansolabehere and Iyengar (1995a) who find that nonpartisans are most turned off by negativity, in the 2008 election it was Democrats who were most angered by our explicit negative campaigning question. As the top panel of figure 3.2 shows, when the phrase "negative campaigning" was included in the question, 77 percent of Democrats were at least somewhat angered compared to 60 percent of Independents and only 49 percent of Republicans ($\chi^2 = 65.6, p < .001$). Other data (not part of our experiment) collected in the post-election survey found that Democrats were far more likely to believe that John McCain was the more negative candidate, while Republicans were more likely to claim that both candidates were equally negative. This clear asymmetry in responses tracks with more objective reporting about the campaign in its final month, which found that McCain's campaign spent a much larger share of its money on negative advertising compared to Obama (Halloran 2008). Thus the finding that Democrats were more likely to be angered by "negative campaigning" in its explicit version during the 2008 election seems to reflect what was happening on the ground in the campaign.

In support of our argument, this partisan difference *disappears* when we remove the phrase "negative campaigning" from the question, as shown in the bottom panel of figure 3.2. In this more neutral treatment of the question, only 35 percent of Democrats were "somewhat" or "very" angered, the same share as both Republicans and Independents ($\chi^2 = 0.07$,

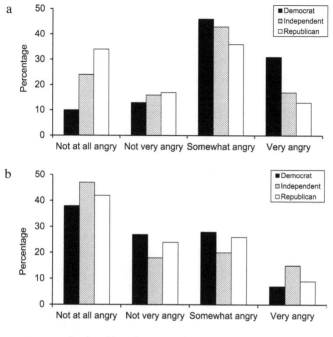

FIGURE 3.2: Partisanship and anger, study I
a. "Negative campaigning" included in question
b. "Negative campaigning" not included in question

$p < .966$). If respondents in the negative treatment were truly reacting to the activity of giving information about an opponent, rather than the use of the phrase "negative campaigning," we would expect the same partisan differences before and after removing the phrase. Instead, we find more evidence that responses to questions asking about "negative campaigning" are more about the word "negative" than the activity of providing information about an opponent.[5]

Study 2: Defining Negativity

The Survey

Study I presents evidence that voters' apparent anger toward negative campaigning may be a reflection of surveys that incorporate the word "negative" (or something akin to it) into their questions. Voters, not surprisingly, appear to be much more negative when confronted with a question that tells them providing information about an opponent is negative campaigning. It is possible that when pollsters ask about "negative campaigns" and "negative advertisements" what voters hear is not as simple as the "talking about an opponent" operationalization that is often used by political scientists in defining negativity for analytical purposes.

Study 2, which surveyed New Jersey voters just before the 2009 gubernatorial election, explores this possibility by allowing some respondents to decide whether certain specific advertising topics are negative. Similar to study 1, for a random half of respondents the question asserted that the topics described were negative. But for the other half, the topics were presented without any cuing as to their negativity, and respondents were asked to determine if running such ads would constitute negative campaigning. Both groups were asked the extent to which the ad topics made them angry. Thus we not only have an expanded version of study 1, with specific topics rather than general "information about an opponent," but we also can find out whether voters themselves think certain topics are negative in the absence of an explicit cue from the interviewer. For study 2 the explicit negative version of the question read:

> Thinking about political campaigns in general now, how would you feel if a candidate used a negative ad to talk about an opponent's [INSERT TOPIC]? Would you feel very angry, somewhat angry, not very angry or not at all angry?

The group not cued with "negative ad" was asked the following:

> Thinking about political campaigns in general now, I am going to describe some ads political candidates have run in the past. For each, tell me if you think a candidate running such an ad would be running a negative campaign. First, a candidate runs an ad that talks about an opponent's [INSERT TOPIC]. Would this candidate be running a negative campaign?

Topics used in both versions were (1) lack of experience, (2) prior record in office, (3) family, and (4) position on issues. The topic order was randomized. Following this question, respondents in this self-defined group were then asked:

> And how would an ad that talks about an opponent's [INSERT TOPIC] make you feel? Would you feel very angry, somewhat angry, not very angry, or not at all angry?

Thus the treatment group was asked first to consider whether a topic was negative and then asked for an affective reaction to it. In this way we mimic the approach taken when the researcher asserts negativity, but allow the respondent to define it for herself one way or the other.

Results

We first assess whether respondents in the explicitly negative condition were more likely to be angered by the various topics than respondents not in that condition, replicating the analysis of study 1 but extending it to specific topics. Table 3.1 shows the percentage of angry respondents for several different conditions. The first column reports subjects explicitly told that all the topics were negative, and the second reports those asked to decide it themselves. As shown in these two columns, for three of the four topics simply removing the "negative" cue reduces anger by 12 points (Experience), 14 points (Record), and 22 points (Issues).[6] This simple comparison reinforces the finding of study 1; when the researcher identifies a topic as negative voters follow along. Even so, for these topics, even when cued with "negative," fewer than half expressed anger. Clearly the cuing of a question as negative has significant impact for topics that otherwise might not be considered negative by real voters. But when the topic of the ad is the opponent's family, voters get their hackles up whether or not they are explicitly told that it is negative. For Family ads, 92 percent of those in the explicit negative condition express anger, as do 85 percent of those allowed to define negativity for themselves.[7]

Just below each topic name in table 3.1, the numbers in brackets show the percentage of respondents who labeled that topic as negative. We find that 34 percent considered lack of Experience to be negative, and for Record and Issues the percentage calling them negative was even lower— 26 percent and 19 percent, respectively. At the same time, Family ads do not just foment anger; they are nearly universally considered negative.

Next we address whether voters' decisions about what is and is not negative trigger different affective responses. In other words, are those who define a topic as negative angrier than those who do not? As the third and fourth columns of table 3.1 show, the answer is clearly yes. Among those allowed to self-define negativity, there are substantial differences across topics both in terms of the likelihood of a topic being defined as "negative" as well as the anger it produces. For example, the first row of the table shows that 57 percent of those defining Experience ads as negative also express anger toward them. In contrast, only 11 percent of those defining

TABLE 3.1. **Effects of defining negativity on anger by topic, study 2**

Topic	Explicit Negative	Self-Defined (All)	Self-Defined as Negative	Self-Defined as Not Negative
Lack of experience [Negative: 34%]	38%	26%	57%	11%
Prior record in office [Negative: 26%]	38%	24%	64%	8%
Family [Negative: 92%]	92%	85%	93%	56%
Position on issues [Negative: 19%]	42%	20%	64%	10%
N =	467	436		

Note: Table entries are rounded percentages of the sample responding "Very angry" or "Somewhat angry." Entries exclude "Don't know" responses.

Experience as not negative are angry. We find a similar pattern for Record and Issues. The vast majority does not consider using them against an opponent to be negative, and only about 10 percent of those who do not call these topics negative are angered by them. On the other hand, majorities of the small numbers who define these topics as negative are angered by them.

Voters' anger toward a topic is heavily dependent on perceptions of whether the topic is negative, and this is true even for the one topic both control and treatment groups were angered by—talking about an opponent's family. Among the 92 percent that find Family to be negative, 93 percent are angered. On the other hand, of the very small group (8 percent) that does not consider talking about family as negative, only 56 percent are angered.

These results show, first, that voters and political scientists are different in their perceptions of what is negative; coding all mentions of an opponent as negative does not necessarily fit with voters' own perceptions. Second, we see again the powerful general effect of cuing respondents to the negativity of an ad topic rather than allowing them to decide it for themselves. The effect works in both directions. Those who self-define a topic as negative are angrier than those explicitly told the topic is negative. For these respondents, reflecting on the topic and finding it to be something distasteful creates a stronger response than simply being told it is negative. But, except for the topic of Family, there are few respondents like this; most find the other topics we provided them to be well within acceptable bounds. Meanwhile those who do not find a topic negative are, not surprisingly, far less angry than those explicitly told that it is. Clearly, the results of this experiment reinforce the idea that some topics are truly off limits; mentioning an opponent's family clearly is perceived to be negative. But other topics are much more legitimate fodder, for instance, issue attacks, which are viewed by more than three-quarters of these respondents as not negative.

Study 3: Exploring Topics in More Detail

The Survey

Our third study was part of a national Internet survey using the 2010 Cooperative Congressional Election Study (CCES).[8] We embedded an experiment into the survey manipulating the description of campaign ads in a manner similar to our first two studies. Using the same question format as in study 2, we asked respondents about specific ad topics. Some were explicitly told the topics were negative, while the others were asked to decide for themselves whether the topics were negative. Subjects were randomly assigned to one of three treatments. In treatment A, the topic was explicitly called a "negative ad." In treatment B, the word "negative" was removed, and the descriptor was simply "an ad." In this version we first asked whether the particular ad topic is negative before asking for cognitive, affective, and behavioral assessments of the ad. Finally, in treatment C the ad topics were again referred to as "an ad" without the word "negative," but the question about whether such an ad would be negative was asked *after* asking for all other responses to it. We did this to address the potential for question order effects of asking about whether an ad is negative.

Respondents were given a range of topics that have been part of recent campaigns. Topics varied by the subject of the attack and relevance to political performance (Fridkin and Kenney 2008, 2011). Five topics were identified:

Lack of experience (relevant to personal qualifications)

Position on issues (relevant to policy)

Convicted of fraud (relevant to character)

Family (not directly relevant)

Atheism (not directly relevant)

Respondents were shown the list of topics in random order and asked the following three questions, each of which was designed to capture the decision-making stage listed in brackets. For each question, the word "negative" was included for one-third of the respondents, while the remaining two-thirds decided for themselves if the topic was negative.

1. [Cognitive] For each of these *negative* ads, how believable would this kind of ad be?
2. [Affective] For each of these *negative* ads, how angry it would make you feel?
3. [Behaviorial intent] For each of these *negative* ads, would it make you more likely to vote for the candidate running the ad, that candidate's opponent, or would it have no impact your vote?

In keeping with our plan to talk about lying and truthfulness in chapter 6, we will postpone consideration of the cognitive response (believability) until that chapter, and instead will focus only on the latter two responses here, affect and vote intention.

Results

Table 3.2 presents the results of our experiment. For the "anger" and "is this negative" questions, we present the differences across the three treatment groups as well as the total for all respondents. We can see that the topics readily divide into two groups: The first three, Issues, Experience, and Fraud, show only small differences between treatments on anger and self-defined negativity. This appears to be because of the decrease in social desirability bias associated with self-administered surveys (like Internet surveys) compared to interviewer-administered (Chang and Krosnick 2009; Holbrook and Krosnick 2010). Compared to studies 1 and 2, the anger levels for Experience (20%) and Issues (16%) ads were quite low among those told that the ads were negative. Among those asked to define for themselves whether these ad topics were negative, respondents said they were not, and this group was even less likely to be angered by them. For the last two topics, Atheism and Family, significant majorities of our respondents were angered and most also self-defined the ad topics as negative. There were no treatment effects for these two topics.

Table 3.2 shows large differences in anger and vote intent across the topics when we look at the full sample. Overall, only 14 percent of respondents were angry about ads on Issue positions, and 18 percent were angered by Experience ads. In the middle, 39 percent were angered by Fraud as a topic, while at the high end 54 percent did not like Atheism and fully

TABLE 3.2. **Effects of negativity on anger and vote by topic, study 3**

Topic	Anger by Treatment				Self-defined as Negative by Treatment		Vote for Candidate	Vote for Opponent
	All	A	B	C	B	C	All	All
Position on issues	14%	16%	10%	13%	12%	16%	28%	6%
Lack of experience	18%	20%	16%	19%	25%	31%	23%	8%
Fraud	39%	42%	33%	41%	46%	58%	22%	12%
Atheism	54%	56%	55%	51%	68%	69%	7%	22%
Family	85%	85%	83%	86%	82%	80%	3%	40%
N =	1,000	330	323	347	323	347	1,000	1,000

Note: Table entries are rounded percentages of the sample responding "Very angry" or "Somewhat angry" combined. Treatments: A = Explicit negative ad; B = Self-defined first; C = Self-defined last.

85 percent were angry about Family as a topic. But rather than evidencing a backlash effect, Experience and Issue ads that talk about the opponent actually appeared to help the candidates' electoral chances, as respondents reported being *more* likely to vote for the campaigner. For the Experience topic, 23 percent were more likely to vote for the campaigner versus 8 percent more likely to vote for the opponent. For Issues, the difference was larger, 28 to 6 percent. Revealing that the opponent was convicted of fraud also improved one's electoral chances (22% to 12%) despite the fact that voters were more angered by that topic (39% overall) than the other two and more likely to claim it was negative (52%).

We also find that some types of negativity are truly disliked and may well create a backlash against the ad sponsor. Only 7 percent of respondents were more likely to vote for a candidate accusing an opponent of atheism, and just 3 percent were more likely to vote for a candidate attacking the opponent's family. In fact, 22 percent (for Atheism) and 40 percent (for Family) were more likely to vote for the candidate being attacked by such a negative ad.

In other words, backlash effects are not consistent across topics. When we look at overall vote intention, the two most unacceptable topics show a probable backlash effect, but the other three topics do not. So we have nuance here, in that voters say they do not like negativity—and in some cases they do not. But they will accept much that is thought of as negative. And furthermore, even those who defined lack of experience, issue position, and fraud conviction as negative were *still* more likely to vote for the candidate using the negative topic than the opponent who is the target of the ad.

Some previous studies—and a great deal of conventional wisdom— suggest that negative campaigning is risky because of the potential for backlash against the candidate going negative. But here we see no *inherent* risk in launching an ad talking about the opponent, because the backlash is predictably tied to the content of the advertisement. It seems very likely that candidates know this—candidates' advertisements almost never attack an opponent's family or brand the opponent as an atheist. Rare exceptions, such as Elizabeth Dole's atheism attack on Kay Hagan in the 2008 North Carolina Senate race, are from candidates who are losing and perhaps view the election outcome as strictly binary (i.e., they are not overly concerned about reputational effects). We will take a closer look at this particular ad and Hagan's response as we examine real ads in the next chapter.

Conclusion

We know from nearly every survey that when voters are asked about "negative campaigning" or its many variants, they react negatively. The dominant theme in both punditry and political science is that negativity is bad by definition; each campaign is worse than the last, and the problem would be solved if candidates would just stop going negative. Furthermore many tend to discount the informational aspect of negative advertising because of aggrandized assessments about the public's disdain for it. But, there appears to be a paradox in which voters react disdainfully toward negative campaigning, yet candidates routinely engage in such campaigns. Using the studies reported in this chapter, we begin to reconcile this apparent paradox with evidence that voters themselves are not as opposed to negative campaigning as previous studies have led us to believe.

Much of the supposed general voter sentiment against negative campaigning is not evidence that voters reject the information negative campaigning can provide them, but instead appears to have more to do with the wording of the questions posed in previous surveys and experiments. Our more neutral treatment may also be a more realistic one—after all, negative advertisements do not explicitly tell voters that they are "negative," and other research has shown voters can be receptive to negative messages deemed more civil or more relevant (Brooks and Geer 2007; Fridkin and Kenney 2008). If we really want to better understand voter opinion toward negativity, we need to measure it more carefully.

A good starting point would be going beyond the standard political science definition of negativity in campaigns, because in some campaigns nearly all advertising talks about the opponent. For example, an article in the *Washington Post* (Grunwald 2006) reported that the National Republican Campaign Committee was dedicating over 90 percent of its campaign budget that year to "negative" advertising. And as we noted in chapter 1, the vast bulk of Super PAC advertising in the 2012 presidential campaign involved "talking about an opponent." If nearly all campaigning is classified as "negative," how meaningful is this term for describing political communication, or for studying it? As we discussed in chapter 2, identifying differences in candidates' approaches to negativity has proven successful in extant research but has been attempted too infrequently.

More important, our findings suggest a revised definition of negativity because voters in many cases fail to connect "providing information about an opponent" with "negative campaigning"; instead, the perceived negativity of an advertisement depends heavily on the topic it addresses. Candidates of course recognize this, and some offer their own definitions of negative campaigning. "Negative campaigning is vicious personal attacks," House candidate Paul Nelson said in the aforementioned *Washington Post* article.[9] Personal attacks—and especially attacks on an opponents' family—are more likely viewed as negative, and are very different from pointing out the shortcomings of an opponent's policy stance or his lack of experience. A study of news articles about negative campaigning found that journalists tend to use "negative" to imply "that a candidate was not only talking about his opponent rather than himself, but campaigning in an inappropriate manner" and use the phrase "negative campaigning" in relation to deception or *ad hominem* attacks (Geer and Lipsitz 2013). As we've shown, voters tend to agree.

In sum, political scientists typically define "negative campaigning" differently from everyone else in the political world. Undoubtedly, there is the advantage of simplicity—there is little ambiguity over whether ads talk about the opponent. On the other hand, the phrase "negative campaigning" contains a value judgment. What happens when these two definitions converge? Political scientists, using a more inclusive definition of negativity, are cited by journalists, who write articles about how nearly every advertisement is negative. For example, a 2012 *Time* magazine article cited two studies showing that 70 percent of the presidential ads in 2012 were negative, and that both candidates had at the time of the article been about 90 percent negative (Greenstein 2012). The story does not mention that both studies used the standard definition of negativity, though we would argue that it doesn't matter much either way. In reporting that nearly every ad is negative, political scientists are handing out misleading information—we are unintentionally telling people that most campaign ads are inappropriate, deceptive, or false. This matters. As we show in later chapters, voters who think that information is negative also tend to underestimate its accuracy.

Regarding the definition of negativity, existing subcategories seem less useful to us with our new understanding that voter responses to such ads depend so much upon the topic. For instance, contrast ads contain both negative and positive messages, generally attacking the opponent first and explaining how the attacker is better. "Contrast" is a useful category for the purpose of assessing the share of negativity across all campaign ads—since a contrast ad is basically two ads (one negative and one positive) that are shown together, not much different from, say, showing a thirty-second negative ad followed by a separate thirty-second positive ad. But that distinction is not sufficient for us, because voters' reactions toward the negative component of a contrast ad are still dependent upon the content of the ad. We need to know something about the topic to understand and predict voter response. In the end, what seems most useful to us is letting voters themselves tell us what they believe is negative.

Similarly, these results indicate a need for studies designed to determine exactly what survey respondents are thinking when they hear the word "negative." We suggested that previous results about voters' dislike of negativity were affected by the social undesirability of assenting to behavior termed "negative." Another possibility is that when the word "negative" is used to describe this campaign activity, voters may inherently assume that the attacks are harsh and personal rather than issue-oriented, and that may be what drives their responses to the general question of negative advertising.

The fact that voter aversion to negativity is less than it may appear is especially relevant to the study of campaign reform since often, calls for campaign reform focus on reducing the amount of negativity. For example, the nonprofit California Clean Money Campaign has argued that public financing of campaigns would have the added benefit of discouraging negative campaigning; presumably limits on attack advertising could be linked to the acceptance of such funds.[10] Alternatively, sometimes candidates are encouraged to sign voluntary pledges to refrain from negative campaigning (Maisel, West, and Clifton 2007). What the public "wants" leads to questions about what might be lost if they get it. As Geer (2006) shows, negativity carries information, often much more than positive messages. Formal models of campaigns as information revelation also show that such a ban leads at best to ambiguous results—the loss of information in the system is not necessarily made up for by any perceived good of banning certain kinds of ads (Mattes 2007; Polborn and Yi 2006). And, as we now show, the public may not desire the elimination of negativity in any case, despite what they say. Our research suggests that in order to understand what the public truly thinks, care needs to be taken when relying on public opinion polling on issues such as negative campaigning. It seems that political consultants who drive campaigns already understand this and discount the claims that voters "hate" negativity. They appear right to do so.

But it might also be that voters react negatively to "negative campaigning" because it brings to mind candidates lying to get what they want. Levels of trust in politicians are endemically low—generally a majority of voters say they trust the government to do what is right occasionally or never.[11] So it may be that identifying an ad as "negative" brings associations with the worst of politics, including that candidates might simply say anything to get elected. This possibility is worth more consideration. Recall that in our first two experiments we asked respondents to consider a case in which the ads were explicitly labeled as true, and in our third survey experiment we asked about the believability of the ad topics we presented. We will turn in chapter 6 to these data to examine the question of negativity and credibility. It seems clear that some ways of talking about an opponent anger voters, who see them as inherently negative, while other topics are only seen as negative when voters are cued to believe this. What we need to better understand is how the truth of a message and its credibility conditions voter responses, whether cued that an ad is negative or not.

But before we turn to this question, we want to better establish the basic findings of this chapter. Our telephone and Internet surveys have the advantage of providing population-based random samples to participate in our survey experiments. But in these surveys we were unable to present actual ads to our subjects, either because of the method of data collection (telephone) or the limitations of our resources for the online survey. In the next chapter we rectify this by using a convenience sample of Amazon Mechanical Turk workers to assess a series of real ads, covering a range of topics and a variety of tones. We asked these subjects to watch the ads and then assess them in many of the same ways we did in our survey experiments, including identifying whether the ad is negative and their responses to the ads. As we will see, the results track very well with our description-based survey experiments, lending strong support to the findings of the population studies reported in this chapter.

CHAPTER FOUR

Examining Voter Response to Real Campaign Ads

Negative campaigning, like beauty, is in the eye of the beholder.—David Mark, *Going Dirty: The Art of Negative Campaigning* (2006)

In the last chapter we showed how voters' dislike of negative campaigning is conditioned at least in part on calling it "negative." People do not seem especially concerned with the activity of negative campaigning, that is, when a candidate talks about his or her opponent. Given that mentions of an opponent are very unlikely to be positive, we suggest these findings argue that negativity is not *per se* opposed by voters. When hypothetical ads are described as negative, voters respond accordingly. When they are not, voters seem less concerned. But we also find that there is some nuance in responses to these hypotheticals. While most topics do not generate much in the way of anger on the part of voters, we found two that clearly did. When ads are described as being about a candidate's family or religion, voters respond with definite distaste.

One key limitation of our first three studies is evident: we did not actually show ads to our respondents. Instead we described the ads in the telephone studies, and respondents read our descriptions of the ads in the online survey. While we are quite comfortable that we properly described the types of ads we wanted to address, it is still not the same as having voters view ads and respond to them. Though our analyses identify a clear social desirability effect, whereby removing the direct reference to "negative" for the most part removes objections to the ads we describe, we need to confirm the this occurs with actual ads, which never assert their negativity. Given that real ads contain a variety of stimuli (images, voice, music, and text) it may be that viewing actual ads triggers different responses, and that voters are quite negative about actual negativity, but rather complacent about hypothetical negativity.

In this chapter we address this issue with a fourth study, analyzing responses to a mix of real-world ads. We asked a national convenience sample of Americans to respond to each of twenty-one ads chosen from past campaigns for US Senate, Congress, and state offices. The ads are a mix of positive and negative messages chosen to cover the range of topics we included in our survey studies. For each ad we collect measures of believability, appropriateness, whether it is negative, how negative, the extent to which it makes the respondent angry, and whether it creates a backlash against the candidate running the ad. We also examine one pair of ads in more detail. These are from the 2008 North Carolina Senate race between eventual winner Democrat Kay Hagan and then-incumbent Republican Elizabeth Dole. Toward the end of that campaign, Dole, behind in the polls, ran an ad which gave the impression that Hagan is an atheist. Hagan, in response, ran an ad that attacked Dole for running that ad. We embedded an experiment in our study where subjects viewed either Dole or Hagan's ad first followed immediately by the other one. This experiment gives us an opportunity to see how context affects attitudes about negative ads and how participants react to candidates' responses to negative ads.

In study 4 we find that, as we would expect, the negative ad videos elicit more negative responses from viewers compared to the positive ads. But we also support our key findings from the population-based survey experiments. Participants in this study differentiate negative ads by topic, and in the main, most of the topics do not bother them very much, even when the ads themselves are perceived to be negative. Our results also confirm that the hypothetical nature of our previous survey questions was not the reason for the overall lack of anger. Rather than being more angered by the real-world ads than by our descriptions of ad themes and topics, participants in study 4 respond with the same equanimity as those in the population studies.

Study 4: Real-World Campaign Ads

DESIGN. We designed a forty-five-minute Internet-based study during which respondents watched twenty-one campaign ads (twelve negative, nine positive) that we drew from real political campaigns over the past few years. The twelve negative ads were selected from among a larger group of ads that were pretested by showing them to classes of undergraduate students and asking the students to identify the topic, how negative the ad was, how angry the ad made them feel, and whether it was an appropriate topic for a campaign ad. The negative ads that were used were chosen to maximize perceptions of negativity within our selected topics. The nine positive ads varied in emphasizing somewhat different themes, but did not appear to need pretesting since in all cases they simply extolled a candidate in broad terms, much as Geer (2006) has pointed out is typical of such ads.

Of the twenty-one ads, these twelve were *a priori* classified as "negative" because they talk about the opponent; this classification was confirmed in the pretest. Of these, we categorized five as defamatory because of the way that they focused directly on personal traits of the attacked candidate. Two of these five focused on religion. One accused the opponent of mocking Christianity [sponsoring candidate: Conway][1]; the other implied that the opponent was an atheist and would support atheistic policies [Dole]. A third ad [Bennet] attacked the opponent on ethics, accusing him of "professional misconduct" and implying illegal activity. A fourth attacked a candidate for supposedly failing to pay child support [Little]. The fifth defamatory ad accused the opponent of marketing dangerous drugs to children and thereby "[putting] his profits ahead of children's health" [Mullin].[2]

The remaining negative ads took on a variety of topics, with three [Young, Patten, Bernero] talking about policy issues, and three others about political incompetence or being out of touch [Reichart, Carnahan, Corker]. Of these, two [Corker, Young] appear to be racially coded; one [Young] attacks a black candidate for being "soft on crime for rappers, lawyers, and child pornographers," and the other [Corker] attacks a black candidate essentially for looking good on television. The last one is Kay Hagan's response to the Dole "atheist" ad [Hagan].

As we discuss the ads throughout the following pages, we need to adopt a convention to differentiate the five defamatory ads from the seven negative but not necessarily defamatory ads. And at times we may need to talk about all twelve attack ads. When talking only about the five defamatory ads, we will use the term "defamatory"; for the seven other attack ads we will use the term "negative." And when we want to talk about all twelve, we will call them "attack ads." The positive ads are simple; we will just call them "positive" whenever we need to refer to them as a group.

None of the nine positive ads mentioned an opponent by name. Yet some of the positive ads had elements of attack, generally against others (in a generic sense) for promoting politics as usual. For example one [Ayotte] implies she is facing rich opponents that are trying to buy the election, and another ad [Shuler] attacks Congress for "not knowing right from wrong." Even so, based on their overall content, we initially classified these as positive, and our subjects agreed. Details on each ad, including its script, are available in appendix A at the end of this book.

To improve comparability with our previous three studies, in which our hypothetical situation did not mention political parties, we sought here to avoid partisan effects. We intentionally chose ads that did not have explicit references to either major political party, and which did not feature patently obvious partisan rhetoric. The challenge, of course, is that such ads are much more difficult to find. One exception to our rule, [Reichart], has text labeling the primary speaker, a voter who supports Dave Reichart, as a Democrat. Though not made clear at all in the ad, the point assumedly is that the speaker supports Reichart (a Republican) despite being a member of the opposing party.

Generally, we chose lower-profile races where the politicians were not particularly well known and ads that were unlikely to have been seen by the respondent. The exceptions to this are the three religion-based ads. In our extensive search of ads to use in this study, we found very few that touched on religion as a theme, and even fewer attacking an opponent's religion or lack thereof. We also wanted to avoid attacks on specific religions. The best three cases, by far, were also higher-profile ads: attacking Rand Paul, Elizabeth Dole, and Kay Hagan. Fortunately, none of the three ads mentioned the candidates' political parties. Later in this chapter, we discuss reactions to the Dole and Hagan ads in detail.

Table 4.1 displays how these ads map onto the questions asked in our population survey-experiments. Note that we classify [Little] as a "family" negative ad, although it does not directly attack the candidate's family. The reason is simple. Try as we might, we could not find a contemporary ad that did so. The worst of such attacks were levied against Andrew Jackson's family in the 1824 and 1828 presidential elections. Newspaper editorials claimed Andrew Jackson's mother was a prostitute and that his wife, Rachel, was an adulterer and bigamist, saying that we should not "place a woman such as Mrs. Jackson at the head of the female society of the United States." Jackson blamed the ferocity of the campaign attacks for Rachel's death in 1828 (Swint 2006).

TABLE 4.1. **Mapping study 4 attack ads on population survey-experiments (studies 1–3)**

Hawkeye Poll	
One general question: Angry if candidate gave information about what opponent had done in office.	[Carnahan, Young, Patten, Bernero]
Rutgers-Eagleton Poll: 12 questions total (4 or 8 per respondent)	
Questions about four topics	
a. Lack of experience	[Corker, Reichart]
b. Prior record in office	[Carnahan, Young, Patten, Bernaro]
c. Family	[Little]
d. Position on issues	[Young, Patten, Bernero]
CCES Poll	
Questions about five topics	
a. Lack of experience	[Corker, Reichart]
b. Position on issues	[Carnahan, Young, Patten, Bernero]
c. Is an atheist	[Dole; Also: Conway, Hagan (General religion)]
d. Convicted of fraud	[Bennet, Little, Mullin]
e. Family	[Little]

Nowadays, while partisans occasionally indulge in such behavior—and then usually only when a family member is actively involved in the campaign—statements attacking a candidate's family are met with swift public admonition by other members of their own political party. For example, in the 2012 campaign, when a Democratic strategist criticized Mitt Romney's wife Ann for "never having worked a day in her life," that same strategist gave a public apology the next day, and furthermore was reproached by Barack Obama, who said, "I don't have a lot of patience for commentary about the spouses of political candidates" (Bingham, Dwyer, and Friedman 2012). Obama had similarly condemned attacks on vice-presidential candidate Sarah Palin's daughter in 2008. He said, "I think people's families are off-limits, and people's children are especially off-limits. This shouldn't be part of our politics. It has no relevance to Gov. Palin's performance as governor or her potential performance as a vice president" (Marquardt 2008). And as we were writing this a new controversy developed as an outside group levied an attack on US Senate Minority Leader Mitch McConnell with a Tweet suggesting that his wife, former Labor Secretary Elaine Chao, was somehow complicit in jobs moving to China because she is Chinese. This led the *New York Times* editorial writer Andrew Rosenthal to write, "The attack seems uncomfortably reminiscent of Lee Atwater's racially charged campaigns."[3]

Our strategy to reduce partisanship effects was for the most part successful in that when we aggregated responses across all ads we found no statistical difference between the expressed anger of Democrats and Republicans, or in their assessments of ads' negativity. Similarly, we found that the anger and negativity assessments of Democratic and Republican respondents were not significantly different when aggregated across the ads favoring Democratic candidates or when aggregated across the ads favoring Republican candidates. There were some differences for a few of the individual ads, though only two—both positive ads [Cooper, Ayotte]—had statistically significant differences between Democratic and Republican respondents for the anger measure. Democrats were less angered by [Cooper], which favored a Democrat, while Republicans were less angered by [Ayotte], which favored a Republican. Also, Republicans thought that [Cooper] was more negative and that [Corker] was less negative; the latter criticized (Democrat) Harold Ford for having no experience outside of Washington, DC. Still, these are exceptions. Across the vast majority of the ads and the assessments our subjects made of them, partisanship has no discernible effect, as we had intended.

PROTOCOL. Participants first answered questions about their voting history, political affiliation, and their trust of government and media. Next, they answered a series of questions about taking politicians' statements out of context, which included an embedded experiment, after which they were shown the twenty-one ads. Given the expected number of respondents and the large number of combinations of twenty-one ads, along with the limitations of our software, we created ten randomized ad orders. For each of the ten possible orders, the order of the twenty-one ads was generated by a random number generator without replacement. Participants were then randomly assigned to one of the ten ad orders. The order of the ads was randomized as presented, with one exception. The two North Carolina US Senate ads were independently manipulated so that subjects randomly viewed either the [Dole] or [Hagan] ad first and then immediately viewed the other. The placement of these two ads was randomized within the full set of ads.

Immediately after viewing each ad, subjects were asked a series of questions:

What was the ad about? (open-ended text)

Have you ever seen this ad before? (yes/no)

How believable is this ad? (four-point scale, "very believable" to "not at all believable")

How appropriate is the subject matter of this ad for a political campaign? (four-point scale, "very appropriate" to "very inappropriate")

Did watching this ad make you very angry, somewhat angry, not very angry, or not at all angry?

Would you be more likely to vote for a candidate who ran an ad like this, more likely to vote for that candidate's opponent, or would it have no effect on your vote?

Thinking about the ad you just saw, do you consider it to be a negative ad? (yes/no)

On a scale of 0–5, with 0 being "Not at all negative" and 5 being "Extremely negative," how negative do you consider the ad you just watched to be?

All questions were asked for each of the twenty-one ads. In the data analysis, we dropped cases where subjects said they had seen the ad before, and we dropped subjects who appeared to have paid little attention by virtue of their answers to the open-ended question about ad content. Mean responses to each question for each ad are provided in table A.2, in appendix A.[4]

After all the ads were shown, a series of questions asked about the subject's ability to recognize when candidates are not truthful, about perceptions of types of attacks, and how helpful different kinds of campaign information might be. A final set of demographic questions concluded the survey. The complete questionnaire is available in the online appendix available at http://www.press.uchicago.edu/sites/mattes/.

PARTICIPANTS.   We used Amazon.com's Mechanical Turk (MTurk, www.mturk.com) service to recruit 235 respondents from across the United States. Participants were recruited in batches over several days, with the batches made available at varying times to ensure that respondents from across the United States would potentially be available. The study took place in early October 2012, during the height of the 2012 election campaign.

Mechanical Turk is an online marketplace for short-duration temporary work and is used for a wide variety of business tasks from audio transcription to detailed research. Its chief benefits are on-demand work and scalability. Rather than hiring a large temporary workforce, one can post the tasks—called Human Intelligence Tasks (HITs) on MTurk—avoiding much of the expensive and time-consuming recruitment phase. Payments are generally inexpensive and given to the workers only upon successful completion of the HITs.

For many of the same reasons, MTurk has rapidly gained traction in the research community, as it provides an inexpensive yet reliable means of subject recruitment for experiments. As with any new approach, the question is whether or not it produces samples that are of sufficient quality or validity for research. Thorough investigations in psychology (Buhrmester, Kwang and Gosling 2011), economics (Horton, Rand, and Zeckhauser 2010) and political science (Berinsky, Huber, and Lenz 2012) have shown support for using MTurk workers as a convenience sample. For example, Berinsky, Huber, and Lenz (2012) find that MTurk samples are a good substitute for other convenience samples (such as college students), that Mturk samples are more representative of the US population than standard Internet samples, and that data obtained from MTurk samples are just as reliable as that from using traditional methods; they also successfully replicate important published experimental work using MTurk samples.

Upon clicking on our HIT, participants were sent to a consent screen that provided information about the study, including its anticipated length and payment for completion. The study was fielded using Lau and Redlawsk's (2006; Redlawsk and Lau 2013) Dynamic Process Tracing Environment (DPTE, http://www.processtracing.org).[5] Upon completion participants were provided with a code that could be entered into the HIT to claim payment.[6] In this chapter we focus specifically on the responses to the ads that were viewed. In chapter 6 we will take up many of the other questions we asked this group of respondents when we address the question of credibility and negativity.

As a convenience sample of MTurk workers, we know our participants are *not* a representative sample of American voters. Thus the disadvantage of this sample is that we cannot directly generalize it to the voting population. However, that is not our goal here. Rather we wish to establish that the basic findings of our text-based population studies hold when we replace ad descriptions and topics with real ads. To the extent that our findings here support our population studies, we have more confidence that those results, which are generalizable, tell us something about how voters respond to negative ads in real election campaigns.

TABLE 4.2. **Demographics of Amazon Mechanical Turk respondents**

Gender		Age	
Male	44%	18–29	38%
Female	56%	30–44	42%
		45–64	18%
Partisanship		65 and over	2%
Republican	16%		
Independent	38%	Race	
Democrat	46%	White	80%
		Black	8%
Ideology		Asian	3%
Conservative	20%	Other/Mixed	9%
Moderate	20%		
Liberal	60%	Hispanic (all races)	6%
Education			
HS or less	10%		
Some college	41%		
College grad	35%		
Post-grad	14%		

Table 4.2 reports the basic demographics of our sample. Respondents come from forty-four states and the District of Columbia. The sample is, not surprisingly, significantly younger and whiter than the voting population, in addition to being much more Democratic and less Republican. Ideology follows this, with a majority identifying as at least somewhat liberal. The sample is also well educated, with 49 percent having graduated from college or with an advanced degree. Most of the others are probably in college now. Respondents are also somewhat more likely to be female than voters in 2012 actually were.

While we are not so much concerned with generalizing to a larger population here, we do want to put to rest concerns that sample we use is somehow anomalous. The primary concern comes if key sample demographics are related to attitudes toward our dependent variables, in particular assessments of negativity and the anger that it generates. We examined our survey data from the Hawkeye, Rutgers-Eagleton, and CCES Internet surveys to see whether demographic factors predict key outcomes. To put it simply, for the most part they do not. We specified regression models using age, race, gender, partisanship, education, ideology, and religiosity to predict perceptions of negativity and reported anger, across all of our ad topics. Only race consistently predicted responses, and only for anger. In our survey-experiments white respondents were consistently angrier than nonwhites. When we included indicators for the topics of our ads, these indicators were highly significant in predicting perceptions of negativity and anger; among the demographics once again only race predicted anger, while none of them predicted assessments of negativity. Our goal in this analysis is to set a baseline to which to compare the study 4 respondents.

We replicated the analysis for study 4, with the same finding. Race predicts anger, with whites more angry than nonwhites, all else equal, but no other demographic factors predict the level of anger in study 4. Furthermore, the regression using only demographic factors is not statistically significant ($F_{(9, 232)} = 1.15, p < 0.32$).

Again, while we would prefer in a perfect world to have a random sample of the population of interest in the study of real-world ads, we simply do not have that. But we are confident that given the lack of direct effects for demographic measures, the sample we do have for study 4 gives us insight into whether the findings we reported last chapter for our population surveys hold up when we use real-world ads as the stimuli.

Results

Recall from chapter 3 that when we asked whether ad descriptions that were explicitly called negative made people angry in our telephone surveys, the mean level of anger was generally much higher than when voters were not given the explicit cue. Moreover, when we allowed respondents to determine for themselves whether an ad topic was negative, for topics other than Family, voters were unlikely to say that the topics were negative, even though the ads were described as a candidate talking about an opponent. When voters did think an ad topic was negative, they were much more likely to be angered by it than when they did not think it was negative. We interpreted these findings to say that much of the reported negativity toward attack ads is driven by the way the questions are usually asked, that is, providing explicit cues that the ad should be disliked. But of course it is possible that respondents are simply not connecting "talking about an opponent" with attack ads.

DO ATTACK ADS GENERATE ANGER?   We start with data from study 3, the CCES Internet study in 2010, which we have not yet discussed. Prior to the survey-experiment in that study we asked all participants whether "political ads" made them angry. We did not categorize the ads as negative or positive and said nothing about opponents

TABLE 4.3. **Do ads make participants angry?**

	Study 3, 2010 "Political ads"	Study 4, 2012 12 attack ads
Very angry	11%	12%
Somewhat angry	43%	32%
Not very angry	29%	27%
Not at all angry	16%	29%
N =	727	232
Mean (4 = very angry)	2.49	2.27 (12 attack ads)
		1.80 (all 21 ads)

or topics. We simply asked how angry they felt about political ads, and found the mean level of anger around the midpoint of the scale. Results in table 4.3 highlight an interesting phenomenon: Our study 4 participants who viewed real-world ads were *less* angry about those ads than respondents in study 3 asked to think hypothetically about political ads. Across all twenty-one video ads (57% were attack ads) in study 4, which was carried out during the heat of the 2012 campaign, the mean level of anger was 1.80 (coding responses from 1 = not at all angry to 4 = very angry). But in 2010, during the midterm election, our hypothetical question about "political ads" generated more, not less, anger among those respondents (mean = 2.49). In fact, these CCES respondents were more upset by "political ads" than were the study 4 participants by the twelve actual attack ads as a group, for which the mean level of anger was only 2.27. In other words, simply asking voters about political ads appears to bring to mind ads that they do not like.

Figure 4.1 displays the levels of anger for the study 4 ads on a chart grouping across the *x* axis by the categories of positive, negative (exclusive of defamatory), and defamatory ads. For simplicity, we do not label the individual ads in the figure, since we are primarily interested in the pattern. Different shapes represent the types of ads. We find that there is a clear distinction between positive and attack ads. However, we also find that participants react with far more differentiation within the category of attack ads than within the positive ads. All of the positive ads rate low on the scale, between 1 (not angry) and 1.5. The attack ads are broadly distributed from 1.5 to 3 on the four-point scale, with the subset of defamatory ads ranking particularly highly. On the whole, attack ads *do* make our participants angrier than positive ads, but on the whole, they still do not get all that angry. Only three ads crossed the midpoint of the anger scale:

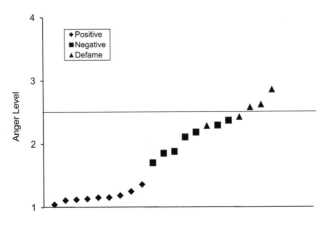

the two religion ads—[Dole] and [Conway]—and the ad accusing the opponent of not paying child support [Little]. Reported anger does not completely distinguish negative and defamatory ads because two ads angered
respondents more than the [Bennet] ad, which implied that the opponent
engaged in illegal activity. The two negative ads that actually made participants angrier than [Bennet] were [Bernero], which accuses the opponent of outsourcing jobs, and [Young], which has the most overt use of
race in the group.

We next address whether real-world attack ads in study 4 generated
anger in a way that our hypothetical attacks in the survey experiments
failed to do. Table 4.4 lays out the mean levels of anger across all of our
studies. We look again at the findings in chapter 3, where we described
the activity and topics of hypothetical ads before asking respondents how
angry the ad made them feel, as a kind of benchmark. While the sample in
this chapter is different, and thus we need to be careful in our assessments,
the fact that the differences in demographics do not seem to predict responses to the ads makes us reasonably comfortable making comparisons
between the studies, since to the extent they differ on demographics, those
differences do not correlate with our dependent variables.

In study 1, our national pre-election survey-experiment in 2008, the
mean anger level for those in the explicit negative condition was 2.65 (on
a scale from 1 to 4, with 4 being "very angry"), while for those not cued
to negativity, the mean was 2.01. In the 2009 New Jersey poll (study 2),
across topics, participants in the explicit negative condition were also an-

grier (2.50) than those where the ad was not explicitly described as negative (2.16). Finally in the 2010 CCES study 3, the overall level of anger for
the explicit group was 2.29 and 2.25 for the nonexplicit groups.

In study 4, during the 2012 election, the mean level of anger across the
real-world attack ads was 2.27 on our four-point scale. For comparison
purposes, study 4 is most analogous in methodology to study 3's third
group where we described an ad topic, asked a series of questions about the
topic (including anger), and then asked whether the topic would be negative. In study 4, of course, participants viewed actual ads, after which they
were asked questions (including anger), followed by the "is this negative"

TABLE 4.4. **Mean levels of anger across studies (1–4 scale)**

	Study 1 National	Study 2 New Jersey	Study 3 National	Study 4 National (Attack ads only)
All topics				
Explicit	2.65	2.50	2.29	
Self-defined first	2.01	2.16	2.18	
Self-defined last			2.33	2.27
Topics				
Issues				
Explicit		2.20	1.60	
Self-defined first		1.73	1.44	
Self-defined last			1.57	2.17
Experience/record/qualifications				
Explicit		2.11	1.78	
Self-defined first		1.84	1.66	
Self-defined last			1.77	2.09
Family				
Explicit		3.58	3.30	
Self-defined first		3.31	3.26	
Self-defined last			3.35	2.63
Atheism/religion				
Explicit			2.56	
Self-defined first			2.50	
Self-defined last			2.58	2.53 (2.73)[a]
Fraud				
Explicit			2.24	
Self-defined first			2.04	
Self-defined last			2.30	

[a] Not including the Hagan religion ad in a response to Dole's claim of atheism.

and "how negative" questions. Across these two different samples, in very different contexts, overall anger at attack ads is neither very strong, nor is it absent. Instead, it is somewhat below the midpoint, leaning toward "not very angry" when we consider all attack ads as a group.

In the hypothetical ad studies, anger was generally significantly greater when the respondent was told the ad was negative than when they were not. When not cued, anger was attenuated. The point here is that when viewing real-world ads, levels of anger seem closer to self-defined hypotheticals than ads explicitly cued as negative. Moreover, the mean across all of the ad topics is no higher when participants see an actual attack ad than when we describe the topic of a hypothetical ad by calling it a negative ad up front.

But if we disaggregate our results by topic, we see some interesting differences. On the two attack topics that generate lower levels of anger— Issues and Experience-related ads—respondents who saw real ads on these topics were made angrier about them than those who only heard descriptions of the topics. Both of these areas certainly seem more reasonable when described in words. After all, talking about an opponent's (presumably bad) position on issues or (lack of) qualifications seems like a reasonable thing for a candidate to do. But when confronted with an actual ad that does these things, anger seems to be increased, most likely because of the emotional component of such ads (Brader 2006), which is not evident in simple textual descriptions.

Our three real-world religion ads generate about as much anger as our description in the CCES study 3. But if we remove the Hagan ad, which has a special status because (1) it was a response to the Dole attack, and (2) we randomly manipulated whether Hagan's ad was seen before or after Dole's, mean levels of anger increase but remain closer to the study 3 results than the other topics. And while it looks like the text descriptions of ads about a candidate's family seem to generate more anger than the actual ad we showed with this topic, this is most likely an artifact of our classification. The hypothetical questions had posited a direct attack on a candidate's family, which made people clearly uncomfortable. But, as we explained earlier, the only family ad we ran in study 4 was one accusing the opponent of failing to support his family by not paying alimony.

So while the magnitude of anger may have been somewhat increased by the actual viewing of ads versus listening to descriptions, in study 4 mean anger levels remain below the center of our 1–4 scale. Moreover, the ordinal placement of ad topics matches well in the two studies using very different samples. In the end, the level of anger expressed at these attack ads—which we believe are quite representative of the topics and types of such ads run across most levels of American elections—really does not seem so great for the most part, given the conventional wisdom that Americans just cannot stand negativity. Instead, we suggest that while attack ads raise some hackles, for the most part the findings of our text-based population studies seem supported here. Negativity is recognized, yes, but does not generate a great deal of anger.

Because we had a national sample, we were able to test the hypothesis that living in a "battleground" state during the presidential campaign played a role in perceptions of these ads (which are not related to the 2012 campaign). If people do in fact get disgusted by the ever-increasing onslaught of negative advertising, then we would expect participants in competitive (and hence, ad-intensive) locales to be more fed up with ads than their fellow citizens in states with less intensive campaigning. But this turns out not to be the case. We see no differences between battleground and nonbattleground respondents. Mean anger was 1.78 in a presidential battleground state, and 1.80 otherwise.[7] One possible explanation is that nearly everyone was inundated with ads regardless, for other elections such as US House or Senate. Another is that the presidential ads were quite easy to find online and the most negative were often discussed and presented in the national media, so the physical location where the ad was targeted was less relevant than we might think.

ARE NEGATIVE ADS REALLY NEGATIVE?   Maybe participants in study 4 were not particularly angered by negative ads because we failed to pick ads that were truly perceived as negative. If our attack ads were not thought to be negative, then we might expect to find limited anger. But that turns out not to be the case. As one of the final questions about each ad, respondents were asked whether the ad was negative. Table 4.5 shows the distribution of the ads with each one flagged by its *a priori* designation. It is immediately evident that participants perceived the ads as we (and our pretesters) did. With one exception, there is complete separation between the ads classified a priori as negative and those we classified as positive. Eight out of the twelve attack ads were perceived as negative by 90 percent or more of respondents, while another three were seen as negative by 80 to 89 percent. Eight of the nine positive ads were viewed as positive by 90 percent or more of respondents, while the remaining one was considered positive by 87 percent. Only [Hagan], which we did not

TABLE 4.5. **Percentage calling ad negative or not negative, study 4**

Negative				Not Negative		
90%+		80–89%	Other	80–89%	90%+	
Carnahan	N	Corker	N	Hagan	N	Shuler	P	Ayotte	P
Bennet	D	Patten	N	(41% Neg)				Coakley	P
Little	D	Reichart	N					Cooper	P
Dole	D							Fetterman	P
Young	N							Roskam	P
Conway	D							Sanford	P
Bernero	N							Skorman	P
Mullin	D							Webster	P

Note: D = Defamatory; N = Negative, not Defamatory; P = Positive.

pretest, is mixed. Again, this is the ad that responded to Elizabeth Dole's ad (seen as clearly negative) implying Kay Hagan is an atheist. Standing alone, Hagan's ad appears negative (and we classified it as such since it talks about Dole), but when seen after the Dole ad, participants were much less likely to call it negative, resulting in this mixed finding. It is clear that we initially classified nearly all our ads correctly, in the sense that respondents viewed them as we did—the attack ads (except [Hagan]) were always viewed as negative, while the positive ones were seen in that light. Again, given the pretest, and the generally dark and menacing tone of the negative ads we chose, this was no surprise. Some ads are negative enough to make the political science and voter definitions of negativity converge.

As described earlier, anger toward the attack ads was clearly stronger than toward the positive ads, which on one hand suggests that jettisoning the current definition of negative ads entirely could be a mistake. On the other hand, the reactions to the attack ads generally viewed as "negative" had a *much* larger range than did reactions to the positive ads, so clearly the basic definition of talking about an opponent misses a great deal of variance. We believe that calling all ads talking about an opponent "negative," which for most people carries a value judgment, implies a magnitude of dissatisfaction on the part of voters that simply does not exist.

Of course, what we are interested in is the impact of these ads, including just how negative they are seen to be. It is one thing to say an ad is negative; it is another to consider it highly negative versus just a little negative. We asked respondents to tell us how negative each ad (both positive and attack) was on a scale from 0 (not at all) to 5 (extremely negative) after indicating if it was negative or not. Even those who said an ad was "not negative" were asked this question.

The results again reinforce our *a priori* expectations about the ads. Those that we expected not to be seen as negative averaged only 0.3 on the 0–5 scale, while the attack ads overall scored 3.5, over the midpoint but not extremely so. When we categorize the ads as either defamatory or negative, a clear difference arises. Participants viewed defamatory ads as much more negative (mean of 4.2) than the nondefamatory attack ads (3.0). In some ways this may seem like a trivial finding—negative ads are viewed negatively—but it is very important that we know whether our expectations in using the ads we chose were correct so we know that we included ads providing the potential range of responses we need to assess their effects.

Figure 4.2 displays the ads by the level of "how negative" responses coding each for positive, negative, or defamatory. The picture is quite clear. No positive ad gets a mean above 1 on the 0–5 scale, while the defamatory ads are all near or above 4 on the scale, representing significant agreement that they are highly negative. As we would expect, the rest of our ads, negative but not defamatory, fall a wide range in between.

Differences are most visible when we look at ads by topic. Attack ads focused on political issues and personal qualifications each average about 3.4 on the 0–5 negativity scale. But the two ads focused on religion—leaving out the special case of the Hagan ad—are viewed more negatively, as is our one family ad [Little], all at 4.3. So there is nuance here, as not all negative ads are created equal. Those that seem to focus on what we would consider relevant questions—issue and candidate qualification oriented—are not seen to be as negative as those focused on the target's family or religion.

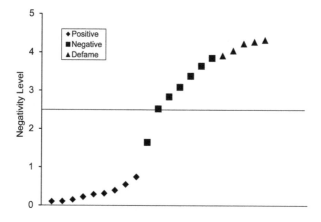

FIGURE 4.2. Perception of negativity by type of ad, study 4

Knowing this, and knowing that the topics were chosen to roughly correspond with topics addressed in the population survey experiments, we turn again to the impact of these ads. In addition to the question about anger, we have a measure of vote intention, asking if the respondent would be more or less likely to vote for the candidate who ran the ad. We also have measures of appropriateness and believability, which we will leave until chapter 6 when we look at credibility more generally. Since our *a priori* assessment of the negativity (or lack of) for all but one of the ads is borne out in the responses we got, we will use this assessment in examining differences between positive and attack ads.

IS THERE A BACKLASH?   It may be that even if negative ads only generate moderate levels of anger, voters are motivated by them to respond negatively to the attacker, creating a backlash effect. If voters really prefer candidates not use negativity, then attacking one's opponent carries a risk that voters will respond not by accepting the attack as legitimate, but instead by refusing to support the attacker. But as we noted in chapter 3, where we described potential negativity in our study 3 CCES experiment, we saw very little backlash; few said an attack on issues or candidate experience would make them vote against the attacker. Such ads actually resulted in more votes for the attacker than for the opponent. Religious attacks—accusing an opponent of being an atheist—were more risky, with just over one in five saying such attacks would lead them to support the opponent, still a small share of all respondents. Attacks on family, however, pushed the envelope—40 percent said they would vote for the opponent while virtually no one supported the attacker in this case. So backlash is certainly possible.

But again, since the CCES study provided only brief topic descriptions, we might suspect more backlash if voters saw the actual negative ads in all their glory. So we asked our study 4 subjects about this as follows:

> Would you be more likely to vote for a candidate who ran an ad like this, more likely to vote for that candidate's opponent, or would it have no effect on your vote?

Our data show a strong relationship between anger and backlash. Fifty-four percent of those who are "very angry" also choose "vote for the opponent." But overall, ads making someone "more likely to vote for the opponent" were uncommon in the set of ads we used.[8]

The most common response across all twenty-one ads was that the ad would have no effect on their vote (48%), while on average 35 percent said they would vote for the ad sponsor and half as many—17 percent—for the sponsor's opponent, representing backlash. Out of the twenty-one ads (both positive and attack) only three had a net backlash effect, two of which were ads about religion. For the Dole attack on Hagan, 51 percent said it would drive them to vote for the opponent (Hagan), while only 15 percent supported Dole. Another 33 percent said the ad would have no effect. Faring little better was the ad from the 2010 Kentucky US Senate race [Conway] in which Jack Conway attacked Rand Paul for forcing a woman to bow down to "Aqua Buddha." A plurality (45%) said the ad would have no effect, while 42 percent said it would make them more likely to vote for the opponent (Paul), and 13 percent said the ad would make them more likely to vote for Conway.

Finally, an ad from the 2006 US Senate race in Tennessee [Corker] polled the worst in terms of support for the attacking candidate, with only 11 percent saying it would make them more likely to support the attacker, Bob Corker. Most said the ad would have no effect (60%), while 31 percent said it would move them vote for the opponent, Harold Ford. But this ad was not the most controversial one from this campaign. Another Corker ad, which we could not use because of its overt support of partisan conservative issues, showed a woman flirtatiously telling us "I met Harold at the Playboy party!" and later saying "Harold, call me!" It ended with white letters on a black screen that read: "Harold Ford. He's just not right" (Files 2006). Amid backlash against the racial overtones, Corker denounced the ad and asked television stations not to run it. Corker won the election; Ford actually had been to a Playboy party.

Looking more broadly across all of the ads we tested, both positive and attack, figure 4.3 displays the mean backlash response for each ad, which for graphing purposes we coded as 2 = vote for the candidate running the ad, 1 = no effect on the vote, and 0 = vote for opponent. As before, different shapes represent the three types of ads: positive, negative, and defamatory. The most obvious result is that the positive ads, of which [Ayotte] received the most favorable score (1.56), were more likely to generate a vote for the sponsoring candidates than any of the attack ads. Reinforcing our expectations, our participants saw the positive ads as positive and responded accordingly, with the attack ads generally separate from the positive ones. The three ads at the low end of the scale are the three discussed above, the worst being [Dole] with an average rating of 0.64; there

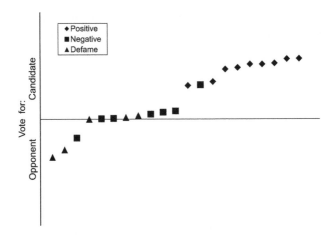

FIGURE 4.3. Voter backlash in response to negativity, study 4

is little differentiation between defamatory and other negative ads for the
rest. But perhaps most telling, for the other nine of the twelve attack ads,
the mean score is 1.0 or higher, suggesting at the worst that, rather than
a backlash, they generated more of a "so what" response. Fifty-four percent of participants said these nine ads would not affect their voting decision, 26 percent favored the attacker, and 20 percent preferred the target.
Among those who subjectively described an ad as negative—an indicator
of the harshest critics in our previous studies—27 percent responded with
backlash and 20 percent preferred the attacker. Even here though, if we
remove the three worst offenders [Corker, Dole, Conway], we find that
slightly more chose the attacker (23%) over the target (22%), and most
did not care (56%).

These results add some weight to our initial studies suggesting backlash effects are modest for the most part. Only when an ad steps over
some boundary is there some backlash. And the fact is, we think candidates know this, which is why ads attacking an opponent's family are virtually nonexistent while ads on religion are exceedingly rare (and probably even more so after the obvious failures of the two we report on here).

WHO FINDS ADS NEGATIVE?   As we noted earlier in looking at
the nature of our sample, a multivariate analysis suggests for the most
part that we cannot identify individual demographic differences in responses to negativity. Here we examine those models in more detail. We

look at two dependent variables: how negative an ad is perceived to be and how angry an ad makes viewers. For both dependent variables we do three analyses. First, we look only at positive ads, followed by an examination of all attack ads, and finally, attack ads with an indicator allowing us to specifically consider the defamatory ads. Each model predicts the dependent variable with a relatively standard set of demographic measures, including party identification (using independent as the base category), gender (female), ideological self-placement (five-point scale, from "very conservative" to "very liberal"), education (college graduate versus nongraduate), religiosity (four-point scale from "never attend services" to "weekly or more often"), race (nonwhite versus white), age in years, and 2012 election turnout intention (five-point scale from "very likely" to "will not vote"). Because each subject examined nine positive and twelve attack ads, we cluster standard errors on our 235 individual participants.

Table 4.6 displays models for perceptions of the level of negativity in an ad. Column 1 reports the model using positive ads, column 2 uses all attack ads, column 3 includes an indicator for defamatory ads, and column 4 looks only at the defamatory ads. Not surprisingly, we really get little purchase on the "how negative" question for positive ads. There was little variance in ratings of those nine ads, and since all were positive, we should not expect much, which is confirmed.

But our overall model for attack ads (column 2) is not much stronger, explaining just a small part of the variance. Even so, two potentially interesting predictors appear for attack ads. First, partisanship seems to play a small role. Both Republicans and Democrats rate the group of attack ads as more negative than do Independents, all else equal. We also see that religiosity appears to play some role in perceptions of negativity, but in the opposite direction. Those who attend religious services more often rate the attack ads as less negative on average than do those who attend less often. Again, though, the substantive effect is very small and we are honestly not sure what to make of this.

Given our earlier results showing significantly different responses to the "defamatory" ads in our collection, we examine the model by adding an indicator for our defamatory ads in column 3 of table 4.6. Now we seem to be getting somewhere. In particular, defamatory ads on average are viewed as much more negative (by 1.17 points, all else equal) than other negative ads. At the same time, adding this indicator does not eliminate the effects of partisanship and religiosity, and adds a significant (but again relatively small) effect for college graduates, who are more likely

TABLE 4.6. **Predicting "how negative" for campaign ads, study 4**

	Positive Ads Only	Attack Ads Only	Attack Ads Only	Defamatory Ads Only
Defamatory ad	—	—	1.1680***	—
			(.0422)	
Gender: Female	-.1347	-.0757	-.0716	-.1618*
	(.0699)	(.0986)	(.0984)	(.0985)
Republican	.0567	.2773**	.2720**	.2156*
	(.0944)	(.1307)	(.1306)	(.1297)
Democrat	.1013	.3063*	.3017*	.1706
	(.1120)	(.1712)	(.1713)	(.1545)
Ideology	.0362	-.0081	-.0075	-.0193
	(.0512)	(.0599)	(.0600)	(.0575)
College graduate	.0768	.3024	.3063*	.2486
	(.0796)	(.1837)	(.1835)	(.1845)
Religiosity	.0763	-.2261*	-.2254**	-.2535**
	(.0645)	(.1078)	(.1077)	(.1113)
Race: Nonwhite	.1620	-.1508	-.1524	-.1669
	(.1245)	(.1401)	(.1400)	(.1529)
Age in years	.0038	.0030	.0029	.0035
	(.0030)	(.0051)	(.0052)	(.0052)
Turnout likelihood	-.0007	-.0147	-.0148	-.0551
	(.0354)	(.0650)	(.0647)	(.0619)
Constant	.0893	3.2356***	2.7435***	4.2420***
	(.2167)	(.3187)	(.3820)	(.3846)
Adj. r^2	.023	.024	.180	.042
N	Subj. = 235	Subj. = 235	Subj. = 235	Subj. = 235
	Obs. = 2096	Obs = 2786	Obs = 2786	Obs. = 1163

Note: Robust standard errors in parentheses. DV = How negative, 0–5 scale; higher values are more negative.
*$p < 0.1$.
**$p < 0.05$.
***$p < 0.01$.

to rate the set of ads highly on our how negative scale compared to non-graduates.

Turning to the five defamatory ads only, we once again see relatively little going on in the model, again most likely because there is a high degree of agreement that these ads are very negative, resulting in limited variance. Women seem to be slightly less negative in their ratings than men, though the coefficient is just barely significant at $p < 0.1$. And Republicans seem to find the defamatory ads somewhat more negative than Independents. Finally, those who are more regular attendees at religious services actually rate the ads as less negative, on average, an interesting finding given that three of the five ads reference religion in one way or another.

We next look at whether we can identify individual differences in the

levels of anger generated by these ads. We use the same analytical strategy, substituting our anger scale as the dependent variable, which we report in table 4.7. Given that positive ads were not viewed as negative by
our subjects, we should not be surprised that we cannot predict anger
for those ads either. As with the question of how negative, the positive
ads did not generate any significant variance in anger, and thus there is
simply nothing to predict (column 1). Turning to the full group of attack
ads (column 2), we also find it difficult to predict levels of anger at negativity. In fact, the only individual difference we can detect is based on race:
as we noted earlier, our nonwhite respondents were less angered by the
attack ads than were whites. The effect is about one-quarter point on our
1–4 scale, so it is not very large, though it is clearly there. And the effect
exists despite seeing no racial group difference in how negative people

TABLE 4.7. **Predicting anger for campaign ads, study 4**

	Positive Ads Only	Attack Ads Only	Attack Ads Only	Defamatory Ads Only
Defamatory Ad	—	—	.4984*** (.0295)	—
Gender: Female	−.0456 (.0342)	−.1016 (.0878)	−.0999 (.0876)	−.0637 (.1019)
Republican	−.0095 (.0611)	.1024 (.1082)	.0995 (.1083)	.1301 (.1226)
Democrat	.0436 (.0432)	.0494 (.1371)	.0476 (.1369)	.0253 (.1586)
Ideology	.0317 (.0334)	.0184 (.0541)	.0190 (.0541)	−.0190 (.0615)
College graduate	.0007 (.0695)	.0561 (.1436)	.0569 (.1432)	−.0091 (.1757)
Religiosity	.0201 (.0397)	.0765 (.0869)	.0771 (.0869)	.0771 (.1018)
Race: Nonwhite	.0548 (.0629)	−.2800** (.1109)	−.2798** (.1108)	−.3933*** (.1246)
Age in years	.0004 (.0030)	.0004 (.0039)	.0003 (.0039)	−.0000 (.0045)
Turnout likelihood	−.0076 (.0187)	−.0657 (.0525)	−.0656 (.0524)	−.0624 (.0615)
Constant	1.1033*** (.1771)	2.3512*** (.3197)	2.139*** (.3182)	2.967*** (.3725)
Adj. r^2	.007	.020	.079	.030
N	Subj. = 235 Obs. = 2096	Subj. = 235 Obs. = 2785	Subj. = 235 Obs. = 2785	Subj. = 235 Obs. = 1162

Note: Robust standard errors in parentheses. DV = How angry, 1–4 scale; higher values indicate greater anger.
*$p < 0.1$.
**$p < 0.05$.
***$p < 0.01$.

thought the ads were. But more interestingly, even though we found that partisans rated these ads as more negative than did Independents, the ads did not make them angrier, all else equal. On the other hand, while those who frequently attend religious services were less likely to rate the ads as negative, they were not made any less angry by doing so.

When we add in the indicator for defamatory ads (column 3) we get a slightly more robust model but things really do not change much. Defamatory ads do, all else equal, generate more anger (0.498 points on the 1–4 scale) than nondefamatory negative ads. And nonwhites remain less angered overall. When we turn to the defamatory ads only (column 4) we are again faced with the reality that across all our subjects there is limited variation on levels of anger generated by these ads. The only significant difference we find is that nonwhites express less anger at these ads, all else equal.

Finally, we take a look at the ads by topic. We have four broad topics in this set of ads: issues, character, family, and religion. We enter indicators for the latter three topics, comparing each to the effects of negative ads that are about issues. Recall that respondents in all of our studies were least concerned about issue-based attacks, suggesting that such attacks are among the most acceptable. Table 4.8 reports models predicting "how negative" (column 1) and anger (column 2) using the full set of attack ads. For these subjects, the attack ad with family references scored significantly and substantively higher on the negativity scale than the other three topics. It also generated a greater anger response, even stronger than the response to the religion attacks, which interestingly, are not seen as more negative than issues but do generate more anger. We also find that character ads increase neither the level of negativity assessed for the ads nor levels of anger and, in fact, we find anger is statistically lower for character ads compared to issues.

It turns out that predicting who in particular will find ads negative and how angry they will be at those ads is difficult, at least with the participants in study 4 and the set of ads we chose to minimize partisan cues. We cannot predict differences in response to positive ads simply because there are none. We do have variance across the attack ads generally, yet our models predicting reactions are not very strong. One takeaway may be that assessments of negativity are idiosyncratic: as David Mark notes in the opening quotation of this chapter, what is negative for me may simply not be for you. Another takeaway is that the relationship between assessments of negativity and anger at the ads is not as clear cut as we might expect. Groups more likely to give higher "how negative" scores to ads are

TABLE 4.8. **Ad topics and effects on perceived negativity and anger, attack ads only, study 4**

	How Negative	Anger
Topic: Character	-.0500	-.0783**
	(.0484)	(.0333)
Topic: Family	.8907***	.4544***
	(.0711)	(.0542)
Topic: Religion	-.0603	.3565***
	(.0596)	(.0467)
Gender: Female	-.0747	-.1011
	(.0986)	(.0877)
Republican	.2758**	.0998
	(.1307)	(.1084)
Democrat	.3055*	.0466
	(.1712)	(.1370)
Ideology	-.0074	.0190
	(.0600)	(.0542)
College graduate	.3042*	.0562
	(.1835)	(.1437)
Religiosity	-.2247**	.0774
	(.1078)	(.0869)
Race: Nonwhite	-.1517	-.2809**
	(.1401)	(.1109)
Age in years	.0030	.0003
	(.0051)	(.0039)
Turnout likelihood	-.0145	-.0649
	(.0647)	(.0525)
Constant	3.1920***	2.2547***
	(.3823)	(.3213)
Adj. r^2	.055	.062
N	Subj. = 235	Subj. = 235
	Obs. = 2786	Obs. = 2785

Note: Robust standard errors in parentheses. DV = How angry, 1–4 scale; higher values indicate greater anger.
*$p < 0.1$.
**$p < 0.05$.
***$p < 0.01$.

not necessarily more likely to be angered by those ads, suggesting that despite the correlation overall between ratings of "negativity" and "anger" responses, the connection is not as strong as it might seem.

Experimenting with Religious Attacks: The Case of Kay Hagan and Elizabeth Dole

With Shannon Holmberg

As we have already described, among the ads we showed to subjects was an attack by Elizabeth Dole on her opponent, Kay Hagan, in which Dole made the implicit claim that Hagan was an atheist. Direct attacks invoking religion like this are quite rare, and in our study participants rated the Dole ad among the most negative of all of the ads. Because we had both ads, we carried out an experiment where participants were randomly assigned to first see either Dole's original attack ad or Hagan's response, followed immediately by the other. This allows us to get a better understanding of the back-and-forth in such ads, and how response to one ad may condition response to the next. In this section we give a quick review of the Dole/Hagan campaign and then analyze the results of our experiment.

A telltale sign of a highly competitive election is the waves of negative campaign advertisements that inundate the public. While these ads commonly point out character flaws or poor voting records of opposition candidates, some ads get very personal. One such ad that created an instant uproar was released by incumbent US senator Elizabeth Dole against her challenger Kay Hagan on October 29 in the 2008 North Carolina Senate race.

In this ad Republican incumbent Dole accused Democrat Hagan of being a "godless American." The ad included atheist group leader interviews and footage of Hagan allegedly attending an atheist fundraiser, and ended with a voiceover that a reasonable viewer would assume was Hagan saying, "There is no God." For what it was worth, fact-checkers from the *Charlotte Observer* analyzed the controversial portions of the ad and discovered that many claims were fabricated or used out of context (Zagaroli 2008). The voice at the end of the ad was not Hagan's. The fundraiser was not for an atheist organization, though it was held at the home of an adviser to the Godless Americans PAC. The footage of Hagan at the fundraiser showed her standing next to a retired religion professor who was also her former Bible teacher.

Dole's ad was viewed by many as an act of desperation in the homestretch of the campaign given she had been trailing in polls since mid-September (Walls 2008). Both local and national news outlets commented on the ad and few were in favor of it. Republican strategist Ed Rollins called it, "so despicable and so unlike Elizabeth Dole that she should be ashamed of herself" while GOP consultant Alex Castellanos commented, "When you're making ads that say, 'There is no God,' it usually means your campaign doesn't have a prayer" (Zagaroli 2008). Despite the backlash, a National Republican Senatorial Committee spokesman defended Dole's ad as accurately portraying the fact that the fundraiser was held in the home of a member of the Godless Americans PAC and Hagan had received support and money from the fundraiser.[9] But this was an exception; for the most part Dole's ad was roundly condemned.

Days after the release of Dole's ad, Hagan responded with an ad defending herself and criticizing Dole for lying. Hagan also said in an interview that she had never heard of the Godless PAC until Dole brought it up. Hagan called Dole's ad "politics of the worst kind," and said that it was "fabricated" and "pathetic."[10] In a press release Hagan defended her Christian faith and listed her repertoire of Christian involvement from being a Sunday school teacher to her family's community service.

In the end Dole lost to Hagan 53 to 44 percent. The ad likely was not directly to blame for Dole's defeat because if the race had been closer, it would probably never have been produced. While few candidates have actually run ads like Dole's, in the heat of a campaign candidates—especially those who are trailing—begin to look for anything that might break through the noise. While an ad like Dole's may be extreme, it does fit within a category of negative defamatory ads making it worth a more careful examination as it left behind a negative legacy for Dole and has served as a paradigm of disastrous negative campaign ads.

Table 4.9 displays the responses of our study 4 participants to each of these ads. It is clear that responses to Hagan's ad are highly dependent on whether that ad was viewed before or after the Dole ad. Participants who saw the Hagan ad first—and thus out of context—were much more likely to consider Hagan's ad as negative (56% negative) than those who only saw it after watching the Dole attack (27%). Not surprisingly, the Hagan ad was also viewed as more negative among those who saw it before Dole's (2.08 before, 1.22 after). Those who saw Hagan's ad first were angrier (2.30 on our four-point scale) compared to those who saw it

TABLE 4.9. **Results for Dole and Hagan ads, study 4**

Ad Order	Dole Ad		Hagan Ad	
	Dole First (N = 111)	Hagan First (N = 89)	Dole First (N = 110)	Hagan First (N = 91)
Is negative	99%	98%	27%	56%
How negative	4.34	4.34	1.22	2.08
Anger	2.86	2.92	1.88	2.30
Vote for candidate	21%	9%	59%	31%
Vote for opponent	52%	50%	7%	18%

Note: More complete results for these two ads, including standard errors, can be found in table 6.12.

after Dole's (1.88). Finally, participants were much more likely to vote for Hagan when her ad was shown second (59% versus 31%).

While response to the Hagan ad depends on the context in which it is viewed, the same is not always true for the Dole ad. Indeed, it was all but universally seen as negative whether viewed before or after Hagan's ad. It rated extremely high on the "how negative" scale (4.34 in both conditions) and generated levels of anger much higher than Hagan in both treatments. The backlash to Dole was similar in both treatments, with about half saying they would vote for the opponent; showing the Dole ad second eroded her vote support from 21 percent to 9 percent.

We take a couple points from this analysis. First, as we supposed from our earlier experiments, using religion in an ad—at least in the context of implying your opponent is an atheist—is simply not a good move. While voters for the most part are not bothered much by negativity, it is clear that some topics are essentially off limits, such as claiming your opponent is an atheist when she is not (of course, if she is, that might be a different story). The claim generated anger and backlash among our participants no matter where they saw it in the sequence of ads.

On the other hand, Hagan's ad, while not generating quite so negative a response, was still viewed as negative by a majority when seen out of context, that is, without viewing the Dole ad first. Since this ad also talks about religion and attacks the opponent for being misleading, it reinforces the lower level of acceptability for religion-oriented attacks. But it also shows that an attack in response to another attack—at least an attack as personal as Dole's was—can generate a great deal of sympathy.

Conclusion

We have now described the results from four different experiments, three of which were description-based and one of which used real-world ads. The first three were all probability samples and readily generalizable to the populations from which they were drawn. The fourth was a convenience sample, but the results both reinforce and further develop what we found in the initial studies. In fact, across all of the studies we find similar results. Voters are able to identify negative ads and respond differently to those they consider negative. They are also pretty good at estimating what their responses to real ads would be—in terms of anger and of potential backlash against the sponsor of negative ads—when presented with hypothetical situations and given only descriptions. Using actual ads does increase the level of anger for some topics, but the differences are relatively minor. Our point in all of this is to reinforce our basic contention. While voters are nearly universally opposed to negative ads when they are described as such by pollsters, when the ads are presented without an explicit cue regarding their negativity—that is, voters get to decide for themselves what is negative—the responses are nuanced, recognizing differences across topics and also the negative or defamatory nature of the ads. But, and this is key, there is relatively little evidence of a backlash against the sponsors of negativity, which makes sense if voters see value in negative ads, not just unmitigated useless negativity.

We think that voters are smart enough to assess the ads on their own merits, and to differentiate negative ads that carry relatively little information of value and those that do. Voters can handle negative ads and the worry that such ads somehow damage democracy is overblown. And now, having shown that voters can tolerate negativity, starting in the next chapter we begin addressing the informational value of negative campaigns.

CHAPTER FIVE

Modeling Negativity

A campaign is about defining who you are—your vision and your opponent's vision.—Donna Brazile, political pundit and Al Gore's campaign manager in 2000

So far, we have shown that negative ads are received reasonably well by voters when those ads provide information about relevant topics. Others, of course, have also shown the informational value of negative campaigns, but a trickier question is whether or not, in the absence of negative campaigns, voters would have received similar information and learned about both the candidate's vision and the opponent's. In other words, is negative campaigning really necessary?

To this point we have relied on a number of different empirical methods to try to understand how voters respond to negativity. We have found through random sample telephone survey experiments (studies 1 and 2) that opposition to the basic activity of a negative campaign— talking about an opponent's weaknesses—is not particularly troubling, for the most part. Our Internet-based national panel survey (study 3) reinforces this key point and delves further into differentiating the kinds of ads that do not bother voters from those that might have them saying, "How dare he!" And in the previous chapter we took yet another approach, showing real-world ads to a nonprobability sample of US citizens (study 4), and asking a number of questions about them. Our findings about the kinds of ads that are acceptable and those that are not are supported not only by showing hypothetical ads to a probability sample, but also when a different sample of voters sees the real thing. This methodological triangulation is an important part of our story, and while any one method has its limits, our confidence in the underlying results is enhanced when multiple approaches point the same way.

Here we shift gears slightly. We started out interested in how voters perceive negativity; now we turn to why candidates so often choose to embrace negative campaigning, and why it is actually necessary that informed voters have access to opponents' attacks on each other. In order to do this we need to move beyond the techniques usually employed by researchers interested in negative campaigning, and look instead at the type of models often used by economists to understand situations where multiple actors have varying incentives to make choices about courses of actions. This approach is often referred to as "economic" or "formal" modeling, and fits within a field of study called *game theory*, which essentially is the study of strategic interaction. Here, as we develop and test a formal model (and discuss an extension of it in chapter 7), we will not delve into the guts of game theory or spend a lot of time on various arcane aspects of this formal model. In fact, we would not even venture into these waters except that we believe a formal model—and, more important, empirical tests of that model with laboratory subjects—can help us better understand the decision-making that goes along with candidates' production of negativity. It will help explain why negativity is absolutely necessary to ensure informed voters in a representative democracy.

So we do need to spend time developing and explicating our formal model, which makes up the first part of this chapter. After reading the following section, those who are less interested in the details of the model, or are uncomfortable trying to make sense of the symbols it uses, may wish to go to our experimental test in the second part of this chapter, forgoing the details of the model. It should be possible to make sense of the experiment and to understand its outcome even without focusing on formal modeling details. On the other hand, for readers who wish to better understand where we are headed, a careful reading of the first part of this chapter may be in order, as well as appendix B.

But first, let us summarize our argument. In a world where negative campaigning (however defined) is banned, and candidates are limited to either presenting a positive campaign or not campaigning at all, voter information will necessarily be incomplete. Simply put, negativity is necessary because without it voters cannot deduce the same information from a candidate's failure to positively campaign that they can get from information-filled attacks. A formal model combined with an experiment gives us a way to simplify and control the election environment in order to assess our argument.

We make use of a formal model and experiment because we cannot adequately address our research question with the usual empirical data derived from real campaigns, such as the content of ads and how often they are shown. For one thing, in any given election there cannot be counterfactual data; we *cannot* know what would have happened if a candidate had *not* used negativity (or any other particular strategy). Any real-world campaign is given. So why not simply look at many different campaigns and compare those that use negativity to those that do not (or use it less)? Unfortunately, this would be a mistake since there can be no random assignment to the treatments, meaning we cannot determine causality. Should we just assume that candidates failing to use negativity are doing so because they are facing situations where negativity will not work? Or should we instead assume the candidates are making mistakes? Second, hardly any competitive elections eschew negative campaigning. It would seem that such elections are idiosyncratic, and so it would be hard to justify the assumption that introducing negativity to a positive campaign would be a good test given the unusual circumstances surrounding an all-positive election. And as we have shown, there is a wide variety of negativity. So there would be many variations of alternate campaign strategies to consider as counterfactuals, a situation further confounded by the fact that voters' response toward the ads depends on the topic of the ad (and, as we will show later, its credibility and appropriateness).

So rather than make untenable assumptions about the real world, we model an information environment where it is possible for voters to get the same amount of information from positive or negative campaigning—and where negative campaigning could be giving redundant information to the voters. Whether this happens depends upon whether voters learn any information about topics that candidates do not—but could—address in a campaign. For example, according to the Advertising Project at the University of Wisconsin, John McCain ran 100 percent negative ads in the weeks leading up to the November 2008 US presidential election (Halloran 2008). McCain's ads provided voters with various reasons as to why they should not support Barack Obama. That's fine, but we need to also ask whether a voter might infer something about *McCain* from his failure to positively campaign. In other words, what did a voter learn about McCain from what he *didn't* say? Might a voter think that McCain had nothing positive worth discussing at all? Or, should we assume that voters already knew McCain's positive traits and/or policy positions? Or were Obama's negative traits deemed far more important, hence warranting such attention?[1]

Thus we introduce a formal model as the next step in studying voters' responses to negative campaigns. The first question we ask is: what can voters infer from a candidate's failure to positively campaign on a given topic? For example, suppose that voters in a primary election will only vote for someone who supports anti-abortion measures. Also assume that all candidates who support these pro-life statutes will advertise that fact. Now, if one candidate (Adams) mentions his support and his opponent (Brown) does not, a voter should conclude that the silent candidate (Brown) doesn't support those statutes. The standard for formal modeling in politics is to assume such reasoning, and to many, it seems reasonable to think that a voter could draw this type of inference. But alternatively, a voter might think that candidate Brown's silence conveys nothing—that there is still a reasonable chance he is pro-life.

So, do voters consider implications that can be derived only from information candidates do *not* reveal? In laboratory experiments designed to test our formal model, we find that voters often fail to make such inferences, and that this has an important effect on the campaign information that candidates present to them—it essentially requires candidates to negatively campaign, because it is the only way for voters to learn why a given candidate should not be elected.

In the above example, candidate Adams could explicitly point out that candidate Brown is *not* pro-life, though if he does, inevitably he must pull campaign resources away from other topics. In any case, limited campaign resources (and perhaps, limited voter attention spans) ensure that some things will always be left unsaid or unnoticed (Lau and Redlawsk 2006). That is why the allocation of resources—especially between positive and negative campaigning—is a crucial decision for all political campaigns. As Harrington and Hess (1996) have explained, understanding how and why candidates choose to allocate recourses toward different campaign themes is necessary to explain why "candidates in the same electoral contest might pursue very different campaign strategies."

Bayesian Updating

"I have found out in the course of a long public life that the things I did not say never hurt me," said former president Calvin Coolidge (Fuess 1940). But why would that be true? We have all heard the maxim, "If you can't say anything nice, don't say anything at all." Since Coolidge had a policy of not saying anything at all, shouldn't people have been making negative inferences from his silence?

This simple question leads us to a decision theory concept called Bayesian inference. It's based upon Bayes' theorem of probability, which shows how a belief held with some probability (but not with certainty) should be revised after the introduction of new evidence. Suppose you change your hairstyle and meet up with two friends, both of whom you think will like it (your prior belief). One of them says it looks great, and the second says nothing. Do you now assume that the second friend *doesn't* like it? If so, you have just used Bayesian updating to infer important information from silence. To some degree we all routinely make inferences like this. It seems to us that these inferences are clearer in simple social situations, such as we described with the hairstyle. The question is the extent to which people can do the same in more complex decision environments with multiple actors and ambiguous information. Everyone has limits.

These limits to voters' decision-making ability in a given information environment are often referred to as *bounded rationality* (Simon 1955), and have rarely been considered in formal models of campaigns and their allocation of scarce resources. In many campaign models, the voter is not conceived as a strategic player and/or receives full information thus eliminating uncertainty (e.g., Adams and Merrill 2008; Ansolabehere and Snyder 2000; Aragones and Palfrey 2002; Groseclose 2001; Harrington and Hess 1996; Londregan and Romer 1993; Skaperdas and Grofman 1995). In other models, voters are provided potentially incomplete information by the candidates, and are assumed to be Bayesian updaters when dealing with any uncertainty about that information (e.g., Austen-Smith and Banks 1996; Callander and Wilkie 2007; Coate 2004; Feddersen and Pesendorfer 1996; Kartik and McAfee 2006; Martinelli 2001; Polborn and Yi 2006).

Bounded rationality is important to our understanding of the informational value of campaigns, since it goes to the heart of whether voters need important information to be provided directly or if they can make valid inferences from the absence of important information. So, are voters in fact Bayesian updaters? Alvarez (1998) found supporting evidence from political surveys. Voters given new information about candidates' issue positions during campaigns tended to revise their perceptions and evaluations of the candidates in line with what would be expected of a Bayesian updater. This Bayesian learning did not always occur in a consistent manner. It was much more prevalent whenever the issues were salient, and increased along with voters' uncertain prior information about the candidates. Moreover, risk aversion—the voter's preference for taking or avoiding risks—was important. Voters with a low tolerance for risk tended to prefer candidates who provided more certain information. Other Bayesian learning models have been successful in explaining voters' assessments of their representatives (Husted, Kenny, and Morton 1995) and responses to media exposure (Bartels 1993). But these studies generally are about information provided to voters, not the *absence* of information.

In fact, there is good evidence that voters cannot make the negative Bayesian inferences described earlier. Using a signaling game experiment that modeled political debate, Dickson, Hafer, and Landa (2008) reported that about 60 percent of their subjects chose to send a message in situations where the Bayesian behavioral prediction was to keep silent. Jamieson et al. (2000) found that voter learning is generally confined to the set of topics featured by the candidates and does not extend to topics not given significant focus. And Redlawsk (2002) presents experimental evidence that voters' biases and affective responses preclude even this amount of Bayesian updating. Given these findings, a likely possibility is that voter decision-making *partially* employs such updating. We designed our model with this possibility in mind.

In our model, two candidates, who have "positive" or "negative" traits on two dimensions, campaign by revealing to a voter either positive information about themselves, negative information about the opponent, or nothing at all.[2] The voter, who receives a higher payoff from choosing a candidate with positive traits, votes after receiving campaign statements from both candidates. Before the campaign, the voter only knows the probability that any candidate has a positive trait, a probability that is systematically varied in this experiment. But after the campaigns, and before voting, the voter has an opportunity to deduce other traits by considering the statements that candidates *failed* to choose.

Using this model, we can focus on the interactions between the strategies of candidates and voters. This is especially so because the theoretical equilibrium—and hence the behavioral predictions for both candidates and voters—differs depending upon the extent of voters' Bayesian updating. For convenience, we will use the term *sophisticated voter* to represent the perfect Bayesian updater, and *naïve voter* to represent the opposite—a voter that does not employ Bayesian updating at all. Of course, most real voters lie somewhere in between.

We designed an experiment to test this model, making sure that one of the two dimensions was always more salient to voters, as they received a higher payout from electing candidates with a positive trait on that dimension. We find that candidates "positive" on the more important dimension almost always choose positive campaigns. Yet voters regularly fail to correctly attribute negative traits to candidates who do *not* engage in positive campaigning on the most salient dimension. This in turn increases the effectiveness of candidates' negative campaigning, as the voters tend to disproportionally vote for the attackers. Hence, the relative naiveté of voters leads to an increase in negative campaigning. This provides a different means for understanding why candidates might choose negative campaigning—instead of focusing only on how the campaigns affect voting decisions, we consider how voters' decision-making affects the candidates' campaign choices.

We also find evidence that the incidence of negative campaigning increases as the voters' prior opinions about candidates *improve*. This reasoning—that voters with positive views of politicians are more affected by negativity—may at first seem incongruent with reality. Approval ratings of Congress, according to Gallup polls, were below 40 percent from 1972 to 1998 and have been below 25 percent since December 2009, reaching a low of 10 percent twice in 2012.[3] However, voters' post-election approval ratings of candidates often differ substantially from their opinions of the candidates before the campaign. In fact, evidence shows that evaluations of unknown political candidates (Holbrook et al. 2001), or for that matter any hypothetical person (Adams-Webber 1979; Benjafield 1985), are slightly positive in the absence of information. In accordance, we focus not on voters' views of candidates already in office, but instead on the voters' prior beliefs about essentially unknown political candidates. It is for these unknown candidates that voters still maintain hope.

The tendency to evaluate hypothetical people (or any neutral scenario) as mildly positive is referred to as a *positivity offset*, and treating it as a variable allows us to do an important test. By definition, a naïve voter will assume that prior expectations hold unless they are given specific new information to the contrary. So, a relatively naïve voter with a positivity offset will assume the candidates have favorable qualities or positions unless she is told otherwise—which can only be accomplished through negative campaigns. As the positivity offset increases, we should see an increase in negative campaigning. On the other hand, if the voter is relatively sophisticated, the extent of the positivity offset will *not* affect the frequency of negative campaigns. These voters can better discern that a candidate has unfavorable qualities (or positions) simply from his failure to talk about them. So, by varying the positivity offset and examining the resulting change in campaign strategies, we can better determine where voters lie on the continuum between naïve and sophisticated. What we find is important: voters seem to operate more in the realm of naiveté than sophistication, strongly suggesting that without negativity they are mostly unable to make important inferences about the traits that candidates possess. Negativity, then, allows voters to overcome their limitations. With its explicit focus on information that otherwise would not be revealed, it gives voters something closer to full information than they would have without it.

The remainder of this chapter is organized as follows. In the next section, we present the formal model, discuss the main assumptions, and describe the equilibria. Following that, we outline the experimental design. Finally, we discuss the experimental results, the most important being the relative naiveté of voters, which in turn rewards candidates for choosing negative campaigns. Now is the point at which some readers may wish to skip directly to the "Testing the Formal Model: Experimental Design" section rather than wade through the details of how our formal model works. The results might not be completely clear without a more full understanding of the model, but we try to summarize them in ways that make sense even for readers not versed in the details of game theory.

A Formal Model of Campaigning

The campaigning game takes place between two candidates and one voter. Each candidate has traits on two dimensions, labeled X and Y, which can either be "positive" or "negative"; hence there are sixteen possible configurations of the candidates' traits (four combinations for Candidate A times four combinations for Candidate B). The traits are drawn from a distribution known to all players, but the realization of the traits is only known to the candidates. So, the candidates know each other's traits, but the voter only knows the probability that the traits are positive. The candidates and voter play a three-stage game as depicted in figure 5.1. Candidates learn their traits and the opponents' traits in stage 1 and campaign in stage 2. The voter chooses a candidate in stage 3, after which all players receive payoffs. The details of each stage are explained below.

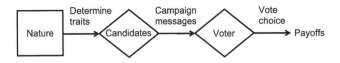

FIGURE 5.1. Campaign game flowchart

In the first stage, each candidate's traits are drawn from the set $\{X+, X-\} \times \{Y+, Y-\}$, so a candidate will draw either a positive $(X+)$ or negative $(X-)$ trait on the X dimension, and independently will draw either a positive $(Y+)$ or negative $(Y-)$ trait on Y. In the second stage, the candidates now know all the traits, and will campaign by simultaneously revealing one of these traits to the voter. Formally, this means that a strategy for candidate ℓ consists of ℓ's campaign message for the sixteen different trait draw possibilities, chosen from the following five campaigning options: revealing one's own X trait (hereafter abbreviated as X), one's own Y trait (hereafter, Y), the opponent's X trait (hereafter, $oppX$), the opponent's Y trait (hereafter, $oppY$), or revealing nothing (hereafter, $\varnothing$). This strategy set is shown in line (1) below.

(1) $s_\ell : [\{X+,X-\}\times\{Y+,Y-\}]^2 \rightarrow \{X, oppX, Y, oppY, \varnothing\}$

In the third and final phase, the voter receives both candidates' messages simultaneously and then elects one of the candidates. The voter's utility function for candidate ℓ is simply additive over that candidate's traits on the two dimensions, as shown in line (2).

(2) $U_V(\ell) = U(X_\ell) + U(Y_\ell)$

The game is defined so a voter receives higher utility from electing a candidate with a positive (rather than negative) trait on any given dimension. Hence the voter's ideal point is reached if the voter elects a candidate with positive traits on both dimensions.

We should note here that our model is predicated on two main assumptions. The first, which we have discussed at length in this book, is that campaigns—including negative campaigns—provide meaningful information to voters.[4] An alternative justification for using this assumption has been offered by Polborn and Yi (2006), who present a similar model of information revelation.[5] They suggest that candidates provide such information indirectly, using advertising to define the debate, that is, putting the spotlight of the media on either their best traits or the opponents' worst.

We also assume that there are limits to this transmission of information. Candidates in this model must choose a particular dimension on which to campaign (or else refrain from campaigning). One can think of this decision as choosing the overall theme of the campaign—that which will be pervasive through all of the campaign discourse. Whether due to financial limitations, voter attention spans, or other reasons, political candidates are constrained, and certainly cannot campaign effectively on every topic. Because of this, they must determine which of the possible messages will most sway voters, and focus specifically on those. Modeling this on a larger scale (for instance, with candidates choosing three topics from any of six dimensions) would complicate the players' strategies but not substantively change the results.

Without loss of generality, let us assume that a candidate positive on dimension X gives a voter a utility of $U(X_\ell) = x$, and a candidate negative on X gives a voter a utility of 0. Similarly, let these values on the Y dimension be y and 0, where $x \geq y$. Before the election, the voter's expected utility for each candidate will be $p(x + y)$, where p is the probability that a given trait is positive.

Voters in this game not only receive the candidates' statements, but also have an opportunity for Bayesian updating—in this case, making inferences about campaign revelations that the candidates do not choose. The formal strategy of the voter, in fact, depends upon her decision-making approach. The naïve voter strategy τ_n maps each of the different pairs of campaign revelations (5 × 5, so 25 combinations) to a choice between the two candidates. This is shown in (3), where R_ℓ and $R_{-\ell}$ represent the campaigns of candidates ℓ and $-\ell$, respectively.

(3) $\tau_n : (R_\ell, R_{-\ell}) \rightarrow \{\ell, -\ell\}$

Having established the game, we turn now to its equilibrium strategies, that is, the strategies that give the maximum payoffs to the players. Because of the differences in assumed Bayesian updating ability, we cannot use the same equilibrium definition for both naïve and sophisticated voters. The concept of *cursed equilibrium* (CE; Eyster and Rabin 2005) helps us here. Like our naïve voter, a "cursed" game player does not take into account how other people's information might have affected their actions. As adapted to our model, in a CE a given voter will act as a naïve voter with some probability and as a sophisticated voter otherwise. This represents uncertainty about the extent to which the voter's Bayesian updating will occur. Later, in our experiment based on the formal model, the CE prediction yields a specific parameter measuring where players' analytical abilities lie on this continuum between perfect updating and ignoring updating altogether. The existence of such a parameter in our model allows us to address the important question of what voters infer about candidates in the context of negative campaigning and the ensuing absence of some information. Recall, we are especially interested in the extent to which voters are sophisticated or naïve in their ability to infer information from silence, since this determines the optimal strategies for candidates. With that in mind, we begin with our equilibrium definition for the game with a naïve voter.

Elections with a Naïve Voter

DEFINITION 1.   Naïve Voter Equilibrium
The equilibrium concept for this game is *fully cursed* in pure strategies (Eyster and Rabin 2005). That is, voters are unable to take into account information not explicitly provided by the candidates. Thus, for each candidate ℓ and for the voter V, the equilibrium consists of:

1. Candidate strategies $\tilde{s}_\ell(\theta_\ell, \theta_{-\ell}) \in \arg\max_\ell \tilde{\tau}(s_\ell, \tilde{s}_{-\ell}(\theta))$
2. Voter strategies $\tilde{\tau}(R) \in \arg\max E_\mu U_V(\tilde{s}, \tau)$
3. Voter posterior beliefs $\mu(\theta | R)$, which are identical to the voter's prior beliefs about the probability distribution unless the candidate location is directly revealed by R.

We designate the function $d_\ell(R)$ as the difference in voter utility between candidates ℓ and $-\ell$ after both have chosen campaign actions $R = (R_\ell, R_{-\ell})$.

(4) $d_\ell(R) = E_\mu(U_V(\ell) | R) - E_\mu(U_V(-\ell) | R)$

PROPOSITION: *In the naïve voter equilibrium, candidates will choose the campaign theme that maximizes $d_\ell(R_\ell)$, the difference in voter utility given candidate ℓ's action only.*

PROOF AND EXPLANATION.   The naïve voter equilibrium always exists in pure strategies. The voter's original expected utility for each candidate,

$U_v(\ell)$, is $p(x + y)$, and any subsequent revelations by the candidates have a measurable effect on her expected utility for one of the candidates. In this proposed equilibrium, the candidates will choose the campaign that provides the greatest increase in the utility difference between themselves and the opponent. The voter strategy is simply to vote for the candidate that yields the highest expected utility given her beliefs. Thus if $E_\mu U_v(\ell) >$ $E_\mu U_v(-\ell)$, then $\tilde{\tau}\,(s_\ell, \tilde{s}_{-\ell}(\theta)) = \ell$.[6] With naïve voting, candidates do not have to take into account the opponent's strategy $s_{-\ell}$, because the voter cannot make any inferences from the campaign messages that either candidate did not choose. Therefore, choosing the option R_ℓ that maximizes $d_\ell(R_\ell)$ is a weakly dominant strategy.[7]

For the naïve voter, each campaign revelation will have an easily measurable effect on her expected utility for one of the candidates. Thus, the equilibrium naïve voter strategies can be derived from comparing the deviations in voter expected utility for each campaign announcement. For the naïve voter game, revealing that one is positive on dimension X will improve voter utility by $(1 - p)x$, and revealing that the opponent is negative on X will lower voter utility for the opposing candidate by px. Similarly, revealing that one is positive on dimension Y will improve voter utility by $(1 - p)y$, and revealing that the opponent is negative on Y will lower voter utility for that candidate by py. Candidates will choose the statement that maximizes this utility change in a direction beneficial to themselves (i.e., revealing only positive information about oneself or negative information about the opponent). If a candidate deviates from the equilibrium strategy, the candidate would necessarily be either choosing a campaign that changes voter utility by a smaller amount (if the campaign is still beneficial), choosing a campaign that is harmful to the candidate, or choosing not to campaign. None of these options would ever improve a candidate's chances of winning the election when the voter is naïve. In equilibrium, the candidates (and the voter) will thus prefer whichever announcement most changes the voter's naïvely adjusted expected utility.

Elections with a Sophisticated Voter

The sophisticated voter, however, will take into account not only the campaign revelations $(R_\ell, R_{-\ell})$ but also the candidates' entire strategies—in other words, what the candidates would have chosen had their actual traits been different. This is shown in (5).

(5) $\tau_n : (R_\ell, R_{-\ell}, s_\ell, s_{-\ell}) \to \{\ell, -\ell\}$

Here we use the concept of perfect Bayesian equilibrium (PBE). In Bayesian games generally at least one of the players has incomplete information that is known by another player in the game. At least part of the game is sequential such that the player with incomplete information has the opportunity to view move(s) by those more knowledgeable. Thus before choosing his own move, the player derives posterior beliefs by using Bayes' rule to determine—given the move(s) of the knowledgeable—more information about the game. PBE places restrictions on beliefs such that at every stage of the game, maximizing expected utility according to those beliefs results in maximizing expected utility of the game.

In the context of our game, it means that the voter, after seeing the two candidates' campaign choices, uses candidates' strategies to update beliefs about the candidates' types. The voter must have specific beliefs about candidate types for every possible message pair. Candidates' campaign decisions are made taking into account the voter strategy and thus what the voter beliefs would be after receiving hypothetical campaign messages.

DEFINITION 2.   Sophisticated Voter Equilibrium
The equilibrium concept for this game is perfect Bayesian equilibrium in pure strategies. Thus, for each candidate ℓ and for the voter V, the equilibrium consists of:

1. Candidate strategies $\tilde{s}_\ell(\theta_\ell, \theta_{-\ell}) \in \arg\max_\ell \tilde{\tau}(s_\ell, \tilde{s}_{-\ell}(\theta))$
2. Voter strategies $\tilde{\tau}(R) \in \arg\max E_\mu U_V(\tilde{s}, \tau)$
3. Voter posterior beliefs $\mu(\theta|R)$ which are a probability distribution derived from Bayes' rule using $\tilde{s}(\theta)$ whenever possible.

The difference between this and definition 1 (the naïve voter equilibrium) is the rule governing voter posterior beliefs $\mu(\theta|R)$, which has been modified so that the sophisticated voter employs Bayesian updating whenever possible. Just as in the naïve equilibrium, the voter must be maximizing her expected utility, and each candidate ℓ must be using a best response to the opponent's equilibrium strategy $\tilde{s}_{-\ell}$. Note also that in equilibrium, candidates' strategies and voter beliefs about those strategies will coincide.

Using Bayes' law "whenever possible" means that there may be certain instances—events that are off the equilibrium path—in which Bayes' rule cannot be used. In our game, there may be message pairs that the voter will never receive in equilibrium. Since the probability of receiving these messages is zero, there is little use for Bayesian updating. PBE still requires that the voter have beliefs about such off-path outcomes, but places no restrictions on voter beliefs in those instances. For those not familiar with game theory, this distinction may appear trivial. It is not, and in fact has ramifications because it increases the number of existing sophisticated equilibria in the game. For those interested, further technical information about the game's PBE and our approach to off-path beliefs can be found in appendix B.

Next, we explain our criteria for limiting the sophisticated equilibria on which we focus. Note that there are four campaign messages that reveal "good" information: "I have a positive X trait," "I have a negative Y trait," "My opponent has a negative X trait," and "My opponent has a negative Y trait." We consider sophisticated equilibria in which candidates prefer to reveal a specific one of those statements—call it statement 1—whenever it is available (i.e., does not reveal harmful information). So in that sense, our approach to sophisticated equilibria is similar to the naïve case. The major difference, however, is that with sophisticated voters, the preferred campaign theme (statement 1) can, but needs not be the one that maximizes $d_\ell(R_\ell)$ for a naïve voter. The other theme on the same dimension will also work as statement 1. So, if "I am positive on X" maximizes $d_\ell(R_\ell)$ for a naïve voter, then both it and "My opponent is negative on X" can be statement 1 in an equilibrium. In some cases, all four messages could serve as statement 1.

We describe the sophisticated equilibria by two statements: statement 1 and one from the other dimension (statement 2), which is essentially the candidate's backup plan for whenever statement 1 is not available. In other words, candidates will choose the primary theme (statement 1) unless it reveals harmful information (i.e., an opponent's positive trait or one's own negative trait). In that case, candidates will instead choose a secondary theme (statement 2), which must be on a different dimension from the primary theme. Because the two themes must be on separate dimensions, there are eight possible sophisticated equilibria that we consider.

We derive the candidates' strategies for a [statement 1–statement 2] equilibrium using the following simple algorithm:

Only use statements that are available, and reveal them in the following order of preference:

1. Statement 1;
2. Statement 2;
3. The other statement on the same dimension as statement 2 (e.g., if statement 2 is "My opponent is negative on Y" [$oppY$], the other statement would be "I am positive on Y" [Y];
4. The other statement on the same dimension as statement 1;
5. Choose not to campaign.

Voter beliefs, then, are that if a candidate bypasses statement(s) for a statement lower on the priority list, the higher-priority statement(s) must not have been available. In general, this means that the voter will end up choosing whichever candidate revealed a statement higher in the preference order. Furthermore, if either candidate reaches step 3 above, or if both candidates choose statement 2, the voter will have full information about the candidates' traits.

There are various possible off-path voter beliefs that support this equilibrium. We have voters derive beliefs by using a straightforward set of rules that works as following: if the campaign revelations are off-path, (1) believe all campaign revelations; (2a) if one candidate revealed statement 1, assume that candidate is positive on both dimensions facing an opponent negative on both, except where this conflicts with (1); (2b) otherwise, believe statements 1 and 2 were not available for either candidate, except where this conflicts with (1).

Given these beliefs, the voter strategy is simply to vote for the candidate who reveals a statement higher in the preference order (provided that the statement does not reveal negative information about the candidate, or positive information about the opponent). If both candidates reveal the same statement, then the voter can randomly choose one of the two.

The sophisticated equilibrium used in the analysis here is the sophisticated $X–Y$ equilibrium, meaning that statement 1 is X (i.e., "I am positive on X"), and statement 2 is Y (i.e., "I am positive on Y"). This is because in the laboratory experiment used to test this model, we chose parameters so that X and $oppX$ were the only possible primary (statement 1) themes in equilibrium. Furthermore, our results show that subjects most often chose positive campaigning over negative when both were viable options

(89% chose X over $oppX$; 78% chose Y over $oppY$). Because of this, we will focus on the sophisticated equilibrium with X and Y as primary and secondary themes. In appendix B, we provide proof of existence for the $X-Y$ equilibrium and show the payoffs for candidates' potential deviations (table B.1). We also show why neither Y nor $oppY$ could be statement 1 in our experiment by providing the existence criteria for the other seven [statement 1–statement 2] equilbria (table B.2).

We can plug X and Y into the algorithm described above to determine the $X-Y$ equilibrium strategy for each candidate:

1. If you are positive on X, reveal X.
2. If you are negative on X, but positive on Y, reveal Y.
3. If you are negative on both, and the opponent is negative on Y, reveal $oppY$.
4. If you are negative on both dimensions, and the opponent is positive on Y and negative on X, reveal $oppX$.
5. Otherwise (i.e., if you are negative on both dimensions facing an opponent positive on both dimensions), choose not to campaign.

Table 5.1 provides details about players' strategies and voter beliefs in the $X-Y$ equilibrium for each of the sixteen possible cases. This table provides a clear summary of what voters *should* believe and *should* do given the candidates' strategies. Our experimental test will examine the extent to which the voters' actual behavior matches these predictions.

The two voter belief columns are derived from the strategies explained above, and show the information that a sophisticated (Bayesian) voter should determine from the campaigns. The question marks (?) indicate that the voter cannot determine a trait with certainty given those particular campaigns and thus will still assume that the prior probabilities hold for that trait. In cases 1, 2, 5, and 6, where both candidates have positive X traits, both candidates will campaign positively on X, which means that the voter will be unable to update her beliefs about either candidate's Y trait. The voter's belief in those cases is that each candidate is (+,?); thus the expected utility difference between the two candidates is zero, and the voter will not have a candidate preference. In the case of a tie, we assume the voter chooses a candidate at random.

What if a candidate in these cases chooses a campaign other than X? A candidate could deviate from the equilibrium and select a different campaign, in essence "tricking" the voter into incorrect beliefs about the candidates' underlying traits. For example, in any of cases 1, 2, 5, and 6, if

TABLE 5.1. **Candidates' choices and voter beliefs in the sophisticated voting X–Y equilibrium**

Case	Candidate 1	Candidate 2	Campaign		Voter Beliefs		Expected Utility Difference (C1–C2)	Vote
			Candidate 1	Candidate 2	Candidate 1	Candidate 2		
1	(+,+)	(+,+)	X	X	(+,?)	(+,?)	0	Tie
2	(+,+)	(+,−)	X	X	(+,?)	(+,?)	0	Tie
3	(+,+)	(−,+)	X	Y	(+,?)	(−,+)	$x - (1-p)y$	C1
4	(+,+)	(−,−)	X	Ø	(+,+)	(−,?)	$x + y$	C1
5	(+,−)	(+,+)	X	X	(+,?)	(+,?)	0	Tie
6	(+,−)	(+,−)	X	X	(+,?)	(+,?)	0	Tie
7	(+,−)	(−,+)	X	Y	(+,?)	(−,+)	$x - (1-p)y$	C1
8	(+,−)	(−,−)	X	oppY	(+,−)	(−,?)	x	C1
9	(−,+)	(+,+)	Y	X	(−,+)	(+,?)	$(1-p)y - x$	C2
10	(−,+)	(+,−)	Y	X	(−,+)	(+,?)	$(1-p)y - x$	C2
11	(−,+)	(−,+)	Y	Y	(−,+)	(−,+)	0	Tie
12	(−,+)	(−,−)	Y	oppX	(−,+)	(−,?)	y	C1
13	(−,−)	(+,+)	Ø	X	(−,−)	(+,+)	$-(x+y)$	C2
14	(−,−)	(+,−)	oppY	X	(−,−)	(+,−)	$-x$	C2
15	(−,−)	(−,+)	oppX	Y	(−,−)	(−,+)	$-y$	C2
16	(−,−)	(−,−)	oppY	oppY	(−,−)	(−,−)	0	Tie

Note:
X = Reveal one's own positive X trait
Y = Reveal one's own positive Y trait
oppX = Reveal opponent's negative X trait
oppY = Reveal opponent's negative Y trait
Ø = No campaign

a candidate switched to Y while the opponent stayed with X, the voter would have to believe that the actual case was either 9 or 10, instead of one of the others. In both, the Y campaigner has a negative X trait, so the voter utility for that candidate is y. The voter would choose the X campaigner, who gives utility of either x or $x + y$. Thus, the deviating candidate would be worse off. In general, because this is an equilibrium, we know that a candidate cannot do better in the election from changing campaign messages—and in this game, the candidate would often do worse. Confirming that neither candidate has such an incentive to deviate is part of proving the existence of this PBE. In appendix B, along with the proof we have included table B.1 which shows, for each of the sixteen trait cases, how candidates' deviations from equilibrium would affect voter beliefs.

Returning to table 5.1, we see that in cases 3 and 7 the sophisticated voter believes that candidate 1 is positive on X (directly from the campaign), that candidate 2 is positive on Y (directly from the campaign), and also believes that candidate 2 is negative on X (indirectly, because of candidate 2's failure to campaign positively on X). The voter cannot determine candidate 1's Y trait. So, voter utility for candidate 1 is $x - py$, and voter utility for candidate 2 is y. The column second from the right gives the voter's expected utility difference between the two candidates. The rightmost column uses the experiment's parameters to determine the voting strategy. If this value is positive—as it is for all three treatments we employed in the experiment—the sophisticated voter will choose candidate 1, and if negative, candidate 2. Cases 9 and 10 are analogous to cases 3 and 7 with the candidates switched. Given the X–Y equilibrium strategies, these are the four cases in which the specific parameters affect the vote.

In the remaining cases, the voter's belief after campaigning is that she has full information about the candidates' traits. As is necessary in Bayesian Nash equilibrium, these beliefs match the candidates' actual traits in each case. In case 4, candidate 2 is believed to be negative on both dimensions (indirectly, from candidate 2's failure to campaign positively on either), and candidate 1 is believed to be positive on X (verified by the campaign) and positive on Y (indirectly, from candidate 2's failure to reveal this trait as negative). Case 13 is analogous.

In case 8, candidate 1 is believed to be positive on X and negative on Y, both directly verified by the campaigns. Candidate 2 is believed to be negative on both dimensions, a belief that is indirectly determined by candidate 2's failure to choose either positive statement. The utility difference favors candidate 1. Case 14 is analogous.

In case 11 the voter believes that both candidates are negative on X (from their failure to campaign positively on X) and that both are positive on Y (directly from the campaign). Case 16 is similar, as both candidates' failure to campaign positively results in the voter's belief that all traits are negative.

In case 12 the voter believes that both candidates are negative on X (indirectly, from their failure to campaign positively on X—but also directly for candidate 1 due to candidate 2's *oppX* campaign). She also believes that candidate 1 is positive on Y (directly revealed from the campaign) and that candidate 2 is negative on Y (indirectly, from candidate 2's failure to reveal a positive Y trait). Case 15 is analogous.

To show one major implication of the difference between naïve and sophisticated equilibria, suppose that the campaign that maximizes $d_\ell(R_\ell)$ is the negative campaign *oppX*. This means that in the case of a naïve voter, candidates' priority in equilibrium must be to reveal *oppX*. However, with a sophisticated voter, in equilibrium candidates could stick with choosing positive campaigning on X as statement 1. This is because once candidate ℓ fails to reveal that he is positive on X, the opponent need not bother with negative campaigning—the sophisticated voter will already know this from ℓ's omission. So instead, ℓ's opponent should campaign on the Y dimension. In many ways, this is the crux of the model. If we assume that voters are sophisticated, then there is no need for negative campaigning. But if voters are not sophisticated Bayesian updaters, if they are unable to infer information not actually given to them, then negative campaigning becomes a necessity if a candidate is going to maximize his opportunity for victory.

Using Cursed Equilibrium to Assess Voter Capabilities

Having examined the two equilibria for both ends of the cursed voting continuum—naïve and sophisticated voters—we can see how the voters' Bayesian updating affects the equilibrium of this game. Candidates generally need not go negative with sophisticated voters because those voters can intuit the information they need from what is not said. But if voters are not sophisticated Bayesian updaters, the story is very different. Thus we need to have a way to allow voters in our game to be either type of voter. To do this, we employ Eyster and Rabin's (2005) cursed equilibrium to determine the extent of voter Bayesian updating. We measure this with a parameter (χ) that indicates the probability that voter posterior beliefs are naïve. We set voter beliefs as naïve with probability χ, and sophisticated with probability $1 - \chi$. Just as with the naïve and sophisticated equilibria, this yields a point prediction for candidate strategy (rather than a distribution across possible outcomes). The strategy is as follows: if $\chi \geq .5$ (the voter tends toward naïve), then follow the candidate strategies from the naïve voter equilibrium; if $\chi < .5$ follow the candidate strategies from the sophisticated voter equilibrium.

The main purpose of our experiment is to test these two competing hypotheses in our formal theory—are voters sophisticated (Bayesian) or naïve?—by determining the equilibrium that best fits the choices of candidates and voters in the experimental sessions. With relatively naïve voting, our theory predicts that for any given draw of candidates' traits, as the probability of candidates having positive traits increases, voters will be more likely to favor candidates who are *negatively* campaigning because of its increasing effects on voter utility. It follows that as p increases there will be more negative campaigning by the candidates. With fully Bayesian/sophisticated voters, neither of these should occur so long as voters and candidates continue to play the same [statement 1–statement 2] equilibrium. Of course we acknowledge that the voting public is neither perfectly naïve nor perfectly sophisticated; thus we include a cursed voting parameter to improve the accuracy of our predictions. Our assumption, of course, is that as long as voters recognize the value of campaign information, *including what it implies*, they will make use of it in rational ways. The implication for our argument in this book is that the less often voters are able to infer what campaign information implies, the more valuable negative campaigning becomes.

Testing the Formal Model: Experimental Design

Formal models generally have a number of uses, including requiring their makers to be very specific about assumptions, which thus improves the rigor of the theory underlying them. More important for our purposes, they can provide testable propositions of the type we have here about the employment of negativity and its informational value. We can assert all we want that negativity is an important and valuable part of the campaign information environment, but the formal model allows us to establish the conditions under which that proposition is true. Our model shows that, given its set of assumptions, our assertion is true if voters are not sophisticated Bayesian updaters, so this is what needs to be tested. What follows is our test of the model, done in a laboratory as most game theory tests are, using subjects who respond to a game designed using the formal model. This test, which we designate study 5, is described below.

Subjects

Study 5 was conducted in May and June 2007 at the California Institute of Technology in the Social Science Experimental Laboratory (SSEL), using software developed at SSEL.[8] Subjects were a convenience sample of undergraduate and graduate students recruited by email from the SSEL subject database. The subjects earned an average of $25 for their participation, with the amount varying in accordance with their performance in the experimental elections.

The final pool consisted of forty-eight subjects, all of whom participated in exactly one of four sessions, with either nine or fifteen subjects participating in each. Each experimental session consisted of sixty rounds, or elections. Detailed instructions were read to the subjects prior to the first round; these included a visual display of example screens from the software application.

Experimental Sessions

Subjects were randomly divided into groups of three with two playing the roles of candidates and one playing the role of voter; roles and groups were reassigned after every election. Since all players were assigned candidate roles in addition to the voter role, the subjects quickly became experienced at making decisions from the candidates' point of view. When voting, subjects had a great deal of information about the likely behavior of candidates since in other rounds, they also *were* the candidates. Because this information was conducive to Bayesian voting, and all subjects had at least some college undergraduate education at a selective university, we would expect that our results are an upper bar on the sophistication level of actual voters.

Following our model, candidates were randomly assigned traits on two independent dimensions, labeled for the subjects as simply X and Y. There were two possibilities for each trait: "positive" or "negative," and three different treatments: the probability p of drawing a positive trait was fixed at either of 30, 50, or 70 percent—respectively representing a negativity offset, no offset, and a positivity offset. Subjects participated in twenty consecutive rounds of each treatment; the order of treatments was varied.[9] This probability of candidates' drawing a positive trait was available on screen to all players, both candidates and voter.

Candidates campaigned by clicking an onscreen radio button next to their desired message, and the content of these messages depended upon the actual traits drawn by the candidates. For example, a candidate positive on X and negative on Y, facing an opponent negative on both, would have the following options: "I have a positive X trait," "I have a negative Y trait," "My opponent has a negative X trait," "My opponent has a negative Y trait," and "I choose not to make a statement." We abbreviate these, respectively, as X, Y, $oppX$, $oppY$, and $\emptyset$. Candidates were not allowed to lie, but were allowed to make self-defeating statements such as "I have a negative Y trait"; these, along with positive statements about the opponent, accounted for fewer than seven percent of all campaign choices.[10]

The voter simultaneously received the campaign messages of both candidates and then was prompted to vote by clicking one of two buttons: "Candidate 1" or "Candidate 2." The vote concluded the round, after which the voters were shown the election results and both candidates' types. Then, all players were reassigned groups and roles for the subsequent round. During the course of the game, a player had available the history of all previous rounds in which he had participated.

The parameters for the study were as follows. Payoffs were contingent upon the results of each round. Voters received a payoff of 80 points if the chosen candidate was positive on dimension X, and 20 points if the candidate was positive on dimension Y. This utility gap ensured that the naïve and sophisticated voter equilibrium predictions were distinct. Because of this sixty-point difference, regardless of the prior probability of being positive (30, 50, or 70 percent), naïve voters would theoretically prefer *any* type of campaign about X traits over those about Y traits, since the X revelations would most change voter utility for a candidate. However, a more sophisticated voter would be more interested in Y traits, as we will explain below. The winning candidate received 100 points, and the losing candidate received 0 points. At the conclusion of the experiment, the points earned were converted to cash and subjects were paid based on their accumulated points.

Naïve Voter Strategies

The equilibrium naïve voter strategies by treatment are presented in table 5.2 and are derived from comparing the deviations in voter expected utility. Note that the 50 percent treatment is excluded from this table since we wish to focus on high and low probabilities of positive traits. In the 30 percent treatment, if a candidate ℓ reveals that he is positive on X, the naïve voter's expected earnings from voting for ℓ increase by 56 (from 30 to 86). Alternatively, if ℓ reveals that his opponent is negative on X, the voter's expected earnings for choosing the opponent decrease by 24 (from 30 to 6). Because the net change in voter utility from revealing positive information is higher, the candidates should prefer positive to negative campaigning. The other utility changes can be compared similarly, and as a result, in the naïve equilibrium for the 30 percent treatment, candidates will choose campaigns in the decreasing preference order of $(X, oppX, Y, oppY, \emptyset)$. In other words, candidates will prefer to reveal themselves as positive on X; if that isn't true they will prefer to reveal that the opponent is negative on X, and so on. Voter utility after the four campaigns will change by 56, 24, 14, 6, and 0, respectively. The naïve voter's strategy will

TABLE 5.2. **Candidates' equilibrium strategies, study 5**

Self	Opponent	Naive Voter 30% Treatment	70% Treatment	Sophisticated Voter
(+, +)	(+, +)	X	X	X
(+, +)	(+, −)	X	X	X
(+, +)	(−, +)	X	oppX	X
(+, +)	(−, −)	X	oppX	X
(+, −)	(+, +)	X	X	X
(+, −)	(+, −)	X	X	X
(+, −)	(−, +)	X	oppX	X
(+, −)	(−, −)	X	oppX	X
(−, +)	(+, +)	Y	Y	Y
(−, +)	(+, −)	Y	oppY	Y
(−, +)	(−, +)	oppX	oppX	Y
(−, +)	(−, −)	oppX	oppX	Y
(−, −)	(+, +)	∅	∅	∅
(−, −)	(+, −)	oppY	oppY	oppY
(−, −)	(−, +)	oppX	oppX	oppX
(−, −)	(−, −)	oppX	oppX	oppY

Note: In this and future tables, traits are listed in the order (X trait, Y trait).
X = Reveal one's own positive X trait
Y = Reveal one's own positive Y trait
oppX = Reveal opponent's negative X trait
oppY = Reveal opponent's negative Y trait
∅ = No campaign

be to vote for candidates in the same order (i.e., to prefer candidates revealing that they are positive on X, followed by candidates revealing that the opponent is negative on X, and so forth).

However, when positive traits are more likely (specifically, when the prior probability of drawing positive traits changes from 30 percent to 70 percent), negative campaigns yield more utility than do positive ones. So in this treatment, the naïve voting equilibrium is for candidates to choose campaigns in the order $(oppX, X, oppY, Y, \emptyset)$. In the 50 percent treatment, either of the 30 percent or 70 percent campaign revelation orders is acceptable in equilibrium, since both X-dimension statements change voter utility by 40, and both Y-dimension statements change voter utility by 10; we use $(X, oppX, Y, oppY)$ in our analysis of the experiment results.

Sophisticated Voter Strategies

The sophisticated voting equilibrium strategies for candidates are also presented in table 5.2. The equilibrium is similar to the naïve voting equilibrium in that candidates' decisions are based upon an ordering of the possible disclosures. Candidates' strategies and voter beliefs coordinate on one particular revelation, the primary theme, which we assume to be positive campaigning on dimension X. If not positive on X, then candidates will instead reveal something from the Y dimension (one's positive trait, if possible, or else the opponent's negative Y trait). They will only choose $oppX$ when they are themselves negative on both dimensions $(-, -)$ and facing an opponent that is $(-, +)$. Finally, candidates will choose not to campaign if they are $(-, -)$ and facing a $(+, +)$ opponent.[11] Notice that for the sophisticated voter equilibrium, the strategies are *not* dependent upon the underlying probabilities (i.e., the treatments of 30, 50, and 70 percent). This is because the sophisticated $X-Y$ equilibrium can be used regardless of the treatment—as mentioned earlier, we set the parameters to ensure this was the case. Thus with sophisticated voting, we should expect negative campaigns to be chosen less frequently, all other things equal. In the sophisticated $X-Y$ equilibrium, the voter will assume that the negative campaigner is $(-, -)$, which should result in that candidate losing the election.

Results of the Experimental Test

We now turn to the results of our experiment. These results will be perhaps easier to follow if the reader waded through the description of the formal model, but should make sense in any case. Again, our goal is to test the expectations of the model and most importantly, to examine how voters respond to the campaigns. We focus on four key findings.

Result 1: Candidates with a positive X trait almost always choose positive campaigning on X. We begin by looking at the choices made by candidates in each situation they faced with table 5.3 displaying the frequency, in percentages, of the candidate campaign decisions. Candidate choices are shown by treatment and by the sixteen possible trait pairs (our cases from table 5.1 above). Because the candidates' choices were often very consistent, we were able to test whether the most frequent campaign choice of candidates in each case was chosen significantly more often than all other options combined. Using this criterion, the choice of X is statistically significant overall when aggregating across every time a candidate had a positive X trait (chosen 92% of the time overall; binomial test $(881/955 = .5, p < 0.001)$) Recall, a positive X trait carried more utility for voters than a positive Y trait.

Moreover, as shown in table 5.3, when separating by case and treatment the choice of X is always significantly different from chance in cases 1 through 8—each of the cases where the candidate had a positive X trait. The best candidate strategy given naïve voting in the 70 percent treatment includes negative campaigning on the part of the candidates in half of these eight cases (namely, 3, 4, 7, and 8). But that assumes a risk-neutral voter; positive campaigning here guarantees the voter a payoff of 80, which is appealing to a risk-averse voter. We are just noting this for now; we address it further when we test for the best-fitting cursed equilibrium.

Result 2: Candidates choose negative campaigning more often as the positivity offset increases. In other words, all other things equal, when the prior probability of candidates having positive traits increased, negative campaigning also increased. This result is consistent with candidates assuming naïve voting but not with sophisticated voting. And remember, each of our candidates also had opportunities to be a voter, so presumably took into account their own likely response to the campaigns. Candidates appear to find it necessary to shift strategies in accordance with the three different treatments. With sophisticated voting, this strategy shift need not have occurred. Since candidates with positive X traits were revealing those whenever possible, negative campaigning on X would provide no new information to the sophisticated voter, who would be able to determine this from the opponent's lack of positive campaigning. Yet

TABLE 5.3. Candidate choices by percentages, study 5

Case	Self	Opponent	Treatment 30%		50%		70%	
1	(+, +)	(+, +)	X	90[†]	X	100[†]	X	96[†]
			Y	10			Y	4
2	(+, +)	(+, −)	X	100[†]	X	94[†]	X	86[†]
			oppY		oppY	6	oppY	14
3	(+, +)	(−, +)	X	100[†]	X	85[†]	X	82[†]
			oppX		oppX	15	oppX	18
4	(+, +)	(−, −)	X	96[†]	X	90[†]	X	87[†]
			oppX	4	oppX	8	oppX	10
					oppY	2	oppY	3
5	(+, −)	(+, +)	X	100[†]	X	100[†]	X	98[†]
							oppY[‡]	2
6	(+, −)	(+, −)	X	97[†]	X	91[†]	X	97[†]
			oppY	3	oppY	9	oppY	3
7	(+, −)	(−, +)	X	100[†]	X	77[†]	X	81[†]
			oppX		oppX	23	oppX	15
							oppY[‡]	4
8	(+, −)	(−, −)	X	93[†]	X	95[†]	X	80[†]
			oppX	5	oppX	5	oppX	20
			Ø	2				
9	(−, +)	(+, +)	Y	86[†]	Y	79[†]	Y	75[†]
			oppY	7	Ø	10	oppX[‡]	11
			Ø	7	oppY[‡]	10	Ø	7
					X[‡]	1	X[‡]	4
					oppX[‡]	1	oppY[‡]	3
10	(−, +)	(+, −)	Y	73[†]	Y	50	oppY	50
			oppY	23	oppY	47	Y	46
			Ø	4	oppX[‡]	3	oppX[‡]	4
11	(−, +)	(−, +)	Y	70[†]	Y	60	oppX	57
			oppX	28	oppX	37	Y	43
			oppY	2	X[‡]	3		
12	(−, +)	(−, −)	Y	84[†]	Y	58	Y	75
			oppX	16	oppX	39	oppX	13
					X[‡]	3	oppY	13
13	(−, −)	(+, +)	Y[‡]	37	Ø	45	Ø	50
			Ø	33	Y[‡]	22	Y[‡]	20
			oppX[‡]	19	oppY[‡]	22	oppX[‡]	13
			oppY[‡]	7	oppX[‡]	8	oppY[‡]	10
			X[‡]	4	X[‡]	2	X[‡]	7
14	(−, −)	(+, −)	oppY	62[†]	oppY	76[†]	oppY	75[†]
			Y[‡]	14	Ø	11	X[‡]	10
			Ø	13	Y[‡]	11	oppX[‡]	10
			oppX[‡]	8	oppX[‡]	2	Ø	5
			X[‡]	3				
15	(−, −)	(−, +)	oppX	93[†]	oppX	91[†]	oppX	63
			Y[‡]	7	Y[‡]	6	Y[‡]	25
					X[‡]	3	X[‡]	13
16	(−, −)	(−, −)	oppX	84[†]	oppX	80[†]	oppX	75
			oppY	13	X[‡]	6	Y[‡]	25
			X[‡]	2	Y[‡]	4		
			Y[‡]	1	oppY	4		
					Ø	4		
Total			670		580		670	

Note: Numbers are percentage of choices made; percentages in a case may add to more than 100 due to rounding.
[†] Campaign choices are significant with a *p* value of .05 or less using a binomial test; the null is that all other options combined were chosen with a probability of 50% or greater.
[‡] Indicates "self-defeating" campaigns (bad information about oneself or good information about the opponent).

candidates did choose to go negative in increasing numbers as the probability of drawing positive traits increased from 30 percent to 70 percent.

Figure 5.2 shows how this percentage of negativity varies by treatment. The nine relevant cases (when a candidate with at least one positive trait faces an opponent with at least one negative trait) are labeled with the focal candidate's type followed by the opponent's type. In every case, the relative amount of negativity in the 70 percent treatment is greater than in the 30 percent treatment. There were a couple of cases in which negative campaigning in the 50 percent treatment was more frequent than either of the other treatments.

Of course the *total* number of negative campaigns was highest in the 30 percent treatment, which is not surprising simply because candidates' traits were more often negative in the 30 percent treatment, so their positive campaigning options were more limited. The overall percentage of negative revelations was 45 percent in the 30 percent treatment as compared to 32 percent in the 50 percent treatment ($\chi^2(1) = 23.0, p < 0.001$) and 15 percent in the 0.7 treatment ($\chi^2(1) = 48.6, p < 0.001$).

Next, we look at vote choice. Table 5.4 reports actual voter behavior, showing the probability of voting for an arbitrary candidate ℓ if the

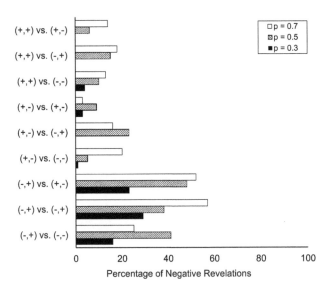

FIGURE 5.2. Relative incidence of negative campaigning by case (candidate traits) and treatment, study 5
Note: p is the probability of drawing a positive trait.

TABLE 5.4. **Voter behavior, study 5**

Candidate ℓ	Candidate $-\ell$	Vote for Candidate ℓ		
		30% Treatment	50% Treatment	70% Treatment
X	Y	1.00	0.93	0.95
X	$opp\,Y$	1.00	0.95	0.93
Y	$opp\,X$	0.84	0.75	0.45
Ø	Any other	0.05	0.00	0.00

Note: Both candidates chose to not campaign only once; this observation is excluded from the table.

opponent $-\ell$ has chosen a campaign different from that of ℓ. The first two rows show that voters overwhelmingly favored the candidate choosing X when the other candidate chose another campaign. Aggregately, the voters chose the X campaigner 97 percent of the time overall in those situations, so positive campaigning on X was in fact the best candidate decision.

Result 3: Voters prefer negative campaigning more often as the positivity offset increases. In another result consistent with naïve voting, voters are more likely to choose the candidate who goes negative as the prior probability that candidates have positive traits becomes greater. Given the candidates' pattern of revealing themselves to be positive on X whenever possible, a sophisticated voter would necessarily infer that any candidate failing to reveal a positive X trait must in fact have a negative X trait. And, if voters think this way, candidates with a negative X trait should campaign on dimension Y rather than choose $oppX$, assuming they have both options. But as we showed in result 2, candidates do not behave as if they think voters are sophisticated. Here we find that candidates are right to assume naiveté.

Note the third row of table 5.4, in which voters face a decision between a candidate revealing any Y trait and a candidate negatively campaigning on X. Revealing any Y trait is better than negative campaigning with a sophisticated voter, yet candidates increasingly favor negative campaigning as the prior probability of positive traits increases. A sophisticated voter should infer that neither candidate has a positive X trait and should know to choose the positive (Y trait) campaigner—because that candidate is known to be $(-, +)$ while the negative campaigner is no better than $(-, +)$ and likely $(-, -)$. But, as table 5.4 shows, notably in the 70 percent treatment, many voters failed to infer this. When given the message pair $(Y, oppX)$, voters chose the negative campaigner 55 percent of the time in the

TABLE 5.5. **Mean difference in voter utility between candidate ℓ and the opponent, study 5**

		Treatment		
Candidate ℓ	Candidate $-\ell$	30%	50%	70%
X	Y	74.61*	78.22*	70.62*
X	$oppY$	76.98*	74.33*	47.78*
Y	$oppX$	18.80*	−2.00	−48.00*

*$p < 0.01$.

70 percent treatment, as compared to only 16 percent of the time in the 30 percent treatment. Yet, in both treatments the majority of naïve voters made the right choices.

Why? Table 5.5 shows the expected utility for the voter in each of the possible voting scenarios, assuming that neither candidate has revealed information harmful to herself. The third row is the relevant row here. It shows the average difference in expected utility for choosing a candidate who uses message Y when the message pair is $(Y, oppX)$. In the 30 percent treatment, the voter would have been better off choosing the positive campaigner, but in the 70 percent treatment, the voter should have chosen the negative campaigner. As we explained above, this is contradictory to sophisticated voting. It is generally not a sophisticated voting equilibrium when voters are better off choosing the X campaigner in the (X, Y) message pair *and* the $oppX$ campaigner in the $(Y, oppX)$ message pair.[12] This is because for one of those two message pairs, the X-dimension campaign will be redundant for the sophisticated voter, who then should choose the Y campaigner. So, candidates were choosing campaigns that would work with naïve voting and backfire with sophisticated voting. Interestingly, in the 70 percent treatment voters in the latter rounds (31–60) were even more likely (80 percent) to choose the negative campaigner. Note also the timing of these $oppX$ versus Y decisions was not confined to the early rounds; over all treatments, 40 percent of all reported $oppX$ versus Y decisions were faced by voters in the last thirty rounds.

Finally we look at the overall success rate of our simplified electoral system, and find that it fared quite well, as the better candidate—the one providing a higher payoff to the voter—won 84 percent of the elections. Subject learning, as measured by the percentage of the time the higher-payoff candidate won, occurred quickly—and well before the treatment shifts in rounds 20 and 40. Sixty-six percent of higher-payoff candidates won in the first five trials, 82 percent of elections in trials 6–10, and 85 percent for the final fifty trials.

Are Voters Sophisticated or Naïve?

Having provided an overview of the experimental results, we now examine where voters lie on the continuum between perfectly naïve and perfectly sophisticated voting. One difficulty we face is that our formal model makes a specific point prediction for each decision, which presents a zero-likelihood problem: any choice that doesn't match the specific prediction is given probability zero, regardless of its plausibility as a mistake. This is especially problematic for our cursed equilibrium parameter since we do not wish to test it as a point prediction. When tested as a point prediction, it states that if a candidate makes *any* assumption that voters are more likely to be naïve than sophisticated, then the candidate must follow strategies from the naïve voter equilibrium. Otherwise the sophisticated strategies are employed. This discrepancy wouldn't matter if the players were infallible, but that's generally not the case in a laboratory experiment even if it is assumed in the formal model. So, we want a structure where the candidates are much more likely to err when they are less certain that voters are naïve than when they are more certain.

A standard method for avoiding such zero-likelihood problems, which we implement here, is to use the quantal response equilibrium (QRE) model as the underlying structure (McKelvey and Palfrey 1995). QRE is a formal model of imperfect play that we use as an extension to PBE in which players do not always choose their best responses. The premise is that people make mistakes, but make them less often when the stakes are higher. The players' decisions are determined by a quantal response function, which assigns a positive probability of choosing every possible action, with the probability of every action monotonically increasing in expected payoffs. So, people are more likely to pick good choices over bad choices and much more likely to pick very good choices over very bad choices. But any choice is technically possible.[13]

QRE applies to the voters in our experiment whenever the candidates' messages are not identical. In those cases, one of the candidates will have a higher expected utility. QRE models the voters' decisions such that they will make the optimal choice more often when the expected utility gap is wider—such as when only one candidate chooses message X. Since QRE allows voters to make such mistakes, it always behooves inferior candidates to minimize the difference between the voter's expected payoffs for each candidate. Also, it means that candidates will be more likely to choose the optimal message whenever using that message creates a large difference in the probability of victory.

TABLE 5.6. **Cursed equilibrium maximum likelihood results, study 5**

Model	Log Likelihood	Λ	q	χ
Cursed	−1116	0.13	0.35	0.73
Naïve	−1255	0.17	0.55	1.00
Sophisticated	−1415	0.07	0.20	0.00

Note: The maximum likelihood results when requiring risk neutrality (q = 0) were: cursed (−1170); naïve (−1607); sophisticated (−1445). In all cases, the log likelihood differences between the risk-averse and risk-neutral models were highly significant (chi-squared test $p < 0.0001$).

We promised earlier that readers who did not wish to wade through the formal model details could come to this section without much loss in ability to follow what is going on. Obviously our employment of QRE adds complexity. So to fulfill our promise, we include in appendix B the details of using QRE, and here continue directly to the results.

Result 4: Voter behavior involves partial updating that tends to be more naïve than sophisticated. Table 5.6 shows the results of modeling using QRE, to determine the best fitting model parameters given the data from study 5. Our goal is to determine whether the data show voters as primarily naïve or sophisticated. Thus the table shows the model fit (maximum likelihood) using the assumptions that voters are partially "cursed" (row 1), completely naïve (row 2) or completely sophisticated (row 3). As row 1 shows, the best fit for the (cursed equilibrium) parameter determining whether voters act as either naïve or sophisticated is $\chi = 0.73$, which weights the naïve model (where $\chi = 1$) more strongly than the sophisticated (where $\chi = 0$), and thus supports our naïve voting hypothesis. This "cursed" model is a better fit than either the purely naïve or the purely sophisticated models (in both cases, $p < 0.001$ for the chi-squared test).[14] This finding of $\chi = 0.73$ suggests that candidates should not assume that very many voters are inferring negative implications from campaign themes (or allocations among themes) that the candidates did not choose. The finding is consistent with other studies that, though not pertaining to elections, have also found χ weighted toward naïve behavior. Eyster and Rabin (2005), in fitting the cursed model to pre-existing experimental datasets, found generally that the best-fitting χ values were above 0.5, thus conferring a stronger weight upon the naïve decision-maker model. Carrillo and Palfrey (2009), in various treatments of a compromise game, found χ values ranging from 0.75 to 0.97, with a pooled average of 0.85.

Including risk aversion improves the fit of the model. If we had required risk neutrality ($q = 0$) the results could have been misleading—the purely naïve model appears to fare worse than the purely sophisticated.

We should not infer that the sophisticated risk-neutral model is better; it is far from an ideal fit, as it cannot explain the candidates' strategy shift across treatments (fig. 5.2 above). In any case, the maximum likelihood results show that including both cursed voting and risk aversion best explains the subjects' behavior.

The probability estimates for voting behavior (table 5.7) and campaign strategies (fig. 5.3) are shown below; these are derived from the predicted χ, λ, and q values at the best fitting Cursed/QRE. In table 5.7 the (Y, $oppX$) message pair shows the effect of naïve voting—voters most often choose the negative campaign in the 70 percent treatment. In figure 5.3 the effect is abundantly clear, as candidates use negative campaigns much more often whenever negative traits are less common.

TABLE 5.7. **Voter behavior in the estimated Cursed/Quantal Response Equilibrium, study 5**

Candidate ℓ	Candidate $-\ell$	Vote for Candidate ℓ		
		30% Treatment	50% Treatment	70% Treatment
X	Y	0.85	0.82	0.78
X	$oppY$	0.93	0.95	0.93
Y	$oppX$	0.63	0.49	0.35

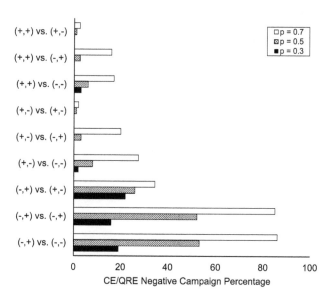

FIGURE 5.3. Incidence of negative campaigns at the Cursed/QRE estimate of λ, χ, and q, by case and treatment, study 5

Conclusion: What Do We Learn from Modeling?

Are Negative Ads Election Promises?

In a recent paper, Geer and Vavreck (2014) hypothesized that a candidate's attack ads are also indirectly campaign promises not to engage in the same behavior.[15] If this is the case—and positive ads conversely imply nothing about the opponent's negative traits—this would make negative campaigning quite attractive. While this is almost certainly the intention of some candidates' attacks, our results here suggest that it is unlikely that many voters are picking up on it. At the same time, candidates routinely attack each other for behavior in which they themselves engage. We saw examples of this regularly in the 2012 presidential election. In a Republican primary debate on January 26, Mitt Romney and Newt Gingrich traded accusations that the other owned stock in Fannie Mae and Freddie Mac, the federally supported mortgage makers accused of contributing to the housing collapse. As it turned out, both did hold stock in the companies, thus each was accusing the other of something true about themselves (CNN 2012). In a debate the next month, Romney and Rick Santorum attacked each other on the question of earmarks, with Romney accusing Santorum of talking the conservative line against them while actually voting for earmarks while in the Senate. Santorum in turn attacked Romney for seeking earmarks as head of the US Olympic Games and as Massachusetts governor. Again, the reality was that the accusations on both sides were true, so both candidates went negative against behavior in which they themselves were engaging (Picket 2012).

Candidates that Don't Bark

In an often-repeated story, Sherlock Holmes considers "the curious situation of the dog in the night-time" to be an important clue because the dog *didn't* bark (Doyle 1894). It seems that voters, however, will rarely draw conclusions about subjects candidates fail to bring up. But the findings here go beyond the completeness of voters' Bayesian updating. For one, this helps us better address whether candidates are framing the debate (Jamieson et al. 2000)—by explaining *why* candidates can frame the debate. Voter decision-making does not involve a large amount of Bayesian inference—so while theoretically, what candidates don't talk about *could* matter, it probably does not. This, of course, includes negative campaigning; candidates may hasten to bring up opponents' flaws simply because many voters won't infer such flaws unless confronted with them directly. This uncovers a core reason as to why candidates go negative. From any candidate's perspective, the flaws of the opponent are important pieces of information. Normatively, this makes sense as well. Voters need to know both the good and the bad about their options. But they clearly cannot infer flaws from the decisions candidates make regarding which information to reveal about themselves. Thus, it is incumbent upon the opponent to make this information available, and thereby "go negative" by talking about the opponent.

Whether these negative campaigns are truthful is a question which we begin to address in chapter 6. For now, it is worth noting that candidates can lie about themselves as well as the opponent; interestingly, Jamieson, Waldman, and Sherr (2000) showed that presidential ads mentioning an opponent were on average more truthful and contained more informational content than self-advocacy ads.

Candidates caught up in the idea of making an opponent looking as undesirable as possible (i.e., 100% negative advertising) have necessarily taken resources away from the promoting of positive information, which may be more preferable to risk-averse voters. These findings suggest why candidates should strike some kind of balance between positive and negative campaigning—candidates who put too much emphasis on themselves or on the opponent will place themselves at an electoral disadvantage.

Above all, we need to think differently about how voters think. The study of voting behavior is not just about voter preferences, for example, whether the voters are conservative or liberal, or whether they prefer valence information or policy information, or whether they vote in their self-interest. Clearly those are important, but we should not overlook how voters' decision-making *processes* affect campaign discourse. A broader understanding of voters' decision-making mechanisms will help improve the direction of future research of political campaigning. For example, not only should we ask how voters respond to seeing a large percentage of negative advertising, but also the extent to which voters' decision-making processes and/or prior beliefs caused these advertisements to come into existence in the first place. We explore this point further beginning in the next chapter with an investigation of ad credibility using our first four studies. Then in chapter 7 we build and test a final formal experiment to tie everything together.

CHAPTER SIX

That Ad Said What?

The Importance of Ad Credibility

John Yarmuth. He plays golf with Saddam Hussein, and snatches toys away from little children.—John Yarmuth campaign ad, 2006

This sounds like a negative ad deserving four Pinocchios, but it is actually part of an ad John Yarmuth ran himself during his 2006 US House campaign. The ad continues:

VOICEOVER: "Ridiculous?"

JOHN YARMUTH: "No more so than Anne Northup's dishonest TV ads. The fact is, Northup and Bush have failed our country, and we need to make a change. Anne won't discuss the real issues. In fact, she won't discuss issues at all. All she'll do is attack and smear, and you deserve better. I'm John Yarmuth, and I approved this ad, because we can't change Washington unless we change the people we send there."

Notice that Yarmuth's complaint is that Northup's negative ads are *false*, not that her attack ads are *negative*. This is not a trivial distinction. "Is this ad negative?" is a separate question from "Is this ad truthful?" We believe that voters care much more about the latter question than the former. This distinction helps explain why some political campaigns magnanimously claim to have refrained from revealing secret scandalous information about the opponent, while at the same time threatening to reveal it later.[1] Why withhold any information until the waning days of a close election? After all, advertisements are only one tactic for conducting a negative campaign; if worried about some sort of backlash campaigns could potentially inoculate themselves by instead passing off such information to media outlets. We suggest that the most plausible reason to completely suppress such "damaging" information is not because it is negative, but instead because either it does not exist or it is a patently false spin on something otherwise less damaging. Indeed, the best time to blatantly lie about an opponent is probably at the very end of a campaign, before there is time for the falsehood to be uncovered—although vague lying about an opponent earlier in the campaign could force the opponent to divert funds in defense, in which case the liar has defined the dimensions on which the campaign will proceed.

While the truth of statements contained within campaign ads is clearly important, it is a separate issue from the style of the campaign. Nearly everyone is in agreement that campaign strategies involving calumny can harm the political system. However, not all negative campaigning is mendacious, nor are all lies negative campaigning. Candidates can just as easily lie (or stretch the truth) about *themselves* as they can present misinformation about their opponents. Davis and Ferrantino (1996) argue that a candidate runs less long-term risk of being caught if she lies about her opponent rather than exaggerates the benefits she will provide if elected. This is because campaign promises can be used against a candidate in future elections, while it is impossible to invalidate claims of what the opposing candidate would have done if elected. At the same time, negative ads nearly always include footnotes and other means to support their claims, while few positive ads have any kind of documentation attached to them (Geer 2006). Thus candidates may be able to engage in puffery without serious consequences, while lying in negative ads carries the risk of rebounding on the liar immediately.

Though desperate and/or unscrupulous politicians may resort to lies, and sometimes these lies are negative campaigns, we should not draw the conclusion that falsehoods and negativity are inexorably linked. Instead, we should strive to separate the effects of false campaigns from the effects of attack campaigns. This distinction between lies and negativity has been written about (e.g., Mayer 1996) but has usually been ignored in surveys and experiments studying negative campaigning. To our knowledge, there is no formal model of negative campaigning that differentiates between true and false types of negativity. And truth is certainly not factored into the working definition of negativity, "talking about the opponent." Kahn and Kenney (1999), however, do make a similar distinction in an empirical study of negative campaigns in US congressional elections. They find that "useful negative information" increases turnout, while "unsub-

stantiated and shrill attacks" decrease turnout; these two categories could
also be classified as "seems true" and "seems false." In the same study,
Kahn and Kenney showed that caustic mudslinging tends to depress turnout. We argue in this chapter that they are on the right track—but it is
our contention that their finding has to do with the fact that the ads were
deemed untruthful, which angered voters. It isn't the attacks themselves
that bother voters—it's when the attacks are seen as inappropriate and/
or unbelievable.

In each of our first four studies, we included questions about voters' reactions to negative campaigns that help us to differentiate between their
dislike of criticism in general and their dislike specifically of false criticism. In this chapter we present results from these questions to go beyond
the relationship between anger and negativity we discussed in chapters 3
and 4. Studies 1 and 2 (our 2008 Hawkeye Poll national election study, and
our 2009 Eagleton Poll of New Jersey voters) look at the question of believability and truthfulness in broad strokes, while study 3 (our CCES experiment) expands the questions to ask about the appropriateness of certain types of ad topics, as well as their believability. Finally, study 4 (our
Mturk online sample) allows us to explore these issues with much more
detail due to our use of real campaign ads and the series of questions following each of them.

The Basics of Truth

Because many studies treat negativity in campaigns as one-size-fits-
all, our first hypothesis was very simple: *false* negative ads upset voters
more than *true* negative ads.[2] Our initial analysis relies on study 1, the
2008 national pre-election telephone survey-experiment we introduced
in chapter 3. Here we considered respondents' reactions to a hypothetical campaign in which one candidate presented "information about what
his opponent had done in office." To test this we asked respondents to
tell us if (negative) campaign ads would be more acceptable if they told
the truth about the opponent. Overall, 30 percent found such ads "much
more acceptable," while 35 percent found them "somewhat more acceptable" and 35 percent said that truthful ads would be "no more acceptable." Overall, truthful attacks were much more readily tolerated among
these respondents.

Of course it is not exactly surprising that some share of voters agreed
that truth would make attacks more acceptable. But with the truth ques-

tion we can also return to our argument that survey wording accounts for much of the public's supposed disdain for negative ads. Here we are interested in whether those who were not cued to think of the ads as "negative campaigning" might be even *more* accepting of the truth. A simple test of the experimental treatment groups supports this hypothesis as well. We coded responses from 1–3, with 3 being "much more acceptable," and found the difference in means between the cued as "negative" treatment (1.96) and the uncued treatment (2.12) to be statistically significant. More specifically, for the cued treatment 30 percent said that truth would make such ads much more acceptable while 39 percent would find them somewhat more acceptable. Only 30 percent said information about an opponent, if it were true, would be no more acceptable. For respondents not cued with the word "negative," truth is an even better rationale for attack. For this group, 43 percent thought truth makes ads that talk about an opponent much more acceptable, while another 31 percent felt they would be somewhat more acceptable. Only 26 percent thought a true statement about the opponent would not be more acceptable. While similar shares of both groups remain unconvinced by the truth (30% and 26%), those not cued to think about negativity are significantly more positive about the effects of a credible ad, by 13 points.

A more detailed examination of the results above (shown in fig. 6.1) uncovers an interaction between anger at negative campaigning and the credibility of the attack. Across both treatments, the angriest respondents were *least* likely to be affected by the credibility of the information. Fifty-two percent of those who were very angry with "negative campaigning" would not be mollified if the information were actually true (fig. 6.1a). On the other hand, only 26 percent of those who were *not* angered by negative campaigning feel the same way; meanwhile, 56 percent say truth would make such ads more acceptable. Results for the neutral version of the question are similar, with 48 percent of those who are very angry at such campaigning unwilling to find truth an acceptable reason, while 57 percent of those who were not angry said truth makes information about the opponent more acceptable (panel 2, fig. 6.1). Thus, conditioned on anger, there is little difference here between the cued and not cued groups. Of course, keep in mind that few respondents in the uncued treatment were very angry at the idea of ads that talk about the opponent (only 9%) compared to 22 percent who were very angry when the phrase "negative campaigning" was included.

These findings suggest that stronger emotional responses toward campaigns are less likely to be altered by future information—so once turned

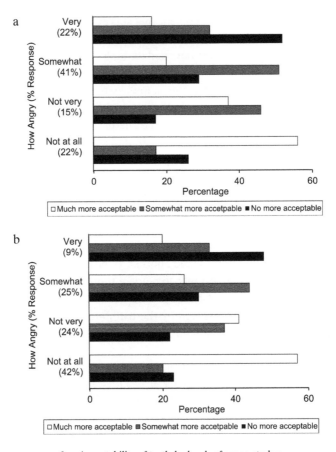

FIGURE 6.1. Acceptability of truth, by levels of anger, study 1
a. With "negative" in question
b. Without "negative" in question

off voters may be less likely to tune back in to the campaign discourse. On the other hand, the subset of voters who are completely nonresponsive (or perhaps negatively responsive) to attack advertising is quite small. We can estimate how many of those who were very angry with the proposed attack campaign were unwilling to waver in the face of its veracity. Even when responding to questions about "negative campaigning," only 11 percent of voters fit this picture. Furthermore, with the negative wording excised, only 5 percent of voters are very angry *and* unwilling to reconsider in the face of truth. In sum, from our question in study 1 we find for many voters truth is a mitigating factor in their anger over negativity, though not necessarily for those who are the most angered by candidate attacks.

Recall that in study 2, our New Jersey sample, we replaced "information about what [the] opponent had done in office" with four hypothetical ad topics, telling half of the respondents the ads were negative and asking the other half to decide for themselves. We asked *everyone* whether the truth would make "negative ads" more acceptable, so we do not expect much of a difference in responses across the two treatments. The results are shown in figure 6.2. As with study 1, truth is clearly important for a significant majority of respondents in study 2, regardless of whether they are cued with the word "negative." Overall, 38 percent believe truth makes a negative ad much more acceptable, 44 percent say it makes the ad somewhat more acceptable, and just 18 percent no more acceptable.

To examine this further, we ran a regression with anger as the dependent variable. We use Issues as the baseline campaign topic, and include variables for the other three topics, the treatment (if negative was cued or self-defined), the importance of the truth, and whether ads are truthful. We also include party identification, religiosity, and the demographic variables such as race that had some level of predictive power in our previous analyses. The regression results are displayed in table 6.1. Anger is coded on a four-point scale with 4 being "very angry," so a positive coefficient means greater anger.

The negative coefficient for the self-defined treatment tells us respondents overall were less angry when they were not told the hypothetical ads were negative. Also, we find that anger toward three of the hypothetical topics (Issues, Experience, and Record in Office) did not differ

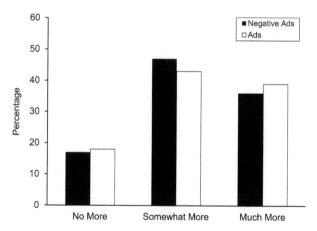

FIGURE 6.2. How much more acceptable are truthful negative ads? Study 2

TABLE 6.1. **Predictors of anger toward negative ads, study 2**

	Coefficient (Std. error)
Self-define treatment	−0.3532***
	(0.0500)
Topic: Family	1.4562***
	(0.0408)
Topic: Record in office	−0.0198
	(0.0346)
Topic: Experience	0.0161
	(0.0379)
Truth more acceptable	−0.0911***
	(0.0347)
Ads generally are truthful	−0.0020
	(0.0248)
Gender: Female	0.0720
	(0.0498)
Age	0.0291*
	(0.0167)
Democrat	−0.0960*
	(0.0581)
Republican	−0.0131
	(0.0647)
Race: Nonwhite	0.1018
	(0.0675)
College graduate	−0.2163***
	(0.0514)
Religiosity	0.0531
	(0.0513)
Constant	2.6395
	(0.1371)
Adj r^2	0.345
N	Subjects = 235
	Observations = 2096

Note: Robust standard errors in parentheses. DV = How Angry, 1–4 scale, higher values are greater anger.
*$p < 0.1$.
**$p < 0.05$.
***$p < 0.01$.

significantly. Family ads, however, generated much more anger. For all of the topics, the multivariate model produces the same results as our single-variable testing did in chapter 3. The one important addition to the model is the introduction of truth as a mitigating factor—shown in the "truth more acceptable" row from table 6.1. This is our strongest indicator yet of voters' concern about the truth of negative ads. Those who believe that truthful negative ads were more acceptable are also more open to negative ads in the first place. Those who don't care about believability react more emotionally to the ads in the first place.

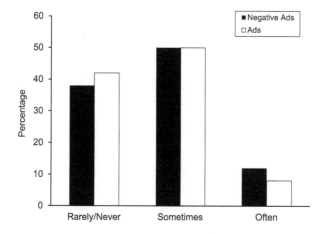

FIGURE 6.3. How often do [negative] ads tell the truth? Study 2

In study 2 we also asked, "How often do *negative* ads tell the truth about the opponent," with "negative" included only for the group that did not get to self-define whether the topics were negative. Figure 6.3 displays these findings. Among respondents just asked about "ads" about 8 percent believe campaign ads "often" tell the truth about an opponent, while just under half think they sometimes do. Nearly as many—42 percent— say such ads rarely or never tell the truth. But, when we add the cue of "negative," we get an unexpected result. Requiring the respondent to think about "negative ads" results in these ads being thought to be truthful *more often* than when we do not include the word negative. Seen as "negative ads," 12 percent say these ads often tell the truth, while 37 percent believe they rarely or never do so. While the p-value (0.09) for the difference in means (t-test) does not quite meet traditional measures of significance, our finding suggests that voters may actually see negative ads as more truthful, echoing Geer's (2006) argument that they carry more information and are better supported by evidence within the ad itself.

Study 3: Examining Believability

Starting with study 3, the 2010 CCES national Internet panel, we asked about the believability of ads rather than the truth of the ads. We are interested in the extent to which negativity interferes with believability, which presumably is an important factor in whether an ad is acceptable. While quite similar in many ways to asking about "truth," believability is a more subjective assessment of credibility on the part of the voter, while truth implies some objective assessment (though left unsaid in studies 1 and 2, it was presented in that way). Recall that in study 3 we expanded the number of topics for the "negative" statements to five, and we split our sample three ways: one group was told that the ad topics were negative, one was asked to assess the negativity of the topics before answering other questions (believability, anger, and vote intention), and the third answered those other questions before they indicated if the ad topic was negative. We have already addressed the anger and vote intention questions in chapter 3; here we will focus primarily on believability with some consideration of how it influences anger.

To get some sense of the data, we begin by describing the distribution of believability responses across our topics, presented in table 6.2. The table shows that believability is highly conditioned on topic, and follows a pattern similar to that of anger, with three of our topics (Experience, Issues, and Fraud) generating at least a "somewhat believable" response from a majority of respondents. The other two topics, Family and Atheism (religion), are widely disbelieved, with nearly seven in ten saying they would find a candidate talking about an opponent's family to be "not very believable" while 61 percent say the same about calling an opponent an atheist.

Our experimental treatments in study 3 are similar to study 2 in that some of our subjects (in study 3, one-third) saw an assertion that the topics were used for "negative ads" while the others were given the opportunity to decide this for themselves. Though table 6.2 collapses across our three treatments, there are significant differences based on whether or not subjects were asked to assess negativity first. In chapter 3 we showed that those who assessed the topics' negativity (the self-defined treatment) were

TABLE 6.2. **Summary results of believability by ad topic, study 3**

	Very Believable	Somewhat Believable	Not Very Believable
Position on issues	27%	51%	22%
Lack of experience	20	52	28
Convicted of fraud	16	44	40
Atheist	6	22	72
Family	3	19	78

Note: Entries are percentage responses from CCES 2010 with "Don't know" responses dropped.

TABLE 6.3. **Believability by ad topic for treatment groups, study 3**

	Group	Very Believable	Somewhat Believable	Not Very Believable
Position on issues	A	27	46	27
	B	30	56	14
	C	23	50	27
Lack of experience	A	20	49	34
	B	25	55	20
	C	18	50	32
Convicted of fraud	A	16	38	46
	B	21	52	27
	C	11	44	45
Atheist	A	5	16	79
	B	9	33	58
	C	4	19	77
Family	A	3	16	81
	B	5	25	70
	C	2	18	80

Note: Entries are percentage responses from CCES 2010 with "Don't know" responses dropped. Treatments: A = Explicit negative ad; B = Self-defined first; C = Self-defined last.

less angry about most of them (except family) than any other group. Similarly, table 6.3 shows the differences between participants who were told the topics were negative ads (treatment A), who decided negativity for themselves before the other questions (treatment B) and who were asked about negativity after other questions (treatment C). Groups A and C look very similar in that they were much less likely to believe all of the topics than were those in group B, who saw every topic as more believable. For every topic, the differences in the mean response between treatments A and B are statistically significant, as are those between treatments B and C.

This makes it very clear that many people, as we expected, link "negative" and "false" (or "unbelievable"), something that the standard definition of negativity does not do. And the voters are making this connection not just when we declare a topic as negative to them—as shown in table 6.3—but even more so if they define a topic as negative. In the latter case, those defining a topic as negative consider it "not very believable" 67 percent of the time, while those defining a topic as not negative think that is so only 19 percent of the time. It appears from the differences between treatments B and C that thinking about these cognitive, affective, and behavioral intention aspects of campaign ads decreased the otherwise positive effect on both anger and believability from thinking the topics were not negative.

In table 6.4 we report the results of regressions with anger and believability as dependent variables. It confirms that respondents are less angry in treatment B, where they were asked first whether each topic was negative. Also those in treatment B found the hypothetical ads to be more believable—our best evidence so far that people are connecting "negative" with "false" in some situations. As for reactions to the topics themselves, note that the default topic in these regressions is Fraud, so the anger regression shows that both Experience and Issues generate less anger than Fraud, while Atheism and especially Family make voters angrier. Similarly, Atheism and Family are less believable, which suggests there is more to voters' dislike of these topics than just whether or not they are relevant. Especially in the case of Atheism, these out-of-bounds personal topics are also less likely to be backed up by incontrovertible evidence. One can check the police record to determine whether a candidate has been arrested for fraud, check former employers to confirm her job experience, and check voting records to gauge her issue preferences. Candidates rarely if ever announce their atheism in public. Finally, unlike study 2, here we find that opinions about whether true (negative) ads are more acceptable have no significant effect on anger, all other things equal. This does matter for believability—those who think that the truth is important are also more likely to say that the attack ads are more believable.

Responding to Real Ads: Study 4

Taken together, the results of our first three studies suggest that there is more to the effects of negativity than a simple assessment of whether people are angered by particular ad topics. Of course, as we have already pointed out, our first three studies do not ask voters to respond to actual ads, just to the description of potential ad topics. But our fourth study, the one with a national convenience sample of participants from Amazon's Mechanical Turk service, used real campaign videos and asked for a wider range of responses for each ad, as described in chapter 4. Here we will explore this study in more depth, leading to a model of affective response to negative ads that will help us understand how credibility conditions negative affect and provides a cushion against the supposed negative outcomes of negativity. In general, when participants in this study see attack ads as credible, they are less likely to be angry at them, all else equal. As always with a sample like this, we cannot make simple generalizations to

TABLE 6.4. **Predicting anger and believability, study 3**

	Anger	Believability
Self-define treatment—pre-question	−0.15*	0.19*
	(0.09)	(0.11)
Self-define treatment—post-question	0.07	−0.22**
	(0.09)	(0.11)
Topic: Family	1.10***	−0.72***
	(0.08)	(0.06)
Topic: Atheist	0.40***	−0.65***
	(.08)	(0.09)
Topic: Experience	−0.45***	0.23***
	(0.05)	(0.06)
Topic: Issues	−0.58***	0.36***
	(0.06)	(0.08)
Truth more acceptable	−0.03	0.12**
	(0.05)	(0.05)
Candidates tell the truth about opponents	0.03	0.23***
	(0.06)	(0.06)
Anger toward ads in general	0.22***	−0.05
	(0.05)	(0.06)
Gender: Female	0.02	−0.05
	(0.08)	(0.09)
Age	0.00	−0.01**
	(0.01)	(0.01)
Democrat	0.06	0.11
	(0.11)	(0.12)
Republican	−0.02	−0.11
	(0.10)	(0.12)
Ideology	0.00	0.05
	(0.05)	(0.04)
Race: Nonwhite	0.12	0.02
	(0.11)	(0.12)
College graduate	−0.06	−0.01
	(0.07)	(0.07)
Religiosity	0.14*	0.04
	(0.08)	(0.09)
Constant	1.60***	1.71***
	(0.31)	(0.33)
Adj r²	0.335	0.250
N	Subjects = 235	Subjects = 235
	Observations = 2980	Observations = 2938

Note: Robust standard errors in parentheses. DV = Higher values are greater anger, more believable.
*$p < 0.1$.
**$p < 0.05$.
***$p < 0.01$.

the population as a whole, but we can learn a great deal about how people respond to real-world ads and, more importantly, we can assess experiments embedded in the study to examine links between credibility and response to negativity. Experiments do not rely on random samples; instead they rely on random assignment and allow us to test how participants respond when we systematically change the information they receive. Moreover, we can assess how specific variables of interest are intercorrelated (using a multivariate analysis) within this sample, and thus see to what degree the findings here support findings from our more readily generalizable studies.

Determining whether or not a given ad is truthful can be quite difficult at times. We begin our additional analysis of study 4 by examining the question of lying using an experiment we embedded in the study where participants were asked to judge political statements taken out of context. To put it simply, taking quotes out of context is lying. It is never done innocently; the purpose is to deceive voters by asserting or implying that the quote means something other than its true meaning. Just as with negativity, taking the opponent's statements out of context has a rich and storied history in American politics, such as in 1934 when an opponent attributed quotes from Upton Sinclair's fictional novels to Sinclair himself (Swint 2006).

Out-of-context statements were particularly visible in the 2012 presidential election, where both Barack Obama and Mitt Romney repurposed each other's quotes in their advertising and were egregiously steadfast in supporting the false claims even after fact-checkers made clear that the ads were taking their opponent out of context. One of Romney's examples is well known; the campaign took a snippet from an Obama speech in which he said, "If you've got a business, you didn't build that," and not only used it in advertising but also built an entire day at the Republican National Convention around it. The Romney campaign incorrectly claimed that the quote was Obama disdainfully rebuking entrepreneurs and businesspeople, telling them they did not deserve to gain from their hard work. The statement, though, came from a much longer comment in which it was clear Obama was referring to the government's role in building the public infrastructure used by business.

For its part, the Obama campaign was not innocent of such activity. In particular, the campaign made every effort to spread the statement by Romney, "I like to fire people," which was said in the context of a larger statement about how the free market works, allowing people to "fire" those (in this case, health insurance providers) who do not give good service and seek out other options. A third example, which we mentioned in chapter 2, comes from earlier in the campaign and was less publicized. The Romney campaign used a clip of Obama saying, "If we keep talking about the economy, we're going to lose." They claimed that Obama was attempting to divert talk about dismal economic conditions. In fact, Obama's quote had come from the 2008 campaign. It was a clip of Obama quoting a statement made by an aide of his opponent John McCain, who had told a reporter that the McCain campaign didn't want to talk about the economy (Shear 2012b). In other words, to be clear, Romney was using a quote from a McCain staffer and attributing it to Obama himself, since the president had spoken it.

The point here is that among attack ads, those that take comments out of context seem to generate a great deal of potential backlash. At a minimum the media fact-checking operations kick into gear in order to make clear that such ads are "lies," while the targets of the ads become quite huffy about having been attacked so unfairly. If there is any kind of ad that should generate a strong negative reaction from voters, this might be it.

An Experiment on Taking Quotes Out of Context

We implemented two simple context experiments after participants had viewed and responded to all of the ad videos. In the first, we used the "keep talking about the economy" statement while the second used a statement where a candidate purportedly said he did not care about unemployment. For both experiments our participants first were asked to imagine that a candidate "ran a TV ad in which he said the following about his opponent" followed by the statement. They were then asked how fair it would be to run an ad with the statement. For the first experiment, the statement was by candidate Tom Smith about his opponent Stu Jones, and read, "My opponent was right when he said, 'If we keep talking about the economy, we're going to lose.' He's done a terrible job dealing with our economic problems." For the second experiment, the statement was made by Jones about Smith, and read: "It is sad that Tom Smith says, 'I don't care what the unemployment rate's going to be.' Smith should care. We all should care." In all cases, respondents saw the comments by Smith before those by Jones.

Following the response to the first statement, participants were randomly assigned to one of two follow-up items that placed the original quote into a context. One of the items showed that the original quote was taken out of context while the other item suggested that it was a reasonably accurate reading of what the opponent had said.

For the "economy" experiment, the two follow-ups were:

A. [OUT OF CONTEXT] Now imagine a fact-check organization has reported that the quote Smith used in his ad: "If we keep talking about the economy, we're going to lose," was part of a longer statement made by his opponent, Stu Jones. Jones' full statement was: "My opponents' campaign actually said, and I quote, 'if we keep talking about the economy, we're going to lose.'" Knowing this, do you still think it was [response to initial statement] of Smith to run this ad?

B. [IN CONTEXT] Now imagine a fact-check organization has reported that the quote Smith used in his ad: "If we keep talking about the economy, we're going to lose," was part of a longer statement about his opponent, Stu Jones. The full statement read: "According to one Jones insider, Jones privately told donors that he needs to change the topic, saying, 'If we keep talking about the economy, we're going to lose.'" Knowing this, do you still think it was [response to initial statement] of Smith to run this ad?

For the "unemployment" experiment, the follow-ups were:

A. [OUT OF CONTEXT] Now imagine a fact-check organization has reported that the quote Jones used in his ad: "I don't care what the unemployment rate's going to be" was part of a longer statement made by his opponent, Tom Smith. Smith's full statement was: "My campaign is about a broader economic philosophy. I don't care what the unemployment rate's going to be. My campaign doesn't hinge on unemployment rates and growth rates. It's about something more foundational— that the government creates an atmosphere for jobs to be created in the private sector." Knowing this, do you still think it was [response to initial statement] of Jones to run this ad?

B. [IN CONTEXT] Now imagine a fact-check organization has reported that the quote Jones used in his ad: "I don't care what the unemployment rate's going to be" was part of a longer statement from his opponent, Tom Smith. Smith's full statement was "I am much more worried about inflation than unemployment. I don't care what the unemployment rate's going to be. Those that need jobs can find them, but if we let inflation get out of control we're in real trouble." Knowing this, do you still think it was [response to initial statement] of Jones to run this ad?

We are interested in several things here. First, do voters respond negatively to ads of this sort, where information is (potentially) taken out of context? Second, once the context is clarified—and in particular when the original statement is viewed as out of context—do voters adjust their opinion of the fairness of such ads? The ad statements make clear these are attacks, although we do not call them that, so here we have a more direct test of our initial text-based studies.

For the "economy" experiment, nearly two-thirds (65%) of participants thought such an ad would be either somewhat or very fair, while 35 percent thought it would be somewhat or very unfair. The ad for the second experiment, on unemployment, was even more acceptable, with 71 percent saying such an ad would be fair while 29 percent disagreed. These results suggest again—as we have shown throughout our studies—that voters really do not react negatively to candidates talking about the opponent, seeing such attacks as fair for the most part.

Do participants who think these attacks are fair revise their opinion when they are shown the quote in context—thereby learning that the initial statement was not accurate? Table 6.5 shows the experimental results by initial response, on a scale with 1 being "very fair" and 4 "very unfair." Initial responses are simplified to a dichotomous fair/unfair. For the first experiment, on the economic statement, when the context is made clear, participants respond accordingly. Those who initially thought the statement was fair but receive the follow-up showing that it was out of context are willing to change their assessment; those given the out-of-context treatment perceive the initial quote as more unfair (mean response of 3.01) than those receiving the in-context treatment (mean 2.23). Likewise, those who thought the initial statement was unfair are more likely to stick with this position when shown that it was taken out of context (mean of 3.05 versus 2.88 if shown to have been in context). More interestingly, among the 35 percent who thought the initial statement was unfair, about 71 percent persist in thinking it is unfair even when shown to be in con-

TABLE 6.5. **Mean unfairness levels by context**

Quote 1: Economy
  All Respondents
    In context   2.459 (.0875) N = 111
    Out of context   3.025 (.0920) N = 122   t(241) = 4.43, p < 0.001

  Initially Fair
    In context   2.225 (.1102) N = 71
    Out of context   3.013 (.1160) N = 80   t(149) = 4.89, p < 0.001

  Initially Unfair
    In context   2.875 (.1198) N = 40
    Out of context   3.048 (.1522) N = 42   t(80) = 0.86, p = 0.19 (ns)

Quote 2: Unemployment
  All Respondents
    In context   2.546 (.0899) N = 119
    Out of context   2.632 (.0918) N = 114   t(231) = 0.66, p = 0.25 (ns)

  Initially Fair
    In context   2.409 (.1055) N = 88
    Out of context   2.423 (.1024) N = 78   t(164) = 0.09, p = 0.46 (ns)

  Initially Unfair
    In context   2.935 (.1533) N = 31
    Out of context   3.083 (.1661) N = 36   t(65) = 0.65, p = 0.26 (ns)

Note: Responses recoded so that in all cases higher numbers represent movement away from fairness, conditioned on their initial response to the ad before context was revealed. 1 = Very fair, 4 = Very unfair.

text. So, only 29 percent of this group was willing to accept the ad once they saw the additional information about it.

The results from the second experiment are not as differentiated. It is possible that the second experiment's attempt to create a context was not as clear to participants, since it addresses an economic tradeoff between inflation and unemployment, but it is no more complicated than real-world examples tend to be. In fact we based it on an out-of-context quote used against Rick Santorum during the 2012 Republican primaries. Santorum said, "I don't care what the unemployment rate is going to be," following with, "my campaign doesn't hinge on unemployment rates and growth rates. It's something more foundational that's going on" (Kaplan 2012). Santorum was arguing that his candidacy was about freedom, transcending economic issues by creating "an atmosphere for the economy to fix itself." Mitt Romney's campaign sufficed with reiterating Santorum's first sentence. "I *do* care about the unemployment rate," he countered. "It does bother me."

However, this second experiment does give us the opportunity to investigate in another way the conditional effect of negativity and context. Our second question flips the candidates so that it is Jones attacking Smith, while in the first question Smith attacked Jones. We can test whether the random assignment to either the in-context or out-of-context versions of question 1 condition the responses to question 2. Table 6.6 presents the results of a regression where the dependent variable is the response about the unfairness of the "unemployment" statement (before it is revealed as either in or out of context). Those who found the "talking about the economy" quote initially unfair also found the second to be unfair, though more so if they had been proven correct in the first quote's follow-up. We also find that when voters started out believing the first quote was a fair attack on the opponent, but then learned it had actually been taken out of context, they were significantly more likely to believe that the second quote (with Jones attacking Smith on unemployment) was fair—before knowing if it was in context. In other words, when having learned that Jones used an out-of-context statement against Smith, participants were more willing to allow Smith to attack Jones, as they were less worried about the fairness of the counterattack.

This experiment allows us to examine how context matters, giving us some sense that participants in the study were not especially bothered by

TABLE 6.6. **Predicting response to second quote by fairness and context of first quote**

	Coefficient (Std. error)
Initial Response to Quote 1: Fair	
Quote 1: Out of Context	−0.2202*
	(.1277)
Initial Response to Quote 1: Unfair	
Quote 1: In Context	0.4422**
	(.1488)
Quote 1: Out of Context	0.8755***
	(.1465)
Constant	1.9577***
	(.0893)
r^2	0.217
N	233

Note: DV = Unfairness of second quote, 1 = Very fair, 4 = Very unfair. The baseline outcome is belief that the quote is fair and learning that it is in context.
*$p < 0.1$.
**$p < 0.05$.
***$p < 0.01$.

negative statements about an opponent (as in our other studies) but were also willing to adjust this assessment given new information. While willing to allow negativity, they saw attacks that were not credible (i.e., taken out of context) to be unfair. Yet, if one candidate attacks out of context there does seem to be some leeway for subsequent attacks made by the transgressed-upon opponent.

Responding to Negativity

We now turn to the many general questions we asked study participants about their responses to attack ads, making use of a rich dataset beyond the basic questions we asked about each ad they viewed. We describe those questions and the overall responses next. While the responses to these questions are interesting by themselves, we later incorporate most of them into a model of affective response to negativity.

Trust: Conditioning How Voters View Politicians, Politics, and the Media

We begin by looking at how voters view the political and media environment through the lens of trust. We asked three questions about trust before our respondents were exposed to any campaign ads: (1) "How much of the time do you think you can trust the government in Washington to do what is right?"; (2) "How much of the time do you think you can trust the media—television, newspapers, online media—to do what is right?"; and (3) "When you think about most candidates for national elected offices, do you think they are usually very trustworthy, somewhat trustworthy, somewhat untrustworthy, or very untrustworthy?"

Each of these taps a different aspect of trust that we suspect is related to how people perceive negative advertising. Those with a lack of trust toward Washington may use that cynical view to simply assume candidates are always lying, and thus may not be particularly bothered by negativity, since it would simply fit into their conception of things. On the other hand, for those with more trust in the federal government, negativity might give them pause. As it turns out, however, as table 6.7 (column 1) shows, there are not very many participants who say they can trust the federal government. The good news may be that few say they *never* trust the government; the bad news is that even fewer trust it always, though more than one in five is reasonably trusting. Still, most of our sample has limited trust in Washington.

TABLE 6.7 **Measures of trust, study 4**

	Trust in Washington DC	Trust in the Media
Just about always	1.3%	1.3%
Most of the time	22.1%	22.3%
Only some of the time	64.4%	67.2%
Never	7.2%	10.2%
	N = 235	N = 235

	Trust Candidates
Very trustworthy	2.1%
Somewhat trustworthy	44.0%
Somewhat untrustworthy	42.3%
Very untrustworthy	11.5%
	N = 235

How about the media? Table 6.7 (column 2) reports those results, and they are no better. In fact, if anything, our participants seem less trusting of the media than they do of the government in Washington, lending reinforcement to our contention in chapter 2 that voters cannot or will not count on the media to police candidate campaigns. Even if the media were to do this, it is not clear that they would be trusted. Though, with this and the question about trust in Washington, we should remain cautious in our interpretation. People may be conditioned to believe they should *say* they distrust the media or the government; to some extent, they could be giving us the socially "correct" answer to these questions.

We also asked respondents to assess the competence of political candidates generally. While not overwhelmed by the idea that political candidates are competent (only 6.4% responded "very competent") most voters in our study give the candidates some credit for competence, with the vast majority—68.5 percent—calling them "somewhat competent." Only 20 percent think candidates are "somewhat incompetent," while a small 5 percent called them "very incompetent." On the whole this suggests a relatively positive view of candidates. In fact, among this set of questions, it is the candidates who come out looking best. While there are still very few who say candidates can always be trusted (table 6.7, column 3), compared to assessments of the federal government and the media twice as many believe candidates are at least somewhat trustworthy. This seems somewhat surprising, given the general sense that citizens are turned off about politics, especially in the context of ever more nasty campaigns. Apparently, those who are supposedly turned off still have a better view of candidates than we might expect and clearly are more positive about

them than they are about "the government" or the media. This lends credence to our chapter 2 argument that candidates may be the best choice
for keeping each other honest.

How Helpful Are Negative Ads?

We've already explored how our respondents reacted to the campaign
ads they were shown, and for the most part, they seemed pretty relaxed
about them. They could identify the negative ones, and were angrier and
less willing to accept the defamatory ones in particular, but the sense is
that these ads were not particularly bothersome for the most part. But
we also have some general, non–ad-specific measures to explore. These
came after our participants viewed the whole series of twenty-one ads, so
to some extent their responses are likely to be conditioned by having just
seen a series of thirty-second campaign ads. We view this as a positive because the recent exposure to so many ads makes the different categories
of ads we ask about seem less hypothetical. Given that the videos were
a mix of positive and negative ads, we are not sure that we would expect
responses to be pushed in one or the other direction, though they might
reflect a certain amount of fatigue with ads after having seen twenty-one
in a row.

We first asked participants to tell us how helpful certain kinds of campaign ads would be to them, including campaign ads that:

talk about an opponent's voting record on the issues (Record)

talk about the differences between the candidates' positions on the issues (Posit-
Diff)

show the inconsistencies of an opponent's position on the issues (PositInc)

talk about why one candidate's positions on the issues are better than the other's
(PositBetter)

criticize the opponent for running a negative campaign (CritOpp)

say the campaign has been very negative (SayCampNeg)

say the opponent's campaign has been very negative (SayOppNeg)

talk about an opponent's faith and religion (OppFaith)

make broad claims about a candidate's future plans for governing (Govern)

Only the final two questions (OppFaith and Govern) were asked of all participants. The last question, about future plans for governing, is really about positive ads, where presumably a candidate is talking about one's own plans for governing. However, we did not make that clear, and so responses need to be taken with a bit of caution.

The other questions were grouped into two experiments, meant to test whether voters were susceptible to different ways of framing the same basic activity. We asked the questions in various ways to rule out the potential effects of question wording. For the first four, the activity is drawing contrasts or criticizing on issues (Record, PositDiff, PoistInc, PositBetter); we described the results of these briefly in chapter 1. Because of the findings from our first three studies, we expected at least a majority of participants would find the first four—ads talking about an opponent—to be helpful. For the next three (CritOpp, SayCampNeg, SayOppNeg) the idea was to test responses to candidates who claim the other candidate has gone negative. Also because of the previous studies, we expected that ads about the negativity of the campaign would not be particularly helpful, since they contain little relevant information on expected job performance and they specifically use the word "negative."

Each participant therefore answered four questions: one from the first four, one from the second three, and then the last two. For all questions, response options were on a four-point scale from "very helpful" to "not at all helpful." The order of the questions was fully randomized, so that there should be no aggregate order effects. Table 6.8 reports the results.

Examining the top panel of table 6.8, we see that 70 percent or more participants do find the ideas of talking about an opponent's record on issues, about differences between candidates, and about why one's positions are better than the opponent's to be at least somewhat helpful. These are all, of course, defined as negative campaigning by most scholars, yet their focus on policy issues means participants find the information potentially diagnostic as they try to choose between candidates. Interestingly though, those who were randomly asked instead about showing an opponent's "inconsistencies" on issues found that type of ad much less helpful, with just 50 percent rating it as at least somewhat helpful, and fewer than half as many calling it very helpful, compared to the other approaches. We suspect that the word "inconsistencies" triggers a more negative reaction. But even here, there are plenty who find this approach helpful. The big picture is that when candidates are negative in a comparative way on issues that define them and their opponents, many find such behavior generally helpful. In fact, as the last column shows, participants

TABLE 6.8. **Responses to helpful battery, study 4**

	Very Helpful	Somewhat Helpful	Not Very Helpful	Not at All Helpful	N
Drawing contrasts or criticizing on issues					
Opponent's voting record	38.10%	33.30%	14.30%	14.30%	63
Differences between candidates	43.10%	33.30%	17.60%	5.90%	51
Opponent's inconsistencies	18.30%	31.70%	28.30%	21.70%	60
One candidate's views better than the other's	37.70%	42.60%	14.80%	4.90%	61
Negative about negativity					
Criticize opponent for running negative	7.90%	3.90%	26.30%	61.80%	76
The campaign has been negative	3.90%	11.70%	31.20%	53.20%	77
Opponent's campaign has been very negative	4.90%	14.60%	25.60%	54.90%	82
Opponent's religion	4.30%	6.80%	16.60%	72.30%	235
Broad claims about future plans	12.30%	26.40%	33.60%	27.70%	235

are more likely to find explicit comparisons helpful than they are to find "broad claims about a candidate's future plans for governing." Such claims—usually presented in positive ads in the real world—are even less helpful than attacking an opponent's inconsistencies. As we have argued, citizens—even those who have just been subjected to twenty-one ads in a row—may well find certain kinds of negativity to be quite useful.

The first three columns of the bottom panel of table 6.8 report responses to a different strategy by candidates, which is to generally attack the tone of the campaign and the opponent. Here the story changes— our participants do not find it very helpful when candidates talk about negativity itself. In fact, all three versions of this question are viewed as distinctly unhelpful, with between 80 and 85 percent saying these types of ads are not very or not at all helpful. Whether complaining about the overall tone of the campaign, or directly criticizing an opponent for being negative, people seem unimpressed. Why? We suspect it is most likely because they see little information in such claims. For one, they undoubtedly know the campaign is negative, and, second, they may well find such negativity to be helpful in the first place. Candidates might do well to consider this point; yet it is routine for candidates to complain about negativity. Finally, the last column simply provides additional support to the basic finding from the campaign ads themselves—participants do not find attacks on religion to be at all helpful, with nearly 90 percent saying so.

Limits to Negativity?

We followed our "helpful" battery with a series of broad questions about ads that could be considered more defamatory. In particular, we asked if "mean-spirited" ads are appropriate and if negative ads attacking a candidate's personal life are appropriate. We also wanted to know if there are ads that are "so nasty I stop watching" and whether ads that attack a candidate's personal life when younger are "interesting." Many of these had socially undesirable answers, so we expected to find little support on the negative side.

Much as Kahn and Kenney (1999) noted in talking about mudslinging, our participants—while quite tolerant of negatively, even finding it helpful sometimes—have their limits. Only about 18 percent either strongly or somewhat agree that "mean-spirited commercials attacking the opponent are appropriate during election campaigns" while 53 percent strongly disagree with the statement. Likewise, they find some ads so nasty they stop watching: 65 percent strongly agreed, while only 12 percent disagreed at all. And participants claim they do not like ads that attack a candidate's personal life, with 90 percent at least somewhat agreeing that such ads are "inappropriate." Interestingly, more are willing to admit that they "find negative political commercials that attack an opponent's personal life as a young person to be interesting," with just under 19 percent saying they agreed somewhat or very much with the statement. Nonetheless, most people denied interest in such ads.

Recall from chapter 4 that study 4 participants were much more likely to say that the defamatory ads they watched were anger-inducing and might cause them to vote for the opponent. These data reinforce that point— there are indeed some ads that go beyond the bounds of decency, beyond what people will accept, even though for the most part they are very accepting of negativity that appears to be useful, such as issue-oriented attacks.

Do People Want to Know about Lies? To Whom Do They Turn to Find Out?

The answer to the former is yes—participants in our study want to know when candidates are lying, with 86 percent telling us it is "very important" to know if there are false claims in a candidate's ad, regardless of whether the ad is negative or positive. Another 12 percent say it is somewhat important to know, while only 2 percent deny the importance of knowing about false claims in ads. This leads to the obvious question of whether voters feel competent enough to figure out when a candidate is lying to them.

We asked two questions to get at this sort of efficacy or self-proclaimed ability to sort through the information candidates present to identify when they are lying.

> With which ONE of the following statements do you agree more? If a candidate tells a lie in an ad: (1) It would be easy for me to find out, or (2) It would be very hard for me to find out.

> With which ONE of the following statements do you agree more? If a candidate tells a lie in an ad: (1) I can usually tell just from watching it, or (2) I usually need someone else to point it out to me.

Results are mixed, as shown in table 6.9a. While 60 percent of participants say they can usually tell a lie when watching a candidate campaign ad, a not-insignificant 40 percent report that they are less sure, needing someone to point it out to them. Fewer think it is easy to find out if a candidate lies; this question is split nearly evenly, with just over 52 percent saying it is easy to find out when a candidate lies, while just 48 percent say it is hard to find this out. There seems to be a great deal of uncertainty as to whether they can actually detect when a candidate lies in an ad. There is little uncertainty about identifying negative ads for what they are, as we showed in chapter 4. But identifying negativity and knowing when a candidate is lying are two very different things, and nearly half felt at least somewhat in need of help to find this out.

So who do participants think they can turn to for this help? Using the

TABLE 6.9. **Finding and reporting candidate lies, study 4**

If a candidate tells a lie, I usually . . .		If a candidate tells a lie, it is . . .	
Can tell from watching it	60.0%	Easy for me to find out	52.3%
Need someone to point it out	40.0%	Hard for me to find out	47.7%

If a candidate tells a lie . . .		If a candidate tells a lie, other candidates . . .	
Media can be trusted to report	29.8%	Should point it out in ads	61.3%
Cannot rely on media to tell me	70.2%	Should let the media point out	38.7%

Note: N = 235 for each question.

same question format, and given statements premised on a candidate lying in an ad, voters were asked if the media can be relied on to point out lying, and if candidates themselves should point out when an opponent lies. Table 6.9b reports these results. In keeping with our earlier questions about trust in media and candidates, it should be no surprise to find that our participants are much more likely to say that candidates should point out each other's lies than they are to think the media will do so. More than 70 percent say they cannot trust the media to point out candidates' lies. This suggests a deep-seated suspicion of the media in this day of talking heads and politicized cable "news." When pitted against candidates to see who should do the honors of identifying lies, participants choose the candidates by a 61 to 39 percent margin. It isn't even close. These citizens are simply far less trusting of the media to get the job of helping them know whether candidates lie than they are of the candidates themselves. Participants in this study, who remember had just seen twenty-one ads, twelve of which were negative, essentially endorse the important role that negative advertising plays in a campaign: keeping candidates honest.

Examining Ad Credibility and Relevance

Now that we have some sense of how our study 4 participants generally perceive negativity, we want to return to the question of ad credibility. As in study 3, we asked how believable participants found a set of ads, but in this case the ads were real campaign videos. As before, when discussing the group of twelve negative ads as a whole we use the term "attack." Within these twelve were five that we determined *a priori* to be defamatory in nature, while seven others were more run-of-the-mill negativity. We will continue to use "defamatory" to denote the former and "negative" the latter. We will also refer to specific ads by the name of their sponsor as in chapter 4. As a reminder, for each of the twenty-one ads, participants answered a series of questions immediately after viewing each ad; table A.2 in appendix A reports the mean responses to each question for each ad. Our participants generally agreed about our three categories of ads, rating the positive ads as "not negative" and rating the defamatory ads generally as the most negative.

Here we look at the two questions that revolve around the relevance and credibility of an ad: whether it was appropriate and whether it was believable. For ads to seem credible they clearly must be believable; these two concepts are pretty well intertwined. At the same time, we believe that in order for a political ad to be credible it must also seem appropriate, that is, the viewer must believe the subject matter of the ad is legitimately brought into play during a campaign.

Following the approach we followed in chapter 4, figure 6.4 plots response to the question of "how appropriate is the subject matter of this ad for use in a political campaign?" against the type of ad for each of the twenty-one ads. Responses are scored 1 = Not at all appropriate, 2 = Not very appropriate, 3 = Somewhat appropriate, and 4 = Very appropriate. Positive ads are clearly differentiated from the negative and defamatory ads. They are all considered more appropriate though there is somewhat less support for the [Roskam] ad, in which the candidate's children heap praise upon him. Negative and defamatory ads are less easily separated from each other, yet seven of these are seen as more appropriate than not. Only five of the twenty-one ads fall below the midpoint (2.5) on our 1–4 scale, and four of these are defamatory ads. Again reinforcing the strong dislike of religious attacks, the two considered least appropriate are the [Dole] attack on Hagan, and the [Conway] "Aqua Buddha" ad that accused Rand Paul of worshipping a non-Christian "god." Also seen as inappropriate was the defamatory attack by Zeb [Little] on Paul Bussman, which claimed Bussman refused to pay child support, suggesting our respondents do not see such personal attacks as appropriate to a political campaign—though still causing us to question to what extent is was considered inappropriate because it seemed unbelievable. Nearer to the midpoint, though still below it, is the attack by Rick [Mullin] claiming that his

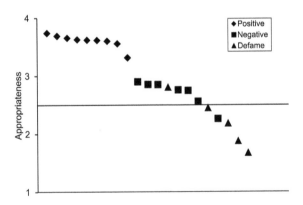

FIGURE 6.4. Appropriateness of ads viewed, study 4

opponent, Rick Bertrand, was an unethical drug salesman who "put profits ahead of children's health." Again, we see an attack that includes children, while also directly attacking ethical behavior outside of the political
realm. Participants in study 4 do not find this line of attack to be particularly appropriate. Finally, the only other ad that falls below the midpoint
is one where Bob [Corker] claimed Harold Ford was from "DC, not Tennessee" and "looks good on TV," an ad that is not especially defamatory
on its face, and which clearly is about politics.

The bigger point here is that the rest of the ads we showed, including
one defamatory ad (Michael [Bennet] attacking Ron Buck on ethics) and
six negative ads, were above the midpoint, meaning that on average they
were seen as appropriate topics for political ads. Though attacks on topics
tangentially or not at all related to politics are considered inappropriate,
by no means do all attack ads fall into this category. On the other hand,
the positive ads were across the board seen as more appropriate than the
attack ads.

A second aspect of these ads is the extent to which citizens find the ads
they watch to be believable. It is certainly the case that we expect people
to respond more negatively to ad topics that seem less believable, as we
found in study 3. Two of the study 3 topics, ads about family and claims
that an opponent is an atheist, were dismissed as unbelievable. Here we
have real videos with a mix of positive, negative, and defamatory ads. Yet
believability responses in study 4 look quite similar to study 3 as shown in
figure 6.5. As with appropriateness, the large majority of these ads, including most of the negative and defamatory ones, are above the midpoint
on a believability scale from 1–4, with 1 being "not at all believable" and
4 "very believable." Only two defamatory ads—[Dole] and [Conway]—
are on average seen as unbelievable. Both are religion-based attacks and
both were also seen as relatively inappropriate. But of the other three
ads that were viewed as inappropriate, only one is seen as unbelievable:
[Corker]. The other moderately unbelievable ad is an attack by Matt [Pat-
ten] on Colleen Gray for "making empty promises for 15 years." Interestingly, that ad is among the most "appropriate" of the attack ads measured.
On the other hand, the two other "inappropriate" ads, [Mullin] and [Ben-
net], are both above the midpoint on believability, with the [Bennet] attack scoring in the top two of the attack ads.

It is the case, however, that all of the positive ads are rated as more believable than any of the negative or defamatory ads with one exception.
The [Hagan] response to the Dole attack rates very high on believability

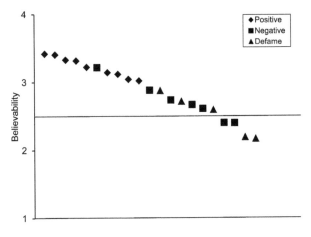

FIGURE 6.5. Believability of ads viewed, study 4

even though it was lower on appropriateness. This is driven primarily by participants who saw the Hagan ad after the Dole ad. We have more to say about this below. Otherwise it is the case that the remaining negative and defamatory ads are all seen as less believable than positive ads, though the difference is quite small for most of the ads.

Modeling Responses to Political Ads

We now turn to building a more comprehensive model of the effect of negative ads. Table 6.10 shows the results of a regression model predicting anger, appropriateness and believability responses for the twelve attack ads in study 4. The independent variables we use are as follows. For the questions about ad helpfulness, we combined into a single variable the responses to each of the four questions in which the candidate was giving information about the opponent (PositDiff, PositInc, PositBetter, CritOpp). The response "very helpful" is coded as 4 and is highest on the four-point scale. We also include measures from questions about finding and reporting lies. These include whether candidates should point out lies in ads (coded 0) or leave it to the media (coded 1), along with the question if it is easy (0) or hard (1) for voters to find out if a candidate tells a lie. We also include a variable for the belief about political candidates' competence on a scale of 1 (not at all competent) to 4 (very competent), and another for whether the participant believed that mean-spirited ads attacking the opponent were okay (four-point scale with "strongly agree" scored as 1 and "strongly disagree" as 4). Participant ideology is measured on a seven-point scale with higher numbers meaning more liberal. Turnout is scored from 1 "very likely" to 4 "very unlikely"; note, however, that 77 percent of our sample said they were likely to vote in the 2012 election, and another 14 percent said they were "somewhat likely." We also include dummy variables for party ID (default is Independent), whether the ad was defamatory or negative (not defamatory) and the ad topics (with Issues as the baseline). Finally, a series of demographic variables— race (nonwhite), age, gender (female), education (college graduate) and religiosity—are included as controls.

In the first column of table 6.10 the dependent variable is the anger judgment, ranging from 1 ("not at all angry") to 4 ("very angry"). The model confirms that defamatory ads made participants angry, all else equal. Those who found information about the opponent to be helpful are also more likely to be angry at our ads. The only other significant variable is a participant's self-efficacy in rooting out candidates' lies. Those who can "usually tell from watching it" are less angry. With the exception of race—nonwhites are less angry—the demographic and political attitude variables are not significant.

In the second column believability is the dependent variable. Again the content of the ad matters, as defamatory ads are seen as less believable. Otherwise, as compared to predicting anger, we find that with believability some different measures are now important. Those who find ads critical of the opponent to be helpful also find the ads from our experiment to be more believable. Those who think that mean-spirited ads are okay also think our ads are more believable. Finally, those who believe candidates are generally competent find our ads to be more believable as well.

In column 3 we present the regression results using the same independent variables but now with appropriateness as the dependent variable. Just as with the others, participants were affected by the defamatory ads, here saying that the defamatory attacks are less appropriate. The other significant variables are the same ones that affected believability.

In sum, for all three of these judgments, we see that there is much to attitudes toward negative campaigns that goes beyond the question of whether an ad is negative or not. The results here echo the simpler analysis we presented earlier, for instance in figures 4.2 (anger), 6.4 (appropriateness), and 6.5 (believability). There we showed that there is definitely

TABLE 6.10. **Predicting anger, believability, and appropriateness responses to attack ads**

	Anger	Believability	Appropriateness
Defamatory	0.4975***	−0.1959***	−0.5033***
	(0.0298)	(0.0265)	(0.0298)
Mean ads are okay	0.0614	−0.1687***	−0.2542***
	(0.0479)	(0.0448)	(0.0438)
Ads about opponent are helpful	0.0781*	0.1201***	0.1045***
	(0.0438)	(0.0343)	(0.0314)
Candidates should let media point out lies	−0.0766	0.1267*	0.2073***
	(0.0915)	(0.0692)	(0.0681)
I can tell if candidate is lying	−0.1558*	−0.0624	0.0708
	(0.0855)	(0.0659)	(0.0641)
Candidates are competent	−0.1193	0.1331**	0.1179***
	(0.0758)	(0.0511)	(0.0446)
Gender: Female	−0.1064	0.0691	0.0679
	(0.0871)	(0.0645)	(0.0617)
Democrat	0.1068	−0.0092	0.027
	(0.1062)	(0.0857)	(0.0833)
Republican	0.1281	0.0074	−0.0812
	(0.146)	(0.1192)	(0.1028)
Ideology	0.0448	0.0163	−0.049
	(0.055)	(0.0477)	(0.0442)
College graduate	0.0499	−0.0526	−0.0503
	(0.087)	(0.0657)	(0.0642)
Religious	0.078	0.0629	0.1071*
	(0.0879)	(0.065)	(0.0648)
Race: Nonwhite	−0.2775**	0.0501	0.0358
	(0.1075)	(0.069)	(0.0753)
Age	−0.0018	0.0025	0.0022
	(0.0039)	(0.0033)	(0.0035)
Turnout	−0.063	0.0765*	0.0362
	(0.0613)	(0.0448)	(0.047)
Constant	2.179***	2.1402***	2.6583***
	(0.4033)	(0.3692)	(0.337)
Adj r²	0.0972	0.0984	0.1721
N	Subjects = 235	Subjects = 235	Subjects = 235
	Obs. = 2761	Obs. = 2761	Obs. = 2761

Note: Robust standard errors in parentheses. DV = higher values are greater anger, more believable, more appropriate.
*$p < 0.1$.
**$p < 0.05$.
***$p < 0.01$.

a negative reaction to negativity, but the reactions among our participants are muted for all but the worst ads. At this point, considering the results above and from previous chapters, we feel quite confident in saying both that there is a large variance in reaction to the ads generally categorized as negative, and that the differences can be gauged from looking at both the ad content (e.g., the topic, whether the intent is defamatory) and attitudes about dealing with false ads.

But that leaves us with one key question, perhaps *the* key question—how does all of this affect voting? With some sense of how the ads performed in terms of credibility we can now try to put everything from study 4 together to address this. Our intent is to put all of these measures into a basic model of response to campaign ads, including both our negative and positive ads, but ultimately focusing on attack ads to examine how this set of study participants saw the big picture. Our thinking is as follows. In encountering a political ad, voters assess if it is positive, negative, or defamatory, primarily based on the topic of the ad as we have identified in several of our studies. The type of ad, combined with individual differences including existing attitudes towards candidates and the political system as well as demographic background factors, condition assessments of appropriateness, believability, and the extent to which the ad generates an anger response. Using these we determine the extent to which all of these cause voters to consider voting for the target rather than the sponsor of the ad. In one sense this is measuring backlash, but we hesitate to use that term because all but three of the ads had a net positive vote gain (see fig. 4.3). More accurately, we are measuring the change in vote intention, which mostly ranges from positive to neutral.

Our expectation is that when we look at all these factors combined, emotional response—anger—will not be the most salient predictor. Instead people care more about whether the ad—positive or negative—is believable than they care about whether they are angry because the ad is negative. If our thesis is right—that negativity about negativity is more a reaction to the way we ask voters about attack ads rather than some true dislike of negative ads—we should see that while anger may well matter, it will not be the most important factor driving responses.

We first build simple models in which we use the three measures (anger, believability, and appropriateness) in a linear regression to predict vote intention, which ranges from 1 (more likely to vote for the opponent) to 3 (more likely to vote for the candidate supported by the ad). The results are in the first column of table 6.11, labeled as model 1, and show that while all three responses are statistically significant, believability and appropriateness have a much larger effect than does anger. Model 2 is the same as model 1 but for the attack ads only, and again we see that credibility and appropriateness are more salient than anger.

Of course, there is some degree of collinearity across the three cognitive and affective measures we use as independent variables in the first two models. One method of addressing such a concern is to use instrumental variables methods such as two-stage least squares (2SLS), which

TABLE 6.11. **Effects of ad assessments on laboratory vote, study 4**

	Model (1) All ads	Model (2) Attack ads	Model (3) All ads 2SLS	Model (4) Attack ads 2SLS
Anger	−.0583***	−.0363**	−.1735***	−.1392***
	(.0152)	(.0163)	(.0603)	(.0567)
Believability	.2348***	.2174***	.3830***	.2748***
	(.0170)	(.0204)	(.1191)	(.1414)
Appropriateness	.2170***	.2012***	.0513	.0978
	(.0155)	(.0194)	(.0922)	(.1037)
Constant	.9723***	.9848***	1.2442***	1.326***
	(.0641)	(.0722)	(.2801)	(.2742)
Adj r²	0.3589	0.2699	0.3170	0.2123
N	Subjects = 235	Subjects = 235	Subjects = 235	Subjects = 235
	Obs. = 4841	Obs. = 2761	Obs. = 4841	Obs. = 2761

Note: Table entries are unstandardized coefficients; robust standard errors in parentheses.
***$p < 0.01$.

replace the collinear variables with instruments that are uncorrelated with the error term in the regression. The 2SLS method is quite appropriate here since, as we described above, our model for how voters process ads is a two-stage model. First, both details about the ad and individual differences among subjects affect cognitive and affective responses to the ad. Second, those responses affect voting decisions.

We combine the simple regression models and estimate vote intention using 2SLS. The independent variables from table 6.10 are used in the first stage to predict believability, anger, and appropriateness responses; we also include a dummy variable for "attack ad" whenever we use all of the ads. In stage 2, we regress our main dependent variable—vote intention—using the stage 1 predictions for anger, believability, and appropriateness on the right-hand side as instruments for those independent variables. By doing this, we more accurately reflect our model of how voters process ads, and we reduce some of the effects of collinearity across our three cognitive and affective measures.

The results of the second stage of this 2SLS regression are shown in table 6.11 as models 3 (all ads) and 4 (attack ads only). In these models, believability has the largest effect of our three measures, though anger is a significant predictor in both models. However, the effect of appropriateness on vote intention is not significant. This suggests that while appropriateness of the ads is a good predictor of vote intention, most of the predictive value is subsumed by factors that similarly affect believability assessments. In all, our findings here support one of the main goals of this study—to show the importance of ad credibility in studies of negative campaigning.

However, the two-stage model has its limitations, perhaps the most obvious being that many different formulations of the instruments are possible, that those formulations may also be justifiable theoretically, that it would be quite difficult to choose the "best" two-stage model, and that in any case, the instruments themselves are not perfectly uncorrelated with the error term. At this point, rather than present many more versions of the same regression, we make additional use of our multimethodological approach by moving back to our formal model of campaigning and expanding it to allow us to test in a "game" environment the findings we see among our sample of voters who examined real-world ads. If we can support our hypotheses about credibility using an entirely different mechanism (the formal model and associated experimental test), this should lend credence to our results in a way that the survey questions could not do on their own, especially with the convenience sample we used in study 4.

In making this transition, we need to address how to operationalize whether an ad is "believable." For this we return to the idea of truth, since we essentially mean the extent to which the voter thinks the candidate is telling the truth—or more precisely, the probability in which the candidate is telling the truth given the candidate's campaign statement. We can do this by adding into the formal model that candidates can give false statements as messages—the voter will never know for sure whether a message is false, but can estimate based upon various factors of the game, such as the message chosen and the probability that a candidate's lies are caught by a (credible) fact-checker. When candidates are required to police themselves, the situation just becomes more difficult for the voter to evaluate.

A Brief Return to Dole and Hagan

We will close this chapter on credibility by returning to the 2008 Dole-Hagan US Senate campaign in North Carolina. In chapter 4 we examined voter response to two ads from that campaign, which were both related to religion. In the real world, Dole attacked first, implying that Hagan is an atheist. Hagan responded with a negative ad that attacked Dole's attack. In study 4 we employed an experiment in which we randomized the order in which our participants saw the two ads, so that approximately half saw the Dole ad first, followed by Hagan, and thus the Hagan ad was in context, while the other participants saw the Hagan response ad first, followed by Dole's attack, which meant they viewed Hagan ad out of context. Such an experiment allows us to see exactly what happens when candidates respond to specific types of negativity, in this case, using religion, one of the apparently taboo subjects for such ads. In chapter 4 we addressed affective response to these ads. In brief, when Dole's ad came first, the Hagan ad was seen as less negative, and anger at it was much lower than when the Hagan ad came first.

Here we look at credibility: were these ads, which touch on a topic that in our text versions was seen as very unbelievable, seen as credible here? Was their believability and appropriateness conditioned by context? Table 6.12 reports mean values for believability and appropriateness, along with negativity, anger, and vote intention. Both Dole's and Hagan's ads were thought more believable when the Dole ad ran first. Running first, of course, means that Dole's ad set the stage, and without anything to contrast it to, participants were significantly more likely to rate it higher in believability then when it ran after the Hagan ad. Hagan's ad was more believable in context, that is, after seeing Dole's attack, than it was when it ran first. The same thing happened with appropriateness; both ads were more appropriate when Dole set the stage. In particular, the difference for Hagan is quite large at 0.81, (the believability difference for Hagan is 0.4) suggesting that participants were inclined to see her response as appropriate. In other words, given the attack by Dole, it was appropriate for Hagan to respond, but without the attack, it was less so. In any case, the Dole ad was much less believable and much less appropriate than Hagan's response. As they told us with our text-based topics, attacks on an opponent's religion go well beyond what people are willing to accept.

In chapter 4, we found that 56 percent said the Hagan ad was negative if it was shown before the Dole ad, but only 27 percent saw negativity if Dole's attack came first. A negative ad, like Hagan's, is rated as much less negative when placed in context. This may not be because it is more believable, however, since the difference in means on believability is relatively small, with the Hagan ad only slightly more believable when it came after the Dole attack. So while not seen as negative, it is not so much that Hagan's ad became more believable in context as it was that the Hagan

TABLE 6.12. **Rating of Dole and Hagan ads, study 4**

	Dole Ad		Hagan Ad	
Ad Order	Dole First N = 111	Hagan First N = 89	Dole First N = 110	Hagan First N = 91
Believability	2.34	1.99	3.39	2.93
	(.092)	(.095)	(.066)	(.095)
Appropriateness	1.80	1.49	3.24	2.43
	(.090)	(.088)	(.089)	(.116)
Is negative	0.99	0.98	0.27	0.56
	(.009)	(.016)	(.043)	(.052)
How negative	4.34	4.34	1.22	2.08
	(.097)	(.110)	(.129)	(.167)
Anger	2.86	2.92	1.88	2.30
	(.099)	(.106)	(.097)	(.113)
Vote intention	1.67	1.60	2.54	2.11
	(.076)	(.069)	(.059)	(.071)

Note: Table entries are means; standard errors in parentheses.

ad was simply seen as more appropriate when it was a response. As we saw with anger and the vote intention previously, the context of the ad matters a great deal.

Conclusion

To summarize, the key result from our regression on vote intention was that, of our three main judgments, believability factored most into vote intention. But this tells us little about *how* believability has this effect. In this chapter we showed that voters find negative ads to be less credible, but nevertheless find them to be helpful. We saw this in a limited fashion with our random sample population surveys, and delved into it in more depth with our Internet convenience sample, reinforcing the random sample findings. While, as we have said a number of times, we cannot readily generalize our study 4 findings to the full population of voters, the findings expand on what we learned from the simpler population survey-experiments, and extend our efforts to triangulate on a set of findings that help us better understand the role of negativity.

One result of the apparent conflict between credibility and helpfulness makes it likely that voters are not using the information from negative ads as well as they should—mainly because they are less likely to trust the negative ads. In the next chapter we expand on our earlier formal model to test this hypothesis and, more generally, to study the impact on voter decision-making in environments where we vary the candidates' propensity to lie to the voters. We find voter error is more frequent when negative campaigning is involved but dissipates when voters are more confident that candidates' statements are true. Thus, we will see again how formal modeling nicely reinforces the findings we have reported throughout this book.

How the Possibility of Lies Damages Voter Confidence in Negativity

Liar, liar, pants on fire!—Old children's taunt; also a rating by fact-checking organization PolitiFact

Up to this point we have shown that voters are not as negative about negativity *per se* as is believed by those who wring their hands over the imminent demise of democracy. While some topics are genuinely disliked, for the most part voters do not appear to be particularly angered by negative ads. Though, when asked if they oppose negative ads, voters agree that they do, and when asked if negative ads make them angry, voters also agree. As we have shown in the early chapters of this book, this is as much due to the way the questions are usually asked as to some real dislike of negativity. Instead, negativity carries information that seems to matter to voters, and rather than negative emotions like anger predicting backlash against negative ads, we find that it is the ad's credibility that matters more so than anger or appropriateness or the fact that it takes on an opponent. But, of course, this requires voters to infer from the campaigns whether the candidates are using truthful attacks rather than lies.

Once again, we find that the survey methods we use in earlier chapters are limited in their ability to answer the question of how credibility matters to voters, in that we cannot observe the voters' decision-making processes as they attempt to determine whether or not the candidates have been forthright. So again we turn to a different method from our arsenal, another formal model-based experiment, in which we revise the "game" candidates and voters play in our lab; we allow candidates to lie, with or without being caught, and to provide this additional information to voters.

In the last chapter we examined the role truthfulness plays in making

negative ads more acceptable to voters using our random sample telephone survey data (studies 1 and 2), finding that the more truthful voters perceived an attack, the more acceptable it was, and, in an interesting twist, this effect was stronger when respondents were explicitly told
the ads were negative than when they were not. We also find that negative ads were actually perceived as more truthful in the first place, compared to the question asked about ads without reference to negativity.
Examining the credibility of ads, we find from our national internet panel
(study 3) that the topic matters: ads that hit on religion and family are
generally disbelieved, and thus seen as not credible. We further learn that
when voters examine real ads (study 4), their responses are very similar to
what we find with hypothetical ads in which we simply describe the activity of negative campaigning. Using these multiple methods, we have developed and tested hypotheses about how voters respond to negativity.
But the key point we were left with in chapter 6, that credibility plays a
crucial role in assessments of negativity, is built primarily on a nonrandom
sample Internet study, which, while it included embedded experiments
and also comported with the more basic findings of our random sample
surveys, still leaves questions about how voters do or do not make use of
negativity and what happens when they learn that a candidate is making
claims that are not credible, that is, when a candidate lies.

So in this final substantive chapter, we address the question of credibility from the previous chapter with an extension of our chapter 5 formal model. In that chapter the model allowed us to assess the implications when voters act in a sophisticated manner, as Bayesian updaters,
compared to when they are naïve. Naïve voters are unable to infer much
about campaign topics that are not openly discussed, even when it is possible for them to do so. Thus the information from negative campaigns becomes of greater importance, even necessary to provide voters with something approaching full information. In testing the model, we find voters in
the experiment *did* tend toward naïve, rather than sophisticated, decision-
making, and that they responded as predicted, finding value in negativity.

From the initial model and its experimental test, we not only learn that
negative campaigns are valuable information sources, but we also uncover
the mechanisms behind *why* they are valuable. Here, we extend the formal
model and conduct another experiment to further understand how voters
process information from candidates that might be false. In the original
model candidates were constrained to tell the truth. As a result, they were
faced with some unusual campaign options, such as revealing positive in

formation about the opponent or revealing negative information about themselves. Obviously in reality candidates rarely do either of these. Suppose you are a subject in the experiment and given the role of a (−, −) candidate facing a clearly superior (+, +) candidate. You would probably wonder something like "Why can't I just tell the voter that I have a positive trait? Or, that my opponent has a negative trait?" From the voters' perspective, though, prohibiting candidates from lying was clearly an advantage. Despite the prevalence of voter naiveté in the first experiment, we found that the electoral system was rather efficient. The better candidate won 84 percent of the elections, meaning that candidates were able to transmit useful information to the voters in most of the cases, in part because they could go negative and the negativity had to be truthful. But what happens to this system when we loosen the reins on the candidates?

To determine this, we introduce several changes to our original design; primarily, candidates with a negative trait and candidates facing opponents with a positive trait are always given the option to lie about that trait. This means that regardless of the actual traits, every candidate has the same five campaign message choices. Two of these are positive—one's own positive trait on either dimension. The candidate could also reveal the opponent's negative trait on either dimension, or finally, choose not to campaign.

If there are no consequences for lying, meaning that it is risk-free, we essentially have a cheap-talk signaling game. In other words, from a game theory perspective, there is no theoretical reason to believe that there is any underlying meaning behind the candidates' choices. For instance, candidates with good traits can reveal them just as candidates with bad traits can "reveal" good traits by lying about them.

Once we modified the rules in our model, we carried out a second experimental test of the model allowing candidates to make false statements. One of our treatments is the cheap-talk variant. However, in all of our other treatments, candidates who lie have some probability of being caught by an exogenous monitor. If caught, the voter is notified of the lie, and the candidate also must pay a penalty. This is very different from being able to lie with impunity.

Meanwhile, the ability to lie in this game is encouraging for inferior candidates, who have the option of simply matching the opponent's campaign; this would result in a 50/50 election whenever the opponent is not caught. If the chance of being caught lying is zero, and the voter nonetheless tends to believe some campaign themes more than others, this means that candidates should always choose the same campaign option; which they choose depends largely on voter beliefs whenever the two candidates choose conflicting campaigns.

In this chapter we take a different approach from that of chapter 5, as we are less concerned with determining which (cursed) equilibrium is being played, and more concerned with whether the candidates and voters are making the correct inferences given what actually took place while they were playing the game. This has the advantage, too, of allowing readers to focus on the substantive aspects of our results rather than on the game theory details. For any given pair of messages, if neither candidate was caught lying, the voter has a challenging inference to make, namely how likely each candidate is to have been lying yet not caught. We are most interested in how voters account for this fact in their decision-making. In short, in testing the model we find that voters tend to underestimate the truthfulness of negative versus positive campaigns. This may be the key to what dislike of negativity there is; we found earlier that those who believe negative ads may be true are less likely to oppose them. But the evidence we will show here is that many voters behave as if they doubt the veracity of the information candidates provide them, even when they should not.

In the next section of this chapter, we show the changes made to the formal model to account for the possibility of unverifiable campaign revelations. Then, we similarly review the changes to the experiment and provide information about our experimental sessions. Finally, we present a series of results from the experiment to show how voters and candidates respond when candidates are not constrained to tell the truth. As in chapter 5, those uninterested in the intricacies of the formal model can skip the following section.

Formal Model

The campaigning game in this chapter adds a new stage to the game we introduced in chapter 5, so it is now a four-stage game as shown in figure 7.1. In stage 1, just as before, candidates draw traits from two dimensions labeled X and Y, which can either be "positive" or "negative." They are shown their own traits as well as those of the opponent.

In stage 2, candidates campaign by sending a message to the voter. Regardless of the specific traits drawn, all candidates now have the same

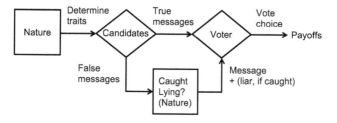

FIGURE 7.1. Campaign game flowchart

five campaign message choices: stating that one's own X trait is positive, that one's own Y trait is positive, that the opponent's X trait is negative, that the opponent's Y trait is negative, or not campaigning. As before, the candidates campaign by simultaneously revealing messages to the voter. Formally, a strategy for candidate ℓ consists of ℓ's campaign message for the sixteen different trait draw possibilities. This strategy set is shown in line (1) below.

(1) $s_\ell : [\{X+,X-\} \times \{Y+,Y-\}]^2 \to \{X, oppX, Y, oppY, \varnothing\}$

Unlike the previous version of the model, candidates here *cannot* make self-defeating statements such as "I have a negative X trait." In this version, positive campaigning is simply stating that one has a positive trait on a given dimension, regardless of whether or not it is true. Similarly, negative campaigning is any statement about an opponent's negative trait.

In stage 3, an exogenous monitor attempts to expose candidates' lies. It is successful in disinterring any lie with probability π; if both messages are false, the probability draws for each candidate are independent. If a candidate is caught lying, the candidate pays a fixed cost κ; the penalty κ can be interpreted as either financial or political. The strategy shown in (1) is specific for a given κ and π, both of which are known by the candidates and the voter before the election begins.

In the fourth and final stage, the voter is given both candidates' messages. If any of the messages has been exposed by the monitor as a lie, the voter is informed of that as well. The voter receives all of this information simultaneously and then chooses one of the candidates. The voter's utility function for candidate ℓ remains additive over the candidates' traits on the two dimensions; there is no extra penalty *per se* in voting for candidates that have or have not lied.

There are nine possible message/monitoring outcomes that the voter can receive from a given candidate. These are the elements of the message set $M = \{X, \hat{X}, oppX, opp\hat{X}, Y, \hat{Y}, oppY, opp\hat{Y}, \emptyset\}$ where the caret ($\wedge$) indicates messages revealed to the voter as false in stage 3, and $\emptyset$ indicates the choice not to campaign. The voter strategy τ_n maps each of the ($9 \times 9 = 81$) possible message/monitoring outcomes to a vote for one of the candidates. This is shown in (2), where M_ℓ and $M_{-\ell}$ represent the message/monitoring outcomes of candidates ℓ and $-\ell$. Voter strategies are specific for a given κ and π.

(2) $$\tau_n : (M_\ell, M_{-\ell}) \rightarrow \{\ell, -\ell\}$$

Changes to the Experiment

To ensure that candidates were aware which campaign choices were lies, we designated false information campaigns by adding "[Lie]," in red text, preceding the message. If a candidate was caught lying, voters were informed with the statement "candidate ℓ has been caught lying" added immediately below that candidate's message.

We also introduced a political context into the game. For campaign topics, we replaced the generic X and Y dimensions with statements about tax policy ("I have a favorable tax policy"; "My opponent has an unfavorable tax policy"), qualifications ("I am competent due to my experience," "My opponent is not competent due to a lack of experience"), and religion ("I believe in God"; "My opponent does not believe in God"). We varied tax policy and qualifications along the X dimension, and varied qualifications and religion along the Y dimension.

We also wanted to encourage candidates to consider using campaigns on the Y dimension, so we raised the utility to voters for candidates positive on Y to 40, and lowered utility for X to 60. We fixed candidates' probability of drawing a positive trait on each dimension to 70 percent, as that treatment in the previous experiment encouraged the most negative campaigning for any given trait draw.

The experiment, which we designate as study 6, was fielded at the Rutgers University Center for Experimental Political Science laboratory in multiple sessions between December 14, 2012, and February 26, 2013. Sessions included a minimum of nine players and a maximum of twenty-one, for a total of 105 subjects, with the modal session including twelve subjects. Most subjects were undergraduate or graduate students at Rutgers

TABLE 7.1. **Treatments, study 6**

Treatment	Odds of Being Caught	Financial Penalty for Being Caught	Expected Cost of Lying	Percentage of Lies
1	0%	0	0	31%
2	80%	0	0	21%
3	20%	20	4	14%
4	80%	20	16	8%
5	50%	50	25	9%
6	50%	100	50	7%

University recruited through classes, social media, and from among student employees at the Eagleton Institute of Politics, although some subjects were nonstudent Rutgers employees. Subjects, 65 percent of which were female, had a mean age of twenty-one. The experiment was fielded using Ztree software (Fischbacher 2007), with each subject participating in eighty rounds of the campaign game. As before, subjects were randomly assigned into groups of three each round, with two candidates and one voter. Four different treatments were used in each experimental session, randomly drawn from the six possible treatments, with the order of the treatments varied across experimental sessions. Subjects earned an average of just over $20 for an hour and a half session. The full instructions for the experiment and the postexperiment questionnaire are in the on-line appendix to this chapter.

Since the focus of our experiment was on believability and vote choice, we varied both the odds of a candidate being caught lying and the penalty for being caught. We used six different treatments, for which we varied the order as listed in table 7.1. The expected penalty to candidates from lying ranged from zero to 50, the latter due to a 50 percent chance of being caught along with a severe penalty equal to the benefit from winning the election (100). All subjects participated in the 0/0 and 50/50 treatments. Of the remaining treatments, forty-eight subjects participated in the 80/20 and 50/100 treatments, while fifty-seven subjects were in the 80/0 and 20/ 20 treatments.[1] Three subjects did not answer the postexperiment survey, so those three are excluded from all subject-level analysis.

Experimental Results

Result 1: Candidates responded to both negative incentives (probability and cost) by lying less often. As shown in the last column of table 7.1, the percentage of candidates' lies in treatment 1, the 0/0 treatment, was 31 percent. Considering that 70 percent of candidates had positive X-dimension traits, and that "positive on X" was the most popular campaign message, a 31 percent lying rate is at about the upper limit of we might expect. It means that most of the candidates in disadvantageous situations decided to reveal false information in this treatment where there was no financial cost and where voters would not know if they had lied. When we introduced small penalties, the rate of lying decreased sharply. In treatment 2, where the expected penalty was still zero but the voter would be notified of the lie 80 percent of the time, the rate of lying was 21 percent. In treatment 3, with a 20-point penalty and only a 20 percent chance of being caught (thus an expected penalty of 4), the rate decreased even further, to 14 percent. For the three treatments with the highest expected penalty for lying, the rate ranged from 7 percent to 9 percent.

To simplify our analyses we will group the set of treatments into three categories based upon expected cost, using the percentage of candidate lies from table 7.1 to aid in the construction of the categories. We leave treatment 1 by itself and will refer to it as the zero-cost treatment since there is neither financial cost nor any chance of voters finding out about a lie. Treatments 2 and 3 comprise the low-cost treatments, with the remaining three considered high-cost treatments.

Result 2: As the costs of lying increased, the distribution of candidates' campaign choices converged toward that of the truth-telling treatment. At the moment, we concentrate on the distribution of candidates' choices, though later we will address what would have been optimal for the candidates, given actual voter behavior in the experiment. Table 7.2 shows for each case the frequency, in percentages, of candidates' choices in each of the treatments. For reference, the rightmost column shows the distribution of choices from the 70 percent treatment in study 5 from table 5.2, which required truth-telling. Candidates' lies are marked with a dagger (†) in the zero-, low-, and high-cost treatments; the same messages are marked with a double dagger (‡) in the verifiable version, since these were not lies, but instead statements revealing information harmful to the messenger.

Overall, candidates frequently chose positive campaigning on the X dimension, especially in the first eight cases when it was true. However, in every one of those eight cases, and for every treatment, they chose *X* less often than in the truth-telling experiment from chapter 5. A close examination of several of the cases shows how this varied according to the incentives candidates were given—that is, the costs of lying.

We first look at case 1, where all candidates' traits were positive. Suppose we are in the zero-cost treatment. Candidates could think of the message choice problem in various ways. Suppose they assume that every other candidate is going to pick the same campaign regardless of the particular trait case. This makes sense considering that lying was costless. Which message? The most common message in the zero-cost case was X, used 58 percent of the time overall (63% in case 1), so that at least seemed to be a natural focal point. So in case 1, choosing X seems reasonable.

Now, suppose the voter also thinks that all candidates are going to choose X, but then gets a different message instead from one of the candidates. Granted, the voter cannot make a mistake in case 1, but the voter does not know it is case 1, and the candidates clearly have something at stake every election. The voter could simply believe that any message apart from X is a lie, which would result a single-message equilibrium (i.e., candidates always choose X because the voter only votes for candidates that choose X).[2] On the other hand, could the voter believe both candidates' statements are true? She cannot if the two messages are X and $oppX$; they are contradictory so one of the two must be a lie.

One reason we used the payoffs of 60 and 40 was to encourage Y-dimension campaigns. Theoretically, when a naive voter believes both candidates, a message of $oppY$ would make that candidate a favorite over a candidate choosing X—the X campaigner would be worth exactly 60, while the voter would have no new information about the $oppY$ candidate, so would still believe the $oppY$ campaigner had an expected value of 70.

Along the same lines, a candidate could choose message Y because the voter would believe it—after all, why would a candidate bother to lie about something on the inferior Y dimension? The voter, believing the Y campaigner, would then value that candidate with an expected utility of 82 (i.e., $40 + .7(60)$).[3] Now, suppose also that the voter believes the (X, Y) message pair reveals nothing about the Y dimension trait of the X campaigner. Then the voter utility for the X campaigner would be $pr(X^+|X,Y) + .7(40)$, where $pr(X^+|X,Y)$ is the probability that message X is true given the (X, Y) message pair. So, if X were true less than 90 percent of the time, the voter would prefer the candidate choosing Y. Now if the voter knows that the other candidates' strategies involve always choosing X, then it seems reasonable that she would infer that the candidate choosing X is simply following the strategy and hence lying 30 percent of the time. If voters think in that way, candidates would do better by *not* choosing the single-message X strategy.[4] Also, note that a Y campaign deviation

TABLE 7.2. **Candidate campaign choices, in percentages, study 6**

Case	Self	Opponent	Zero-Cost		Low-Cost		High-Cost		Verifiable (Chapter 5)	
1	(+,+)	(+,+)	*X*	63	*X*	82	*X*	85	*X*	96
			Y	10	*Y*	10	*Y*	11	*Y*	4
			oppX†	23	*oppX*†	8	*oppX*†	2	*oppX*‡	0
			oppY†	3	*oppY*†	1	*oppY*†	1	*oppY*	0
			Ø	1	Ø	0	Ø	0	Ø	0
2	(+,+)	(+,−)	*X*	52	*X*	61	*X*	71	*X*	86
			Y	20	*Y*	13	*Y*	11	*Y*	0
			oppX†	9	*oppX*†	6	*oppX*†	1	*oppX*‡	0
			oppY	19	*oppY*	20	*oppY*	17	*oppY*	14
			Ø	0	Ø	0	Ø	0	Ø	0
3	(+,+)	(−,+)	*X*	61	*X*	69	*X*	68	*X*	82
			Y	13	*Y*	9	*Y*	4	*Y*	0
			oppX	21	*oppX*	20	*oppX*	29	*oppX*	18
			oppY†	4	*oppY*†	2	*oppY*†	0	*oppY*‡	0
			Ø	1	Ø	0	Ø	0	Ø	0
4	(+,+)	(−,−)	*X*	61	*X*	62	*X*	59	*X*	87
			Y	11	*Y*	19	*Y*	10	*Y*	0
			oppX	24	*oppX*	15	*oppX*	27	*oppX*	10
			oppY	5	*oppY*	4	*oppY*	3	*oppY*	1
			Ø	0	Ø	0	Ø	0	Ø	0
5	(+,−)	(+,+)	*X*	66	*X*	92	*X*	95	*X*	98
			Y†	17	*Y*†	2	*Y*†	3	*Y*‡	0
			oppX†	13	*oppX*†	4	*oppX*†	2	*oppX*‡	0
			oppY†	4	*oppY*†	2	*oppY*†	1	*oppY*‡	2
			Ø	0	Ø	0	Ø	0	Ø	0
6	(+,−)	(+,−)	*X*	69	*X*	88	*X*	79	*X*	97
			Y†	8	*Y*†	0	*Y*†	2	*Y*‡	0
			oppX†	10	*oppX*†	0	*oppX*†	3	*oppX*‡	0
			oppY	13	*oppY*	12	*oppY*	16	*oppY*	3
			Ø	0	Ø	0	Ø	0	Ø	0
7	(+,−)	(−,+)	*X*	63	*X*	76	*X*	65	*X*	81
			Y†	6	*Y*†	2	*Y*†	2	*Y*‡	0
			oppX	25	*oppX*	17	*oppX*	33	*oppX*	15
			oppY†	6	*oppY*†	5	*oppY*†	0	*oppY*‡	4
			Ø	0	Ø	0	Ø	0	Ø	0
8	(+,−)	(−,−)	*X*	62	*X*	84	*X*	63	*X*	80
			Y†	0	*Y*†	0	*Y*†	6	*Y*‡	0
			oppX	24	*oppX*	11	*oppX*	27	*oppX*	20
			oppY	14	*oppY*	5	*oppY*	4	*oppY*	0
			Ø	0	Ø	0	Ø	0	Ø	0
9	(−,+)	(+,+)	*X*†	54	*X*†	36	*X*†	17	*X*‡	4
			Y	33	*Y*	54	*Y*	77	*Y*	75
			oppX†	9	*oppX*†	10	*oppX*†	3	*oppX*‡	11
			oppY†	2	*oppY*†	0	*oppY*†	2	*oppY*‡	3
			Ø	3	Ø	0	Ø	1	Ø	7
10	(−,+)	(+,−)	*X*†	37	*X*†	43	*X*†	9	*X*‡	0
			Y	29	*Y*	45	*Y*	49	*Y*	46
			oppX†	20	*oppX*†	2	*oppX*†	4	*oppX*‡	4
			oppY	14	*oppY*	10	*oppY*	37	*oppY*	50
			Ø	0	Ø	0	Ø	1	Ø	0

TABLE 7.2. (*Continued*)

Case	Self	Opponent	Zero-Cost		Low-Cost		High-Cost		Verifiable (Chapter 5)	
11	(−,+)	(−,+)	$X^\dagger$	41	$X^\dagger$	28	$X^\dagger$	8	$X^\ddagger$	0
			Y	31	Y	48	Y	42	Y	43
			$oppX$	24	$oppX$	20	$oppX$	49	$oppX$	57
			$oppY^\dagger$	4	$oppY^\dagger$	0	$oppY^\dagger$	0	$oppY^\ddagger$	0
			$\emptyset$	0	$\emptyset$	4	$\emptyset$	1	$\emptyset$	0
12	(−,+)	(−,−)	$X^\dagger$	38	$X^\dagger$	14	$X^\dagger$	2	$X^\ddagger$	0
			Y	43	Y	50	Y	43	Y	75
			$oppX$	10	$oppX$	32	$oppX$	49	$oppX$	13
			$oppY$	10	$oppY$	5	$oppY$	6	$oppY$	13
			$\emptyset$	0	$\emptyset$	0	$\emptyset$	0	$\emptyset$	0
13	(−,−)	(+,+)	$X^\dagger$	55	$X^\dagger$	55	$X^\dagger$	42	$X^\ddagger$	7
			$Y^\dagger$	11	$Y^\dagger$	0	$Y^\dagger$	3	$Y^\ddagger$	20
			$oppX^\dagger$	11	$oppX^\dagger$	17	$oppX^\dagger$	6	$oppX^\ddagger$	13
			$oppY^\dagger$	13	$oppY^\dagger$	6	$oppY^\dagger$	3	$oppY^\ddagger$	10
			$\emptyset$	11	$\emptyset$	21	$\emptyset$	47	$\emptyset$	50
14	(−,−)	(+,−)	$X^\dagger$	76	$X^\dagger$	37	$X^\dagger$	20	$X^\ddagger$	10
			$Y^\dagger$	5	$Y^\dagger$	0	$Y^\dagger$	2	$Y^\ddagger$	0
			$oppX^\dagger$	0	$oppX^\dagger$	11	$oppX^\dagger$	4	$oppX^\ddagger$	10
			$oppY$	19	$oppY$	47	$oppY$	65	$oppY$	75
			$\emptyset$	0	$\emptyset$	5	$\emptyset$	10	$\emptyset$	5
15	(−,−)	(−,+)	$X^\dagger$	43	$X^\dagger$	45	$X^\dagger$	6	$X^\ddagger$	13
			$Y^\dagger$	19	$Y^\dagger$	0	$Y^\dagger$	4	$Y^\ddagger$	25
			$oppX$	29	$oppX$	55	$oppX$	81	$oppX$	63
			$oppY^\dagger$	10	$oppY^\dagger$	0	$oppY^\dagger$	0	$oppY^\ddagger$	0
			$\emptyset$	0	$\emptyset$	0	$\emptyset$	9	$\emptyset$	0
16	(−,−)	(−,−)	$X^\dagger$	42	$X^\dagger$	12	$X^\dagger$	40	$X^\ddagger$	0
			$Y^\dagger$	0	$Y^\dagger$	0	$Y^\dagger$	0	$Y^\ddagger$	0
			$oppX$	42	$oppX$	38	$oppX$	55	$oppX$	75
			$oppY$	17	$oppY$	50	$oppY$	5	$oppY$	25
			$\emptyset$	0	$\emptyset$	0	$\emptyset$	0	$\emptyset$	0
N				1,156		1,040		2,448		670

Note: Numbers are percentage of choices made; percentages in a case may add to more than 100 due to rounding.
† Campaign choices that are lies.
‡ "Self-defeating" campaigns (bad information about oneself or good information about the opponent).

as described above would especially appeal to risk-averse voters who (for whatever reason) are convinced that a Y message in the zero-cost game must be true.

Our reason for including the preceding discussion is to provide reasonable arguments for why candidates would consider campaigns other than X, as they obviously do. In case 1, they choose other campaigns with some regularity in the zero-cost treatment (X was 63%). But, as the costs of lying increase, they choose X campaigns more often. In the high-cost treatments, X was chosen 85 percent of the time, much closer to the chapter 5 truth-telling rate of 96 percent. In several of the cases, just as in case 1, much of the convergence toward the truth-telling treatment took place between the zero-cost and the low-cost treatments. Candidates facing case 5—(+, −) versus (+, +)—chose the X campaign only 66 percent of the time when lying was risk-free but 92 percent of the time once costs were introduced.

Case 2, in which a candidate positive on both dimensions faces a candidate positive on X only, saw a steady increase in X campaigns (52% to 71%) across the three treatments. It looks as if we can attribute about half of this shift to the fading allure of choosing a Y campaign. Support for the Y campaign wanes (from 20% to 11%) along with candidates' lies. The strategy shift across treatments did not take place in every case, though. Candidates who were (+, −) facing a (−, −) opponent—case 8—were inclined to reveal their positive X trait in the low-cost condition (84%), just as in the original experiment (80%). However both the zero-cost (62%) and high-cost (63%) treatments featured a considerable amount of negative campaigning on X (24% and 27%, respectively).

In cases when a candidate had a negative X trait, the differences across treatments are more pronounced. In case 9, where X was the only negative trait of the four, lying about X decreased from 54 percent in the zero-cost to 36 percent in the low-cost, and 17 percent in the high-cost scenarios. Choosing Y, which was essentially the only beneficial campaign in the truth-only experiment, was a very reasonable option here, considering the opportunities for error by either the voter or the opponent. The rate of Y message choices rose from 33 percent to 54 percent to 77 percent across the three treatments. In cases 10–12, (−, +) candidates similarly shifted away from lying about their own X trait, opting instead for a mix between Y and a (truthful) negative campaign. Along the same lines, (−, −) candidates not facing (+, +) opponents also tended toward truthful negative campaigns when facing high expected lying costs. We also note that candidate pairs with four negative traits were very uncommon, so there were not enough cases to meaningfully analyze decisions in case 16.

The ability to lie obviously provided opportunities for (−, −) candidates facing (+, +) opponents, but candidates did not take full advantage of them. In the zero-cost treatment there is no theoretical reason why candidates would need to change campaign strategies based upon their actual traits. In other words, here the (+, +) candidate and the (−, −) candidate should really be choosing identical campaigns. But in fact, the (+, +) candidates favored messages on the X dimension; they chose X more often (61% to 55%) as well as *oppX* more often (24% to 11%) than their (−, −) counterparts.

TABLE 7.3. **Voter behavior, study 6**

| | | Vote for Candidate ℓ | | |
		Zero-cost Treatment	Low-cost Treatment	High-cost Treatment
Candidate ℓ	Candidate $-\ell$			
X	Y	68	78	86
X	oppX	66	62	58
X	oppY	79	75	78
Y	oppX	63	62	43
oppX	oppY	40	80	72
Caught lying	Any other[a]	n/a	5	8

Note: Vote cell entries are percentages.
[a] In no cases did a voter have to choose between a candidate not campaigning and a candidate caught lying.

Result 3: Voters trusted negative campaigning more in the high-cost treatments. Just as with the candidates, we find in general that voter behavior also differed depending upon the level of exogenous monitoring. There were six different message pairs for which the voter had to choose between candidates that did not run identical campaigns. Five of these are listed in the first five rows of table 7.3, which shows the percentage of voters that chose a candidate using the message in the first column over a candidate using the message in the second column, given that neither candidate was caught lying.[5] For example, whenever one candidate chose to reveal his or her own positive trait on dimension X, and the other revealed his or her own positive trait on dimension Y, the voter chose the X campaigner 68 percent of the time in the zero-cost treatment, 78 percent of the time in the low-cost treatments, and 86 percent of the time in the high-cost treatments. From a voter's perspective, the logic for this change is that the lower the costs of lying, the more often the X message was a lie than was the Y message. But was choosing Y over X the correct voting decision? It was not, which we will discuss when we examine result 6.

One major difference for voters in this experiment compared to study 5 was that they might face conflicting campaigns about the same trait, meaning that a voter would know that exactly one of the two candidates was lying, but would not know which one. In the zero-cost treatment, the (X, oppX) message pair was actually the most common of the six differentiated pairs. The increased trust in negative campaigning as lying costs increase can be seen in table 7.3 for the (X, oppX) case. Support for the negative campaigner increased from 34 percent (zero-cost treatment) to 42 percent (high-cost treatments). The increased trust in negativity also manifested in the less common Y vs. oppX case, where the voters chose the negative campaigner 57 percent of the time in the high-cost treatment versus 37 percent otherwise.

Result 4: Electorally, the expected cost of being caught lying was nearly certain defeat. As shown in the final row of table 7.3, candidates caught lying lost about 93 percent of elections against innocent candidates. In 92 percent of the cases where a voter chose a known liar over a truth-teller, the liar had chosen a positive campaign, though in 68 percent of the cases, both candidates had chosen positive campaigns.

Interestingly, exposed liars still managed to do better than candidates who chose not to campaign at all (who lost 96% of the time). Not campaigning was rare—only 88 examples occur across all the elections, so each subject on average faced such a voting decision less than once per session. In all four cases when a voter chose a candidate that didn't campaign, the losing candidate had used message *X*.

Result 5: Given a choice, candidates preferred to lie about themselves. To determine this, we looked at cases in which the candidates with a negative X trait were facing candidates with a positive X trait (9, 10, 13, and 14). In these situations, candidates campaigning on the X dimension had a choice between lying via positive campaigning and lying via negative campaigning. Candidates that chose to lie *heavily* preferred the positive over the negative, choosing to lie about themselves 77 percent of the time. In contrast, candidates faced with a choice of truths—whether to tell the truth about one's own positive X trait or the truth about the opponent's negative X trait—revealed their good side less frequently (67%). There were no significant behavioral differences across the treatments. Put differently, when the opponent was positive on X and the candidate was not, instead of claiming the opponent was negative on X, candidates lied about themselves, in essence, putting forth a positive campaign statement where it was undeserved. But candidates were willing to go after opponents *truly* negative on X, attempting to reveal that (truthful) situation by running a negative campaign.

This suggests that voters would benefit from choosing negative campaigners. But, on the other hand, we also find that in the twelve other cases—where candidates did not have a choice between lies—lies on the X dimension were more often negative (67%) than positive (33%). This suggests the opposite—that voters should be wary of negativity. So, if no candidate is caught lying—always the case in the zero-cost treatment—whom should the voter believe is lying? Table 7.4 shows, from the perspective of the voter, how likely the candidates are to have been lying given the messages received by the voter.

TABLE 7.4. **Probability that a candidate is lying, by message pair and given that no candidate has been caught lying, study 6**

ℓ	$-\ell$	Zero-Cost		Low-Cost		High-Cost	
		ℓ Lying	$-\ell$ Lying	ℓ Lying	$-\ell$ Lying	ℓ Lying	$-\ell$ Lying
X	X	0.23	0.23	0.09	0.09	0.04	0.04
X	Y	0.19	0.21	0.10	0.01	0.01	0.02
X	$oppX$	0.34	0.66	0.38	0.62	0.55	0.45
X	$oppY$	0.21	0.40	0.06	0.03	0.02	0.05
X	$\varnothing$	0.14	0.00	0.00	0.00	0.00	0.00
Y	Y	0.20	0.20	0.05	0.05	0.06	0.06
Y	$oppX$	0.13	0.28	0.00	0.07	0.01	0.01
Y	$oppY$	0.50	0.50	0.00	1.00	0.33	0.67
Y	$\varnothing$	0.00	0.00	0.00	0.00	0.09	0.00
$oppX$	$oppX$	0.74	0.74	0.25	0.25	0.07	0.07
$oppX$	$oppY$	0.67	0.08	0.40	0.40	0.00	0.03
$oppX$	$\varnothing$	0.67	0.00	0.00	0.00	0.00	0.00

In the low-cost and high-cost treatments, most of the percentages are quite low. This means that for the most part, an additional Bayesian calculation (What are the odds of a candidate lying with message M, given he or she was not caught lying?) would not meaningfully affect the expected voter utility from the candidates. So voters generally did not need to adjust their strategies to account for potentially false statements. However, they *did* need to judge which candidate was being honest when the message pair was $(X, oppX)$. Only in the high-cost case was the negative campaigner most likely to be the honest one. But, as we discuss in the next result, the optimal choice did not depend upon the treatment. The expected payoff from voting for the negative campaigner was always higher.

Result 6: Voter support for negative campaigning was below what would have been optimal. Table 7.5 shows the difference in mean candidate worth (to the voter), based on treatment, voting case, and message. For each treatment, each cell indicates the difference in voter payoff from choosing a candidate using the message in the leftmost column versus the second column. For example, when faced with the decision between a candidate using message X and a candidate using message Y, voters should have chosen the candidate announcing X. On average for the (X, Y) message pair, the candidate using X was worth 8.3 more points than his opponent in the zero-cost treatment. This difference increased to 19.95 in the low cost-treatments and to 27.59 in the high-cost treatments, making the X versus Y decision more consequential to voter profit, and comporting well with those voters who chose X over Y more often as the lying costs increased. All three of these differences in means are significant at the $p < .05$ level.

TABLE 7.5. **Mean difference in voter payoff between Candidate ℓ and the opponent, study 6**

Candidate ℓ	Candidate $-\ell$	Zero-cost	Low-cost	High-cost
X	Y	8.30*	19.95*	27.59*
X	oppX	−9.66*	−7.62	−27.27*
X	oppY	−1.13	−9.44	3.74
Y	oppX	−13.75*	−13.79*	−30.00*
oppX	oppY	−26.67*	0.00	26.25*
Caught lying	Any other	n/a	−43.50*	−50.82*

* Indicates the difference in mean payoffs between the two candidates is nonzero at significance level $p < 0.05$.

The next three rows speak to the advantage to the voter from choosing a negative campaigner, something that the voters did not do frequently enough. In almost every situation with one negative and one positive campaigner (rows 2, 3, and 4), voting for the negative campaigner would have given the voter significantly higher utility. The one exception was X versus $oppY$ in the high-cost treatment, which favored the X candidate, though this difference was not significant.

Combining all votes when the two campaign messages were different, we find the voter's expected profit from choosing the candidate with the "better" message in a given pair was 79, versus 58 for choosing the other candidate. Overall, as expected, voter profit was highest when the costs of lying were the highest, but the differences were not as great as they could have been. Voters on average earned 71.4 in the zero-cost treatment, 75.7 in the low-cost, and 76.8 in the high-cost treatments. For the zero-cost treatment, 71.4 is a better payoff than a voter would expect in any equilibrium. Since candidates are free to choose any message regardless of traits, they should not be able to distinguish themselves from their opponents, even when holding a trait advantage. Thus, voter profit would simply be 70, the expected utility of choosing a candidate at random. As the next result shows, the candidates in the other treatments were more successful with their campaign choices.

Result 7: With few exceptions, the most popular candidate message choice was also the most profitable given voters' decision-making tendencies. Tables 7.6a–c show the expected candidate profit from using each of the five messages, given the trait case from that candidate's point of view. Table 7.6a shows the zero-cost treatment, with 7.6b showing the low-cost and 7.6c the high-cost.

Each row gives the expected candidate profit for a given message, adjusting one candidate's choice while leaving the others constant. Messages that are lies have the expected profits in italics. The optimal messages,

TABLE 7.6A. **Expected profit for each campaign message, zero-cost treatment, study 6**

	Message				
Case	X	Y	oppX	oppY	Ø
1	**56.8**	41.8	39.0	35.8	0.6
2	**56.4**	39.4	36.9	34.6	0.0
3	**59.2**	42.6	38.6	37.8	1.3
4	**62.6**	45.4	43.2	31.4	5.3
5	**60.5**	39.9	36.3	38.2	0.0
6	**56.7**	37.5	36.1	32.1	0.0
7	**62.3**	44.4	38.3	45.3	0.0
8	**56.4**	34.4	34.4	28.2	0.0
9	**57.1**	41.7	38.7	36.4	0.4
10	**56.7**	41.4	38.5	36.5	0.0
11	**60.5**	45.3	39.1	45.2	0.0
12	**60.6**	44.9	39.4	44.1	0.0
13	**57.1**	41.6	38.4	37.3	0.0
14	**57.9**	40.5	38.0	35.9	0.0
15	**61.9**	43.4	37.1	44.7	0.0
16	**61.3**	46.1	40.8	44.8	0.0

Note: Optimal campaign choices (and those within 0.1 of optimal) are shown in bold. Messages that are lies are in italics.

which are shown in boldface, are the best responses given the candidates' and voters' aggregated mixed strategies. We assume that for the given case and treatment the opponent's campaign will be determined probabilistically using the overall distribution of candidates' messages in table 7.2. This, and whether any candidates have been caught lying, determines the message pair given to the voter. The probability of the voter choosing a candidate was calculated according to actual voter behavior when given that message pair and the lie-monitoring result for a given treatment, as shown in table 7.3. For example, look at case 9 in table 7.6c, in which a $(-, +)$ candidate faces a $(+, +)$ candidate. Thus, the opponent is in case 3. Say we are in the high-cost treatment. From table 7.2, we know that the opponent will choose X 69 percent of the time, choose Y 9 percent of the time, and so forth. If a candidate chooses campaign X, which is a lie, 68 percent of the time the opponent will choose X and the message pair will be (X, X)—giving a 50 percent chance of winning—whenever the candidate is not caught lying. If caught, there is a lying penalty and an electoral penalty—the message pair will be $(\hat{X}, X)$, where the chance of winning is quite small. Instead of choosing X, 4 percent of the time the opponent will choose Y. Now the message pair will be either $(\hat{X}, Y)$ or (X, Y). If the latter, table 7.3 shows us there is an 86 percent of winning.

After similar calculations for the remainder of the opponent's possible

TABLE 7.6B. **Expected profit for each campaign message, low-cost treatments, study 6**

| Case | Message | | | | |
	X	Y	*oppX*	*oppY*	Ø
1	**56.9**	31.9	*25.7*	*15.3*	25.4
2	**54.3**	28.8	*25.5*	28.9	27.7
3	**75.4**	54.1	*50.4*	*16.4*	23.6
4	**72.9**	69.4	**72.8**	63.6	48.6
5	**62.0**	28.2	*30.4*	*17.4*	19.3
6	**54.9**	*19.2*	*26.7*	29.9	24.1
7	**74.6**	*37.1*	*53.7*	*19.4*	24.5
8	**73.9**	52.6	**73.9**	54.6	26.9
9	*34.9*	**36.4**	*25.7*	*13.5*	19.9
10	*34.5*	**35.8**	*27.0*	28.4	23.5
11	*46.8*	**56.1**	*50.7*	*14.8*	18.2
12	*43.2*	**58.1**	56.1	35.9	25.0
13	**36.5**	*22.7*	*25.8*	*12.0*	17.4
14	**32.9**	*18.7*	*25.7*	27.8	23.1
15	*45.7*	*35.9*	**48.6**	*9.6*	8.9
16	*44.4*	*51.1*	**68.1**	40.8	8.3

Note: Optimal campaign choices (and those within 0.1 of optimal) are shown in bold. Messages that are lies are in italics.

TABLE 7.6C. **Expected profit for each campaign message, high-cost treatments, study 6**

| Case | Message | | | | |
	X	Y	*oppX*	*oppY*	Ø
1	**57.5**	22.5	*−9.9*	*−16.9*	11.5
2	**54.0**	19.2	*−10.1*	27.1	13.1
3	**87.4**	57.2	64.5	*−7.1*	17.0
4	88.9	86.8	**91.3**	87.5	60.4
5	**61.1**	*−16.8*	*−9.1*	*−16.3*	8.7
6	**58.3**	*−16.7*	*−8.4*	31.4	11.9
7	**84.5**	*−3.3*	67.7	*−8.3*	10.7
8	**82.2**	3.6	78.5	62.5	23.7
9	*−8.0*	**25.5**	*−10.9*	*−18.1*	7.6
10	*−7.7*	26.5	*−10.4*	**27.1**	8.4
11	*0.2*	50.6	**57.9**	*−12.8*	8.1
12	*−2.2*	53.0	**59.5**	41.0	13.2
13	*−6.9*	*−17.3*	*−10.3*	*−17.6*	**7.0**
14	*−5.9*	*−15.7*	*−8.6*	**30.2**	11.0
15	*−1.2*	*−9.5*	**57.0**	*−14.8*	3.4
16	5.6	0.8	**64.5**	48.6	28.6

Note: Optimal campaign choices (and those within 0.1 of optimal) are shown in bold. Messages that are lies are in italics.

choices, we find that the expected profit from an X campaign in case 9 is −8.0, so the large penalty (an average of 28 across the three high-cost treatments) and high chance of being caught (65% across the three) makes lying unappealing in this case. The truthful announcement Y is a much better option. Going back to table 7.3 we see that, in fact, 77 percent of candidates faced with this decision chose the Y campaign.

In the zero-cost treatment, the best campaign was always X, no matter the case. So, in eight of the sixteen cases, the optimal campaign was a lie. Actual candidate choices were such that X was the plurality choice for all but case 12, in which candidates mistakenly preferred to tell the truth about their positive Y trait. The cost for doing so was 15.5 points of expected profit. Candidates in the zero-cost treatment overall chose the optimal campaign (i.e., message X) 58 percent of the time in this treatment, the lowest success rate of the three treatment categories. As the case 12 result illustrates, candidates were sometimes sidetracked by a desire to reveal a trait advantage, even though the design of the treatment made any type of differentiation theoretically impossible.

Earlier we mentioned that a candidate might think that choosing Y in case 1 was a good idea because it appeared more honest. From the analysis above we show that clearly it was a bad idea. It lowered expected profit in case 1 by 15, 25, and 35 points in the zero-, low-, and high-cost treatments, respectively.

In the low-cost treatments (table 7.6b), lying would have been the optimal campaign in only two of the cases—case 13, which is the worst possible trait draw, and case 14, where the only positive trait is the opponent's X trait. Additionally, in case 9 the expected value calculation actually favored lying in one of the two low-cost treatments (treatment 3, with a 20% chance of being caught and 20 penalty). Despite this, candidates were more truthful (57%) in treatment 3 than in the other low-cost treatment (51% in treatment 2, with an 80% chance of being caught and zero penalty). In the high-cost treatments (table 7.6c), lying would never have been optimal.

The decisions candidates faced in case 4, where the candidate had a trait advantage on both dimensions, were quite meaningful. In the experiment requiring truth a candidate could hardly go wrong, considering the opponent could either not campaign (which nearly always lost) or reveal harmful information (which nearly always lost). Here, the candidates needed to make a decision as if the opponent was a liar, because if the opponent didn't campaign, the decision was not of much consequence.

How does one campaign when one knows the opponent has no intention to be honest? The answer is not very effectively. Candidates in case 4 actually were losers in the zero-cost treatment, only prevailing in 47 percent of elections. Table 7.6a shows that with better campaign choices these candidates would have won about 63 percent of the time. The candidates in case 4 of course won more often in the low-cost (70%) and high-cost (84%) treatments. But as table 7.2 shows, this improvement had little to do with improving their message choices, which varied little across the three treatments. Instead, the improvement was simply due to the opponents' case 13 predicament—lying is penalized while not campaigning nearly ensures defeat.

The possibility of dealing with liars causes people to make mistakes that they otherwise would have avoided. This is a behavioral trend that we will see again when we look more closely at our voters. We are not implying that political elites would make the same campaign errors as our candidates did. But consider two of the presidential debates from 2012 as examples. Though there were many Republican primary debates, the January 28 debate in Florida had particularly high stakes for Newt Gingrich. He had just won the South Carolina primary and was hoping to emerge as the main challenger to Mitt Romney by winning in Florida as well. But Gingrich struggled that night against a forceful, aggressive Romney. "You cannot debate somebody who is dishonest," he said afterward, referring to Romney. "The people say I'm a good debater. I can't debate somebody who won't tell the truth."[6] On October 3, in the first general election debate, Barack Obama often appeared nonplussed instead of engaging with Romney. Afterward, the Obama campaign offered an excuse similar to Gingrich's (though due to absurdity in political coverage needed to avoid actually using the word "liar"). "When I got onto the stage, I met this very spirited fellow who claimed to be Mitt Romney," said Obama.[7] "But it couldn't have been the real Mitt Romney . . ." Obama campaign strategist David Axelrod concurred. He said, "I give Romney an 'F' for being honest with the American people."[8] What is striking here is that the performances of two veteran politicians, by their own admittance, were adversely affected by the prospect of dealing with someone who *in their view* was a liar.

Postexperiment Survey and Subject-level Results

At the end of the experiment, all of our subjects were asked to complete a brief survey, in which they were asked a subset of the questions from our real campaign ads study 4. These included questions about trust of candidates and the media, whether candidates should leave it to the media to point out lies, and whether they found it difficult to determine if candidates were lying. We tested whether these, along with other variables from the experiment, could be used to predict whether subjects would lie when playing the candidate role, and whether they had any effect on a subject's ability to make optimal voting decisions.

Table 7.7 shows the results from a logit with the dependent variable being whether a candidate chose to lie. Of course, this potentially depends on many factors. As we have demonstrated earlier, the traits of the candidates are important, and here we measure this by using separate independent variables for voter payoff from choosing the candidate and the opponent. A candidate was worth either zero (negative on both), 40 (positive on Y only), 60 (positive on X only), or 100 (positive on both). We capture the expected penalty for lying in two separate variables instead of grouping by treatment. As shown in table 7.1, in our six treatments the cost of being caught lying ranged from zero to 100, and the probability of being caught lying from 0 percent to 80 percent.

We next included the political context of the decisions. Recall that in this experiment, candidates were asked not to reveal "X" and "Y" traits, but instead tax policy, competence (due to experience), and belief in God. In the regression, we use two dummy variables to capture the potential effects. One variable is whether tax policy (as opposed to competence) was on the X dimension, and hence worth 60 points to voters. The other is whether religion (also as opposed to competence) was on the Y dimension, thus worth 40 to voters. As mentioned above, we also included the measures of trust, helpfulness of ads, and so on, from the postexperiment survey. Standard errors are clustered by individual subject.

The regression in table 7.7 confirms that the utility difference between the candidates affected the decision to lie, and expands on that to show that candidates did in fact react to both their own lower values and the opponent's higher values by lying to the voter more often. Both of the monitoring variables—the probability for being caught lying and the according penalty—also significantly affect the decisions. But, those were not the only factors.

As we have discussed throughout this book, campaign topics affect reactions to negative ads, especially regarding believability. Here we find that the topics also affected the candidates' propensity to lie, even after accounting for the more recognizable factors of candidate traits and monitoring. For one, candidates were more willing to lie whenever religion

TABLE 7.7. **Logit regression for whether candidate lied, using case and subject variables, study 6**

Round Variables	
Candidate's worth	−.0373***
	(.0026)
Opponent's worth	.0194***
	(.0019)
X dimension = Taxes	.3801**
	(.1525)
Y dimension = Religion	.1982*
	(.1023)
Probability of being caught lying	−2.0897***
	(.2688)
Cost of lying if caught	−.0171***
	(.0029)
Subject Variables	
Candidates not competent	−.4222**
	(.1916)
Distrust media	.5063**
	(.2039)
Media point out lies (not candidate)	−.4474*
	(.1859)
Voted in 2012 election	.4291
	(.2223)
Democrat	−.0085
	(.2675)
Republican	.3893
	(.4244)
Gender: Female	−.1298
	(.1870)
Race: Nonwhite	−.2234
	(.1903)
Constant	.1137
	(.5511)
Pseudo r^2	0.29
N	Subj. = 105
	Obs. = 4449

Note: Robust standard errors in parentheses.
*$p < 0.05$.
**$p < 0.01$.
***$p < 0.001$.

was on the Y dimension. The actual difference in our data was modest—candidates lied 17 percent versus 14 percent when religion was a possible topic choice (χ^2 $p = 0.018$). But the reason for this difference becomes more striking when we look at the specific messages candidates chose overall. When religion was a topic on the Y dimension, our candidates looked to avoid mentioning it, even though the words "I believe in God" or "My opponent does not believe in God" were really just placeholders for "I have a positive Y trait" and "My opponent has a negative Y trait." Candidates chose messages on the X dimension (which was either tax policy or experience) 76 percent of the time if religion was the other topic choice, and 71 percent otherwise ($p < 0.001$). Putting all of this together tells us that candidates—at least in our experiment—would rather lie than talk in any way about religion! On its face this comports very nicely with our earlier studies which show that religious-based attacks generate great anger, and are considered less appropriate and less believable than most other topics.

We also found that candidates tended to lie more when tax policy was an option, though when we looked further at the data we did not find significant discrepancies similar to the religion result above. Demographic and political variables were not significant; in table 7.7 we include those for gender, race, and party identification since those have factored into the discussion of our results in previous chapters.

Regarding trust and candidates' roles, subjects' attitudes matched their behavior. Table 7.7 includes only those attitudes we found to be significant. People who were distrustful of the media's ability to countermand candidates' lies tended to lie more often. Those who believed candidates should hold each other accountable (rather than leave it to the media) also lied more often. Finally, the more people thought real political candidates were generally competent, the more often they lied while playing the candidate role.

With table 7.8 we look at predicting success for a voter. For each message pair we can compute the theoretically correct vote, given the treatment and using the expected utility for the candidate using each message. Since many cases are less interesting—most notably those where candidates' messages are identical—for our analysis we used only six message pairs. These were (X,Y), $(X,oppX)$, $(X,oppY)$, $(Y,oppX)$, $(Y,oppY)$, and $(oppX,oppY)$, all of which require that the candidates' messages are distinct and that neither was caught lying.

Table 7.8 shows the results of a logit with the dependent variable being whether the subject voted for the candidate with the higher expected utility, given the actual aggregate mixed strategy for candidates in each treatment. We look at each voting instance separately, clustering by individual subject. For this logit we include dummy variables for each voting case (i.e., message pair received in that election). The (X, Y) voting case is the baseline. Next, we include a variable for the difference in expected utility between the candidates given the message pair and treatment. Just as

TABLE 7.8. **Predicting whether a given vote was theoretically correct, study 6**

Round Variables	
Message Pair (baseline = (X, Y))	
$(X, oppX)$	-1.3647***
	$(.3683)$
$(X, oppY)$	-1.2475***
	$(.3156)$
$(Y, oppX)$	-1.1667***
	$(.4397)$
$(Y, oppY)$	$-.5766$
	$(.6060)$
$(oppX, oppY)$	$-.6152$
	$(.4081)$
Expected utility difference	$.0100$
	$(.0084)$
Percentage lied as candidate	1.8217
	$(.9775)$
X Dimension = Taxes	$.6285$**
	$(.2413)$
Y Dimension = Religion	$.0787$
	$(.1699)$
Probability of being caught lying	1.2184***
	$(.3236)$
Cost of lying if caught	$.0065$*
	$(.0030)$
Subject Variables	
Hard to find out lies	$-.2971$
	$(.1726)$
Distrust media	$-.5579$***
	$(.1564)$
Media point out lies (not candidate)	$-.4033$*
	$(.1731)$
Voted in 2012 election	$.3438$
	$(.2238)$
Democrat	$-.1304$
	$(.2361)$
Republican	$.5995$*
	$(.2521)$
Gender: Female	$.1902$
	$(.1891)$
Race: Nonwhite	$-.3066$
	$(.1782)$
Constant	1.7301**
	$(.6704)$
Pseudo r^2	0.16
N	Subj. = 105
	Obs. = 1044

Note: Robust standard errors in parentheses.
*$p < 0.05$.
**$p < 0.01$.
***$p < 0.001$.

when we used quantal response theory for equilibrium analysis in the first election game, we here expect that voters are more likely to vote correctly as the expected utility gap widens.

After further investigation, we found that the utility difference between candidates did not reach statistical significance because our five dummy variables capturing the six voting cases acted as a more differentiated measure of the same concept. Without these, the coefficient for the utility difference increases tenfold and becomes highly significant ($z = 6.45$, $p < 0.001$).

The ($Y,oppY$) and ($oppX,oppY$) were comparatively rare, so their lack of significance is not particularly surprising. Otherwise, we find that voters by far did best when one candidate chose X and the other chose Y. Of key importance is that this is the only one of those situations in which neither candidate used a negative campaign. The conclusion should not be that we need to eliminate negative campaigning—the reason that voters received good information in that case is because the candidates were choosing X and Y when the situations warranted, rather than being forced to choose that way.

Attitudinally, we find that those distrustful of the media's ability to uncover candidates' lies and those who think candidates should expose lies both were *less* likely to vote correctly in these potentially ambiguous situations. One commonality between these two attitudes is an increased uncertainty about whether candidates are telling the truth. The first connection is obvious, the second because it implies greater awareness that lying and counteracting lying are a part of campaigning. One might think that such beliefs would provide clarity to a voter. This is not the case. The more salient candidates' potential for lying, the worse voters' decisions become. Tying this with our key results on believability, we can see that it is because voters are misevaluating the honesty of negative campaigns. This is why we argue that, going forward, believability should be a major focus of negative campaigning studies.

Why is believability so relevant? Note one more finding from table 7.8—that the probability of being caught lying and the lying penalty are both positive and significant. Normatively and positively speaking, they *shouldn't* be, because we have already controlled for the message pair, the difference in utility between candidates, and the campaign topics. Given the same amount of differentiating information, voters were less accurate simply because they knew that candidates were more likely to get away with lying, which is unfortunate. Lies disrupt the electoral system even when they are *not* obfuscating things.

Conclusion

Thus we find in this chapter that voters are much more skeptical about the truth of negative campaigns, even when there is no basis for such skepticism. Perhaps it is a form of conditioning from having seen so many real-world positive campaigns that are devoid of useful information, so voters just accept the positive ads—while barely paying attention—and move on. After all, many positive ads look like the nine we showed to voters in study 4; candidates have a tendency to use vague statements giving broad plans for governing. "We need fresh faces and new ideas," said candidate Paul Sanford in one of our nine positive ads. "It's time to put the people back in charge," he continued. "You can count on me to work hard representing you honestly and openly." This is hardly good material for fact-checkers, so it is no wonder that so much fact-checking focuses on negative ads, which more often claim to be presenting facts. The problem, however, is that voter distrust leads to poor decision-making even in cases where it shouldn't lead to poor decision-making.

And as these last two chapters have shown, voters tend to give negative campaigns more scrutiny than positive campaigns. So while voters may continue to protest that negative ads make them change the channel in disgust and refuse to vote out of frustration, it turns out that the negative ads are more engaging, as of course is negative information in general. When we look back at our survey questions about whether candidates are competent, this preference for information from negative ads makes even more sense. Voters, we find, assume that candidates in major elections are capable unless told otherwise. In fact, respondents from this chapter's experiment (study 6)—having already wrestled with difficult campaign decisions in the game—admired the competence of political candidates even more. *None* of the subjects said that candidates for national elected office were generally "very incompetent." So perhaps there simply isn't as much value added from a positive campaign about one's job capabilities. But what if the candidate actually isn't qualified? This would lead us full circle back to chapter 2 and the question of whose job it is to point out candidates' flaws.

CHAPTER EIGHT

Conclusion

Treating your adversary with respect is giving him an advantage to which he is not entitled. The greatest part of men cannot judge of reasoning, and are impressed by character ... treating your adversary with respect is striking soft in a battle.—Samuel Johnson, from Boswell's *Life of Johnson*

Given the unrelenting negative campaigning that characterizes modern political elections, it appears that many candidates subscribe to Samuel Johnson's view and derive utility from attacking their opponents. The use of negative advertising may stem from its necessity in competitive elections, so that those who "stay positive" are striking soft and putting themselves at a disadvantage. Those who recognize that negativity is inevitable often find this state of the world deplorable, viewing negative campaigning as a necessary evil in the short term that will destroy the psyche of fragile voters and perhaps the system itself in the long run. But a growing number of those who systematically study negative campaigns are not as pessimistic. An increasing number of studies (e.g., Freedman, Wood, and Lawton 1999) find that voters can distinguish between different topics or tactics in negative campaigns and respond to the attacks accordingly. Both William Mayer (1996) and John Geer (2006) actively defend candidates' negative campaigning with Geer stressing the informational content that such ads convey to voters.

In this book, our goal has been to show why voters need this information. We started with a simple premise—that voters are not as upset by negative campaigning as conventional wisdom suggests—and built on it through subsequent chapters. Because voters are not particularly bothered by negativity, they are potentially receptive to the information it provides, even as they tell survey researchers how much they dislike "negative campaigning." Whether they use the information that these ads can provide effectively, though, depends on the extent to which voters can count on candidates being merely biased as opposed to blatantly dishonest. So our intent here has not been to defend negativity—we do not see any reason to do so—but instead to comprehend how voters understand negative ads, getting past the standard concern that because they complain when asked, they must be turned off by negativity.

Voters are not as bothered by negativity as many seem to think they are. Much of the disdain voters express in survey questions about negativity is an artifact of the way they are asked about it. Many people oppose "negative campaigning" because the word "negative" is in the phrase. There are so many reasons to dislike "negative campaigning"—social desirability bias (wanting to give the interviewer the "correct" answer), dissonance (feeling bad about yourself for supporting something negative), or just agreement with the predetermined value judgment (if it's called "negative," it must be a bad thing). We find a great reduction in purported voter anger toward negativity just by removing "negative" from the questions we ask. We are not suggesting, however, that voters look forward to the deluge of negative ads every two years. In fact, we find that voters recognize ads talking about an opponent as negative, at least when shown the entire ad beforehand. And they are less angered by positive ads to be sure, but this is just a relative difference; the overarching point is that the negative ads do not make them all that angry. Voter backlash to negativity, where they hate the sponsor more than the target—is limited and quite predictable because it is tied to criteria such as the topic of the attack or the believability of the ad. We find this in reactions to both real and hypothetical ads.

Voters need negativity because they appear unable to make inferences in the absence of positive information. As our experiments show, voters generally fail to recognize that candidates are unlikely to discuss topics unfavorable to them. Thus, the absence of a positive statement is generally not recognized as a signal that the topic is one on which the candidate may be vulnerable. Without negativity from the other side, undiscussed topics carry no information at all. Thus, in some cases, voters may well welcome negative information, with negativity being especially important for voters who are less engaged and have better things to do than search around for reasons why a candidate should not be elected. Why is it difficult to imagine that voters might prefer a candidate who both highlights her own experience and criticizes her opponent's failures rather than one who stays visibly positive and simply hopes negative inferences, subtle hints, and suggestions of her opponent's limitations are recognized by voters?

Looking at this another way, if candidate Adams attacks candidate Brown for raising taxes, Adams has probably made an indirect promise not to raise taxes. Such implications of negativity are so often true that exceptions seem noteworthy, for instance, Newt Gingrich and Mitt Romney accusing each other of investing in Fannie Mae and Freddie Mac, as they did in a primary debate, when both actually had such investments. But, as we learned from our formal model-based experiment, voters do not seem to recognize such implications. In the example above, candidate Adams would not be held accountable for this implicit campaign promise. People just don't think about politics that way. Perhaps the only answer, without negativity, would be somehow to retrain voters to see these implications. That, of course, is unlikely.

We have made much of the fact that the topics of attack ads affect voters much beyond the simple fact that the ads talk about the opponent, and we corroborate that finding when we look at real ads from real elections. In study 4, the five defamatory ads—which were not just harsh but also very personal—generally garnered the worst reactions, being judged less appropriate and more negative. But another problem with those ads—for example, Rand Paul worshipping Aqua Buddha—is that they just *seemed* false. In the two-stage regression at the conclusion of chapter 6, we show that much of the variation in vote intent among the attack ads can be attributed to variations in believability, more so than emotional response, and instead of assessments of appropriateness. Considering the wealth of negative advertising, it is actually very encouraging that voters are more discerning of negative versus positive ads, but that still leaves the problem of whether the voters will be able to correctly gauge the ads' credibility; the more dubious they are of candidates in general (or the more salient the possibility of candidates' dishonesty), the more likely they will make a mistake by choosing a candidate offering lower expected utility. But eliminating negativity would only exacerbate the situation.

Does the truth matter? In general, a major difficulty with studying truth in elections is the lack of counterfactuals. Because of this, we have stressed experimental research over field research. In the lab experiments, we always know whether or not candidates are being honest, and what would have happened if the voters had elected a different candidate. We actually provide this information to voters in the laboratory after the elections in which they participate. Also, we suggest that one of the reasons for the mixed effects in the extant negative campaigning studies is that the idiosyncrasies of individual campaigns make it difficult to compare across different campaigns. Since we do not know what the election results (or turnout) would have been had the candidates used different campaign strategies, these have to be estimated using results from other elections. We believe that it is more effective to conduct our study in the laboratory so that we can isolate our research interest—voters' attitudes toward negativity—from both campaign-specific details and voters' predispositions.

Truth, of course, is often viewed through the lens of relativity—many have noted that those in power can define the truth. In our formal model, we take the position that the truth of a statement can be learned by the voter retrospectively (i.e., after the election). Extending this point to the economy as an example, we do not know *now* if the economy is moving in the right direction, but we would argue we *will* know the answer about today's economy, say, by the next election—provided, of course, that we agree beforehand on a specific measurement for "right direction." But in any case, the major foci of our truth and negativity model are topics for which (1) there *is* a truth (e.g., voting records, arrest records, past religious affiliation, ethics violations), and (2) it would be unrealistic to expect the voter to conduct her own research to validate the truth. Our results show that, ultimately, when voters conflate "negative" and "false" their decision-making ability suffers. Distrusting voters tend to lose more faith in negative rather than positive statements. Truth does matter, and it is important that candidates be held to some standard. But who should do it?

In chapter 2, we argue that the media fail in a watchdog role, and thus it becomes the candidates' responsibility to reveal negative information about the opponents. Candidates, though, are quite good at stretching the truth. When revealing information about their opponents, candidates are going to do so in as biased a manner as possible (just as they do with information about themselves—when analyzing candidates' positions, scholars often tend to assume, incorrectly, that candidates provide accurate information about themselves and inaccurate information about the opponent). In any case, there are still limits to negative campaigns, and we argue that these limits are directly tied to the severity of the attacked candidate's weakness. For example, an opponent in 2012 could have attacked Mitt Romney for a lack of political experience, since he had spent only four years in elected office. We're sure that a quality advertising team, by stretching the truth, could make that seem like a liability. It's hard to imagine backlash against negative ads that accurately, albeit aggressively, attacked a candidate's experience.

But the 2012 Obama campaign did not try to go there. Instead, they focused on different "flaws," primarily using Romney's business experience to paint him as uncaring and out of touch. Candidates can go negative on anything they want, but different attacks yield different returns. In the Romney example, his opponents also could have pushed the envelope and lied by stating that Romney had "no political experience." Obviously this is easily refutable and risks voter backlash, but that's our point. If Romney *really* had zero years of experience, the advertising team would undoubtedly create a less risky and much more effective negative ad.

Of course, in real life, truth about the past can *still* be a matter of perspective, or even undeterminable. For example, in the 2012 Republican primaries, one of stalwart conservatives' complaints about Mitt Romney was that the "true" Romney was too liberal, was falsely claiming to hold more conservative positions, and would abandon conservatism if elected. But since Romney lost to Obama, we will never know what Romney would have done in office and thus will be unable to evaluate whether he was telling the truth about his conservative issue positions.

In the end, our point about truth is both simple and complex. Voters assess the believability of advertising, both negative and positive, through whatever lens they wish to use. In doing so, they use that assessment to determine at least in part whether a particular negative ad goes too far, beyond some personal limit they themselves know. That is fairly simple. But of course, that limit will be greatly affected by the lens that is used, and in American elections that lens is usually one of partisanship. So we should certainly expect Republicans to be less trusting of claims by Democrats and vice versa. But it is not unanimous. Not all Republicans will always deny the truth of a Democratic statement; nor will all Democrats feel the other way. We find that even after controlling for partisanship, the believability of a negative ad has a significant impact on the likelihood of a voter backlash against the ad's sponsor.

To our knowledge, few if any scholars have examined credibility as a basis for assessment of negativity. The research we examined for this book instead focused on other areas, especially the tone of the ads (ranging from civility to musical selection), whether the ads were personal or policy-based, and whether the ads were appropriate or relevant to political discussions. All of these are important, but as we showed in chapter 6, ignoring credibility leaves out an important piece of the puzzle.

So why is there so much negativity? As we look back at the 2012 presidential campaign, it seems clear that the negativity has persisted, and that every campaign seems to be more negative than the last. Geer (2012) argues that the media have incentivized politicians to use negative advertising. The media seem obsessed with negativity even though, as we show in chapter 2, we really cannot count on them to replace opposing candidates as watchdogs over the campaign. It does seem to make sense for the media to have this obsession. For one thing, psychologists have shown that people give more weight to negative information than to positive information. Second, as we have noted several times, negative ads are comparatively more informative than positive ones. This point hit us first-hand while screening real political advertisements for our study 4. Many of candidates' positive ads we endured really *were* devoid of campaign relevant information. Why would the media rebroadcast ads that show a candidate fishing, or ads that show a candidate's children talking about what a great dad he is? They need to bring eyeballs to the screen or to the page; you cannot do that without controversy. Positive ads just don't create compelling media stories. If reformers had their way and negativity was suddenly abolished from all American campaigns, it is hard to imagine what the media response would actually be, given that so many hours, pages, and pixels are filled with stories about negativity. Perhaps they would have to focus on the substantive issues of the campaign instead!

This leads us to a brief thought about the inherent contradiction in calls by reformers for the elimination of negativity in political campaigns. The very same pundits who rue negativity also generally complain that many elections are not competitive. They complain about gerrymandering, worry that incumbents rarely face quality challengers, and believe such a lack of choices is inherently undemocratic. We imagine these reformers are not great fans of the incredible incumbency advantage enjoyed especially by members of the US House of Representatives. Recent history tells us that even in those rare years in which large numbers of incumbents go down (1994 and 2006, for example), more than 85% of incumbents who choose to run for reelection win. We would certainly take those odds any day.

Now, let's imagine a world without negativity. How much more competitive would elections be? Not at all, we suspect. In fact, banning negativity could be the ultimate in incumbent protection as challengers would find themselves fighting with one hand tied behind their backs. Incumbents usually have more money, certainly have more name recognition and press coverage, and have the potential advantage of a record to extol (perhaps even by stretching the truth about their accomplishments, which the opponent would be unable to counter). So where is the challenger left in such a world?

The most likely effect of banning negativity would be eliminating the ability of challengers to effectively campaign against incumbents. If a challenger cannot talk about her opponent, cannot describe what a miserable failure he is, and cannot explain to voters why they should not vote for him again, what is left for the challenger to do? Certainly every challenger has to explain to voters why they should consider change, and it is hard to do that without being allowed to do exactly what the word "challenger" suggests is the core task: challenge the incumbent.

Is it really worse to have a candidate attack an opponent on issues, when the attacks are accurate, than it is to have that same candidate make false statements about his or her own record in presumably positive ads? Banning negativity does not ban falsehoods. One can easily lie in a positive ad. But it does eliminate the ability of an opponent to respond to such lies. So we would be left with a media that appears relatively unable to police the situation and which itself is actually less trusted than are candidates who presumably turn off voters by going negative. The only conclusion to draw about those who would reform the system to eliminate negativity is that any attempt to do so would be an attempt to make the system more democratic by making it less democratic. A contradiction indeed.

So where do we stand now? The 2012 presidential election appears to have once again outdone all others in negativity, at least if media reports are accurate. A November 4, 2012, Politico.com story reported that the election set "a record for the most negative campaign ads in presidential election history" (Slack 2012). Who are we to disagree with the story's statistics, which, according to the Wesleyan Media Project, identified 86 percent of Obama's TV ads and 79 percent of Romney's as negative? This was up from 69 percent for Obama and John McCain combined in 2008 and just 58 percent of George W. Bush and John Kerry ads in 2004. All we can say is "wow."

Actually, we can also say "so what?" To our minds the issue has never been some onslaught of negativity; it has instead been the content of those negative ads. And it is the extent to which voters find them either credible or not as they attempt to learn relevant information about both sides of the debate. Would voters have been better off if zero percent of ads had been negative? We highly doubt it. What we do know is that they would most definitely not have had the opportunity to learn as much as otherwise, since the campaign information environment would have been vastly less informative. Did candidates lie sometimes? Of course. Were all their lies in negative ads? Probably not. Eliminating negativity would not eliminate lying, but it would eliminate valuable information as John Geer (2006) so clearly shows. So we need to get beyond our penchant to buy into the knee-jerk response that negative advertising is inherently bad for voters, bad for candidates, and bad for the system. Instead, we would be doing more of a service to our understanding of campaigns if we focused more on how negativity does or does not engage voters, and delved even more deeply into understanding the conditions under which voters accept negative advertising as one of many useful sources of information versus when they recognize that it is, in fact, beyond the pale and should be ignored. Understanding how voters make use of negative ads and examining voters' ability to distinguish useful, accurate information from false, inaccurate, valueless information should be our next steps. We need to go beyond simply being negative about negativity.

Details of Video Ads Used in Study 4

Transcripts of ads used in study 4, by sponsor name, with on-screen text in brackets.

Ayotte

AYOTTE: "I'm Kelly Ayotte. My family's proud to serve New Hampshire. My husband Joe flew combat missions in Iraq, and I served as attorney general fighting to put criminals behind bars, and when our state faced payoffs, I refused a pay raise. Public service is rewarding but sure doesn't make you rich. Now some of my opponents can buy all of the commercials they want but, I approve this message because shouldn't our next Senator have the biggest commitment to serve and not just the biggest bank account?"

Bennet

VOICEOVER: [Ken Buck's Secret, news headline highlighting "rebuke"] "Ken Buck's secret: he was rebuked for professional misconduct, left the Justice Department under a cloud. Buck gave inside information to lawyers for an illegal gun dealer, then the dealer donated money to Buck's campaign. The official reprimand said, 'Buck showed reckless disregard for his obligations' and Buck was ordered to attend ethics class. But you don't learn right from wrong in class, and you certainly don't learn ethics in Washington, DC" [most of the spoken words were also written on the screen, sentence by sentence].

TABLE A.1. **Details and classification for each advertisement used in study 4**

Sponsor	Party	Opponent	Party	Winner	Position	State
Positive Ads						
Kelly Ayotte	Republican	Paul Hodes	Democrat	Ayotte	US Senate	NH
Martha Coakley	Democrat	Scott Brown	Republican	Brown	US Senate	MA
Jim Cooper	Democrat	Gerard Donovan	Republican	Cooper	US House	TN
Adam Fetterman	Democrat	Michael DiTerlizzi	Republican	Fetterman	State Rep.	FL
Peter Roskam	Republican	Tammy Duckworth	Democrat	Roskam	US House	IL
Paul Sanford	Republican	Jeff Enfinger	Democrat	Sanford	State Senate	AL
Heath Shuler	Democrat	Keith Smith	Libertarian	Shuler	US House	NC
Richard Skorman	Nonpartisan	Steve Bach	nonpartisan	Bach	Mayor	CO
Daniel Webster	Republican	Alan Grayson	Democrat	Webster	US House	FL
Negative Ads						
Virg Bernero	Democrat	Rick Snyder	Republican	Snyder	Governor	MI
Robin Carnahan	Democrat	Roy Blunt	Republican	Blunt	US Senate	MO
Bob Corker	Republican	Harold Ford	Democrat	Corker	US Senate	TN
Kay Hagan	Democrat	Elizabeth Dole	Republican	Hagan	US Senate	NC
Matt Patten	Democrat	Colleen Grady	Republican	Patten	State Rep.	OH
Dave Reichert	Republican	Darcy Burner	Democrat	Reichert	US House	WA
Robert P. Young	Republican	Denise Langford Morris	Democrat	Young	State Supr. Ct	MI
Defamatory Ads						
Michael Bennet	Democrat	Ken Buck	Republican	Bennet	US Senate	CO
Jack Conway	Democrat	Rand Paul	Republican	Paul	US Senate	MA
Elizabeth Dole	Republican	Kay Hagan	Democrat	Hagan	US Senate	NC
Zeb Little	Democrat	Paul Bussman	Republican	Bussman	State Senate	AL
Rick Mullin	Democrat	Rick Bertrand	Republican	Bertrand	State Senate	IA

TABLE A.2. **Mean scores for each ad in study 4**

Sponsor	How Negative	Believable	Angry	Appropriate	Is Negative	Vote
Positive Ads						
Kelly Ayotte	0.55	3.41	1.15	3.62	0.09	2.56
Martha Coakley	0.23	3.32	1.13	3.69	0.00	2.51
Jim Cooper	0.15	3.33	1.12	3.66	0.01	2.56
Adam Fetterman	0.29	3.04	1.11	3.62	0.02	2.51
Peter Roskam	0.11	3.02	1.19	3.32	0.02	2.31
Paul Sanford	0.32	3.14	1.15	3.63	0.03	2.35
Heath Shuler	0.75	3.22	1.36	3.60	0.15	2.48
Richard Skorman	0.10	3.42	1.04	3.74	0.00	2.52
Daniel Webster	0.40	3.12	1.25	3.56	0.04	2.47
Negative Ads						
Virg Bernero	3.64	2.89	2.29	2.75	0.96	2.06
Robin Carnahan	3.38	2.61	2.18	2.56	0.93	2.00
Bob Corker	3.09	2.40	1.88	2.26	0.88	1.82
Kay Hagan	1.65	3.22	2.11	2.85	0.41	2.32
Matt Patten	2.84	2.40	1.85	2.85	0.86	2.04
Dave Reichert	2.53	2.74	1.70	2.90	0.81	2.07
Robert P. Young	3.85	2.67	2.37	2.76	0.97	2.00
Defamatory Ads						
Michael Bennet	3.92	2.88	2.29	2.81	0.97	2.03
Jack Conway	4.23	2.17	2.58	1.88	0.98	1.71
Elizabeth Dole	4.28	2.20	2.86	1.68	0.98	1.64
Zeb Little	4.33	2.72	2.62	2.19	0.99	2.00
Rick Mullin	4.05	2.60	2.42	2.45	0.98	2.01

Note: "How Negative" is scored from 0 (not negative) to 5 (extremely negative). "Believable," "Angry," and "Appropriate" are scored from 1 (not very) to 4 (very). "Is Negative" is scored 1 for yes, and 0 for no. "Vote" is scored from 1 (more likely to vote for the opponent) to 3 (more likely to vote for the candidate running the ad).

Bernero

VOICEOVER: [Snyder made $14 million] "We know Snyder made a fortune at Gateway."

SNYDER INTERVIEW: "I created jobs when I was at Gateway and I'm very proud of that record."

VOICEOVER: "[Proud?] Snyder's leadership was called [a complete disaster], [a total failure]." [2001: 3,000 Layoffs] "2001, Gateway lays off 3,000 workers. 2002, Gateway cuts another 2,250 jobs. 2004, Gateway slashes 1500 jobs." [Gateway Sold to Chinese] "2007, Gateway sold to the Chinese, another American company gone. That's not change, that's business as usual." [Snyder: Business as Usual]

Carnahan

ELDERLY WOMAN: [Here in Missouri] "Roy Blunt's been gone some time now. Probably doesn't know how tough folks here in Missouri have it."

YOUNG WOMAN: [Back in Washington] "Roy is the life of the party in DC His wife, great, a powerful tobacco lobbyist . . ."

ELDERLY WOMAN: "Jobs sent overseas, schools heading downhill."

YOUNG WOMAN: "Roy's building a new million-dollar home in DC's best neighborhood."

ELDERLY WOMAN: "My nephew lost his house."

YOUNG WOMAN: "That's how you know he's made it here."

ELDERLY WOMAN: "Roy Blunt's just forgotten Missouri."

Coakley

COAKLEY: "You know we tell kids don't talk to strangers, but now the stranger might be right in their room. I'm [Martha Coakley] and I led a national effort to keep children safe online" [Protected children online] "and won passage of the law to keep sex predators behind bars longer." [Coakley bill "a victory for child protection."] "In the Senate, I'll work to [strengthen cyber security] and give our parents and police new tools to keep our kids safe." [New tools for parents and police, visit marthacoakley.com for more information.] "I approve this message because I know what it takes to protect children and that's what I'll do in the Senate." [Martha Coakley A Different Kind of Leader].

Conway

CONWAY: "I'm Jack Conway, I approve this message."

VOICEOVER: [Rand Paul's College Society Mocked Christianity] "Why was Rand Paul a member of a secret society that called the Holy Bible [a hoax] that was banned for mocking Christianity and Christ? Why did Rand Paul once tie a woman up, tell her to bow down before a false idol, and say his [God was Aqua Buddha]? Why does Rand Paul now want to end all federal [faith-based initiatives] and even end a [deduction for religious charities]? Why are there so many questions about Rand Paul?"

Cooper

WOMAN 1: [disaster] "I was just so devastated I didn't think anybody could help me."

WOMAN 2: [bureaucracy] "FEMA denied me, until I contacted Jim Cooper."

WOMAN 1: [response] "He stood up to the big banks and never stopped."

MAN 1: [accountability] "It was Cooper who was takin' on the Army Corps of Engineers."

MAN 2: [CooperForCongress.com] "Asking the tough questions and demanding answers."

MAN 3: [recovery] "You know Jim Cooper's not just a congressman."

MAN 2: "Jim worked to bring this whole community together."

WOMAN 1: "He was a neighbor when I needed him."

MAN 3: "He was a friend."

WOMAN 2: I was able to get my home repaired."

WOMAN 1: "I got back in my house."

MAN 2: "Jim Cooper is always on my side."

COOPER: "I'm Jim Cooper and I approve this ad."

Corker

MAN 1: [Memphis: where they know Harold Ford Jr. the best.] "Whoo, he looks good on TV!"

WOMAN 1: "Didn't he grow up in DC?"

WOMAN 2: "Went to some prep school in DC, didn't he?"

MAN 2: "Harold's from DC, not Tennessee."

MAN 3: "Our mayor says the Ford family is trying to tie up every political slot in Tennessee."

WOMAN 3: "Has Junior ever had a job outside of politics?"

MAN 4: "The Ford family business is politics."

WOMAN 2: "But he does look good on TV."

BOB CORKER: [Bob Corker] "I'm Bob Corker, and I've approved this message."

Dole

DOLE: "I'm Elizabeth Dole and I approve this message."

VOICEOVER: [Kay Hagan Godless Americans Fundraiser, Boston 9/15/08] "A leader of the Godless Americans pact recently held a secret fundraiser in Kay Hagan's honor." [Godless Americans?]

ELLEN JOHNSON: [Executive Director Godless Americans] "There is no God to rely on."

INTERVIEWEE: "There is no Jesus."

BILL O'REILLY: "Taking 'under God' out of the Pledge of Allegiance, you're down with that?"

DAVID SILVERMAN: "We're down with that."

BILL O'REILLY: "In God We Trust, you're gonna whip that off the money?"

DAVID SILVERMAN: "Yeah we would."

VOICEOVER: "Godless Americans and Kay Hagan, she hid from cameras, took Godless money [What did Hagan promise in return?]"

FEMALE VOICE, presumably Hagan: "There is no God."

Hagan

KAY HAGAN: "I'm Kay Hagan and Elizabeth Dole's attacks on my Christian faith are offensive. She even faked my voice in her TV ad to make you think I don't believe in God. Well, I believe in God, I taught Sunday school, my faith guides my life and Senator Dole knows it. Sure, politics is a tough business but I approve this message because my campaign is about creating jobs and fixing our economy, not bearing false witness against fellow Christians."

Little

VOICEOVER: "We expect fathers to provide for their children. It's what any dad should want to do, especially one who makes over [$200,000 per year]. But that's not how state Senate candidate Paul Bussman sees it. He [refused to pay thousands of dollars of family support] until a judge finally forced him to do so. Incredibly, the judge even had to force him to pay his children's [medical bills]. [Paul Bussman failed his children] [Can we trust him] to represent us in the state Senate?"

Mullin

[Rick Bertrand, Drug Salesman for Most Unethical Company in the World] "Rick Bertrand said he would run a positive campaign." [Bertrand False Attacks]

"Now he's falsely attacking Rick Mullin. [Why?]" [Bertrand's Company Marketed Sleep Drug to Children] "Because Bertrand doesn't want you to know he put his profits ahead of children's health." [Rick Bertrand Drug Salesman for Most Unethical Company in the World] "Bertrand was a sales agent for a big drug company that was rated the most unethical company in the world." [Major side effects include behavior changes such as self-harm.] "They singled out Bertrand's company for giving a dangerous sleep drug to children. [Rick Bertrand: broken promises . . . a record of deceit.]"

Patten

WOMAN: "Education is a mess in Ohio. I think Matt has a great plan to fix it and that's why we're working so hard to win."
WOMAN 2: "Isn't Matt's opponent on the state school board?"
MAN 1: "Yeah she's part of the problem."
WOMAN 1: "[Colleen Grady is the problem.] I'm a special education teacher and there's no funding to do what we need to do." [No funding for education] "People like Colleen Grady have been making [empty promises] for fifteen years."
PATTEN: "Look, guys, that's in the past. We need to focus on the future of our children if we're gonna get anywhere. That's what I'm gonna do when I'm elected state representative."

Reichert

DENISE SPENCER: "We've seen enough. With Darcy Burner trying to tear down Dave Reichert, at a time when our country's hurting? Burner really scares me. [No experience.] [No record.] [Burner doesn't have an economic degree from Harvard.] She's kind of making it up as she goes along. But Dave Reichert knows what to do, and his plans to fix the economy really make sense. Darcy Burner's running negative ads to help herself. Dave Reichert's working to help us. We better get this right, or we're all in trouble."

Roskam

FAMILY: [Meet the Roskams] "We're the Roskams,"
STEVE (son): "and we're gonna tell you about our dad."
GRACEY (daughter): "You may have heard about him, he's running for Congress."

FRANKIE (daughter): "He's been a state senator, so he's got experience." [State Legislature 13 years]

GRACEY: [Peter Roskam Cut Taxes] "He talks about cutting taxes all the time. It's kind of boring but he's really into it."

PETER (son): "He talks a lot about protecting Social Security, too." [Protect Social Security].

GRACEY: "That helps my grandma and grandpa." [Grandpa and Grandma Roskam]

FRANKIE: "But really, you should know how great of a dad he is."

AJ (son): "And he's losing his hair."

PETER ROSKAM: "Hey! I'm Peter Roskam and I approve this message."

Sanford

SANFORD: [Paul Sanford State Senate] "I'm Paul Sanford, candidate for Alabama Senate. We need fresh faces and new ideas in legislature, and that's why I'm running. For far too long, special interest groups have controlled the agenda and it's time to put the people back in charge. You can count on me to work hard representing you honestly and openly." [Paul Sanford Common Sense Uncommon Conviction] "I'm Paul Sanford and I appreciate your vote on June 9th because public service should be about integrity and trust."

VOICEOVER: "Vote June 9th, Paul Sanford for State Senate, no longer politics as usual."

Shuler

[Heath Shuler for Congress]

SHULER: "Congress doesn't seem to know right from wrong, but we do. It's not right when big insurance companies write healthcare laws and millions can't afford to see a doctor. It's not right when big oil companies write energy laws and gas prices skyrocket. It's not right when Congress passes trade bills that send our jobs overseas. Congress won't change until we change the people we're sending to Washington."

Skorman

VOICEOVER: "Colorado Springs' first strong mayor will be setting the stage for generations to come."

SKORMAN: "This is no time to experiment. I'm Richard Skorman. As a small business owner, former city councilman and vice mayor, and a proven leader, I have the experience, leadership, and vision to chart a new course for Colorado Springs." [SkormanForMayor.com] "Please read my plan, Opportunity Springs, for creating jobs and jumpstarting the economy. And thanks for your vote."

Webster

WEBSTER: [Daniel Webster] "I'm Dan Webster. Why should we care so much about fixing Washington?" [Civility and Statesmanship–*Orlando Sentinel*] "Because like you, Sandy and I are concerned about the direction of our country." [Respected–*CNN*] "Because we want our sons and daughters to find a job, buy a home, and raise a family." [Webster is a Class Act–*West Orange Times*] "And like you, we want our grandchildren to have a future of enormous promise, not endless debt." [Effective ... we endorse Webster—*Orlando Sentinel*] "I'm Daniel Webster and I approve this message because America's not broken, Washington is."
VOICEOVER: "Send Congress a message. Daniel Webster."

Young

VOICEOVER: "[Judge Denise Langford Morris has been soft on crime for rappers, lawyers, and child pornographers.] For a rapper, facing a [gun charge while on probation], Langford Morris let him walk free. For a city attorney who crashed while driving 100 with cocaine in his car, Langford Morris [gave him probation]. And for a special ed teacher convicted of child pornography crimes, [just one day in jail]. Tell Judge Denise Langford Morris, get tough on convicted criminals." [Call Judge Denise Langford Morris 248–858–0360. Get Tough on Convicted Criminals.]

Appendix to Chapter 5

On the Sophisticated Voter and Perfect Bayesian Equilibrium

Either candidate has the opportunity to deviate to a different campaign strategy, in essence "tricking" the voter into incorrect beliefs about the candidates' underlying traits. To confirm that the strategies in shown in table 5.2 of chapter 5 are part of a perfect Bayesian equilibrium, we must show that neither candidate has such an incentive to deviate.

The voter's off-path beliefs, described in this chapter for [statement 1–statement 2] equilibria in general, are important here. They consist of the following: if the campaign revelations are off-path, (1) believe all campaign revelations; (2a) if one candidate revealed X, assume that candidate is positive on both dimensions facing an opponent negative on both, except where this conflicts with (1); (2b) otherwise, believe statements 1 and 2 were not available for either candidate, except where this conflicts with (1). These off-path beliefs immediately rule out deviations to not campaigning, revealing positive information about the opponent, or revealing negative information about oneself; after such a choice, the voter will believe that the candidate is negative on both dimensions, and will never lower her assessment of the opponent, so no candidate would make these campaign choices. Table B.1 shows every other possible deviation and its effect on voter beliefs.

As the strategies are symmetrical, deviations are provided for candidate 1 only. The rightmost columns show the change in the expected utility difference if candidate 1 deviates to the strategy listed in that row, and the voter's strategy, given her beliefs and not being aware of the deviation. For example, in case 1, candidate 1 could deviate to reveal Y, after which the voter would believe it was case 9 or 10, and would vote for candidate 2.

In no case does a deviation favorably change the vote for candidate 1, given the parameters x, y, and p. Thus, the X–Y equilibrium exists for the game in the experiment.

What about for other values of x, y, and p? In the X–Y equilibrium, the only deviations that might yield positive incentives are switches from X to Y in cases 1–3, as these are the only entries in the expected utility difference column that are not negative. For example, in case 1, a candidate could switch to revealing his positive Y trait instead of his positive X trait. This will cause the voter to assume that we are in either case 9 or case 10.

In each of the three cases, this deviation from X to Y lowers the voter's utility for candidate 1 by x, since candidate 1 is now "known" to be negative on X from his failure to campaign with X. But in return, it raises the voter's utility for candidate 1 by $(1 - p)y$, because candidate 1 is known to be positive with certainty on dimension Y. In cases 1 and 2, this could change the result from a tie to a win for candidate 1. But, if $(1 - p)y - x \le 0$, then candidate 1 does not have an incentive to deviate, and so the X–Y equilibrium exists. For the experiment conducted in this paper, x and y were 80 and 20, respectively, and p was one of 30 percent, 50 percent, or 70 percent (depending on the treatment). In all treatments, $(1 - p)y - x \le 0$; thus, the X–Y equilibrium exists for the given values of x, y, and p.

Similarly, we can derive existence criteria for the seven other potential equilibria of the [statement 1–statement 2] type, which we denote as X–$oppY$, $oppX$–Y, $oppX$–$oppY$, Y–X, Y–$oppX$, $oppY$–X, and $oppY$–$oppX$. The Y–X existence criterion is the most straightforward to determine, since all of the strategies would work in an analogous way to the X–Y equilibrium, just with the x and y variables switched. This yields $(1 - p)x - y \le 0$ as the criterion for existence. Note that this equation is false for all three values of p used in the game in this paper, so the Y–X equilibrium does not exist in our game.

In fact, for all eight of these potential [statement 1–statement 2] equilibria, we can determine the criteria because they are analogous to the results from table B.1. In other words, the only profitable deviation would be going from statement 1 to statement 2, such as from X to Y in the X–Y case. Table B.2 lists the existence criterion for each of the eight. Notice that whether statement 1 is positive or negative campaigning affects the strategies of the candidates, but it does not affect the criterion for existence.

From the four distinct equations in table B.2 we can show that at least four of these eight equilibria must exist. Either $(1 - p)y - x \le 0$, in which case the first two in the table (X–Y and $oppX$–Y) exist, or $(1 - p)y - x > 0$.

TABLE B.1. **Results from Candidate 1 deviation in the X–Y equilibrium**

Case	Candidate 1	Candidate 2	Campaign		Voter Beliefs		Believed Case(s) after Deviation	Change in Expected Utility Difference (C1–C2)	Vote[a]
			Candidate 1	Candidate 2	Candidate 1	Candidate 2			
1	$(+,+)$	$(+,+)$	X	X	$(+,?)$	$(+,?)$			Tie
			Y		$(-,+)$	$(+,?)$	9 or 10	$(1-p)y - x$	C2
2	$(+,+)$	$(+,-)$	X	X	$(+,?)$	$(+,?)$			Tie
			Y		$(-,+)$	$(+,?)$	9 or 10	$(1-p)y - x$	C2
			$oppY$		$(-,-)$	$(+,-)$	14	$-x - py$	C2
3	$(+,+)$	$(-,+)$	X	Y	$(+,?)$	$(-,+)$			C1
			Y		$(-,+)$	$(-,+)$	11	$(1-p)y - x$	Tie
			$oppX$		$(-,-)$	$(-,+)$	15	$-x - py$	C2
4	$(+,+)$	$(-,-)$	X	$\varnothing$	$(+,+)$	$(-,-)$		0	C1
			Y		$(-,+)$	$(-,-)$	$(12)^{b}$	$-x - y$	C1
			$oppX$		$(-,-)$	$(-,-)$	$(16)^{b}$	$-x - y$	Tie
			$oppY$		$(-,-)$	$(-,-)$	$(16)^{b}$		Tie
5	$(+,-)$	$(+,+)$	X	X	$(+,?)$	$(+,?)$		n/a	Tie
6	$(+,-)$	$(+,-)$	X	X	$(+,?)$	$(+,?)$			Tie
			$oppY$		$(-,-)$	$(+,?)$	14	$-x - py$	C2
7	$(+,-)$	$(-,+)$	X	Y	$(+,?)$	$(-,+)$			C1
			$oppX$		$(-,-)$	$(-,+)$	15	$-x - py$	C2
8	$(+,-)$	$(-,-)$	X	$oppY$	$(+,-)$	$(-,-)$			C1
			$oppX$		$(-,-)$	$(-,-)$	15	$-x$	Tie
			$oppY$		$(-,-)$	$(-,-)$	16	$-x$	Tie

9	(-,+)	(+,+)	Y	X	(-,+)	(+,?)		n/a	C2
10	(-,+)	(+,-)	oppY	X	(-,-)	(+,?)		-y	C2
11	(-,+)	(-,+)	Y	Y	(+,+)	(-,+)	14	-y	C2
			oppX		(+,-)	(-,+)	15		Tie
12	(-,+)	(-,-)	Y	oppX	(-,+)	(-,-)			C2
			oppX		(-,-)	(-,-)	(16)[b]	-y	C1
			oppY				(16)[b]	-y	Tie
									Tie
13	(-,-)	(+,+)	Ø	X	(-,-)	(+,+)		n/a	C2
14	(-,-)	(+,-)	oppY	X	(-,-)	(+,-)		n/a	C2
15	(-,-)	(-,+)	oppX	Y	(-,-)	(-,+)		n/a	C2
16	(-,-)	(-,-)	oppY	oppY	(-,-)	(-,-)	(16)[b]	o	Tie
			oppX						Tie

Note:

X = Reveal one's own positive X trait

Y = Reveal one's own positive Y trait

$oppX$ = Reveal opponent's negative X trait

$oppY$ = Reveal opponent's negative Y trait

$\emptyset$ = No campaign

[a] Assumes that $x > (1 - p)y$ and $x > py$, which is true for the game parameters (x, p, y) used in this study.

[b] Denotes that the pair of revelations is off-path, so the listed case has been determined using the voter's off-path beliefs.

TABLE B.2. **Existence criteria for all [statement 1–statement 2] equilibria**

Equilibrium	Existence Criterion
X–Y	$(1 - p)y - x \leq 0$
$oppX$–Y	$(1 - p)y - x \leq 0$
X–$oppY$	$py - x \leq 0$
$oppX$–$oppY$	$py - x \leq 0$
Y–X	$(1 - p)x - y \leq 0$
$oppY$–X	$(1 - p)x - y \leq 0$
Y–$oppX$	$px - y \leq 0$
$oppY$–$oppX$	$px - y \leq 0$

If the latter is true, since $0 \leq p \leq 1$, it is also true that $y - (1 - p)x > 0$. Thus $(1 - p)x - y \leq 0$ and so the Y–X and $oppY$–X equilibria exist. Similarly, if $py - x \leq 0$ then both X–$oppY$ and $oppX$–$oppY$ exist. But if $py - x > 0$ then $y - px > 0$. Thus $px - y \leq 0$, and so the Y–$oppX$ and $oppY$–$oppX$ equilibria exist. Note that it is possible for all eight to exist, for example if $x = y$.

For the experiment conducted in this study, both $(1 - p)y - x \leq 0$ and $py - x \leq 0$ are true for all three values of p, and so the first four equilibria listed in the table (X–Y, X–$oppY$, $oppX$–Y, and $oppX$–$oppY$) all exist. Those with a Y-dimension strategy as statement 1 (i.e., the primary theme) do not.

As shown, this game always has multiple equilibria, though they are not limited to the ones presented above. One of the drawbacks to using perfect Bayesian equilibrium (PBE) in a signaling game is that it places very weak restrictions on the off-path (zero-probability) events. For example, the following is an equilibrium in this game. All candidates do not campaign. If they do (which is off-path), the voter believes the campaign, but also that the unrevealed traits are negative for the campaigner and positive for his opponent.

A more relevant consideration is whether there exists a sophisticated voting equilibrium in which the campaign actions of the candidates in each case are exactly the same as in the naïve voter equilibrium. It could, but requires constructing off-path beliefs in which the sophisticated voter uses vastly different reasoning off-path than she does on-path. Below, we show this for the 30 percent treatment. In the naïve equilibrium the candidates prefer to reveal, in decreasing preference order, (X, $oppX$, Y, $oppY$). This is actually just a [statement 1–statement 2] equilibrium in which we relax the restriction that the two statements must be on separate dimensions. Here, both are on the X dimension. The on-path equilibrium strategies would look like those in table B.3.

TABLE B.3. **Perfect Bayesian equilibrium with statements 1 and 2 on the X dimension**

Case	Candidate 1	Candidate 2	Campaign		Voter Beliefs		Expected Utility Difference (C1−C2)	Vote[a]
			Candidate 1	Candidate 2	Candidate 1	Candidate 2		
1	(+,+)	(+,+)	X	X	(+,?)	(+,?)	0	Tie
2	(+,+)	(+,−)	X	X	(+,?)	(+,?)	0	Tie
3	(+,+)	(−,+)	X	Y	(+,?)	(−,+)	$x-(1-p)y$	C1
4	(+,+)	(−,−)	X	∅	(+,+)	(−,−)	$x+y$	C1
5	(+,−)	(+,+)	X	X	(+,?)	(+,?)	0	Tie
6	(+,−)	(+,−)	X	X	(+,?)	(+,?)	0	Tie
7	(+,−)	(−,+)	X	Y	(+,?)	(+,?)	$x-(1-p)y$	C1
8	(+,−)	(−,−)	X	oppY	(+,−)	(−,+)	x	C1
9	(−,+)	(+,+)	Y	X	(−,+)	(+,?)	$(1-p)y-x$	C2
10	(−,+)	(+,−)	Y	X	(−,+)	(+,?)	$(1-p)y-x$	C2
11	(−,+)	(−,+)	oppX	oppX	(−,?)	(−,?)	0	Tie
12	(−,+)	(−,−)	oppX	oppX	(−,?)	(−,?)	0	Tie
13	(−,−)	(+,+)	∅	X	(−,−)	(+,+)	$-(x+y)$	C2
14	(−,−)	(+,−)	oppY	X	(−,−)	(+,−)	$-x$	C2
15	(−,−)	(−,+)	oppX	oppX	(−,?)	(−,?)	0	Tie
16	(−,−)	(−,−)	oppX	oppX	(−,?)	(−,?)	0	Tie

Note:

X = Reveal one's own positive X trait

Y = Reveal one's own positive Y trait

oppX = Reveal opponent's negative X trait

oppY = Reveal opponent's negative Y trait

∅ = No campaign

[a] Assumes that $x > (1-p)y$ and $x > py$, which is true for the game parameters (x, p, y) used in this study.

Eight of the sixteen cases result in tied elections. In four of these (cases 11, 12, 15, and 16), candidates are both choosing *oppX* campaigns even though the voter's belief that both candidates are negative could come solely from the candidates' failure to reveal positive X traits. In each of these cases, the voter learns nothing about the Y dimension, so we need to check whether candidates can do better by deviating and instead choosing something on the Y dimension (instead of negative campaigning on X).

Any deviation, however, would be off-path; the voter should never see an announcement pairing of (*Y, oppX*) or (*oppY, oppX*). The most straightforward off-path belief in this case would be to believe the Y-dimension campaigner and make no other updates. Both candidates' failure to campaign positively on X still implies that they both have negative X traits. But with those beliefs, the voter should vote for the deviating candidate, meaning that this would not be a PBE. So, we will need a different set of off-path beliefs to sustain the equilibrium.

Say that candidate 1 deviates to *Y* in case 11 or 12. The voter believes (directly from the campaign) that candidate 1 is (−, +), but must generate beliefs for candidate 2. There are only two possibilities for off-path beliefs that make candidate 1's deviation nonprofitable. First, the voter could believe that candidate 2 has some possibility of being positive on X, *even though he failed to campaign positively on X*. While this belief is allowable in PBE, it essentially requires the voter to have naïve off-path beliefs.

The second possibility is that the voter believes that this is case 11 with certainty; that in case 12, candidate 1 would *never* deviate. While this is allowable in PBE, if the voter instead believes that there is a very small $\varepsilon > 0$ probability that the deviation was from a candidate in case 12, the voter should vote for candidate 1, meaning that this equilibrium would not exist. Furthermore, in this setup, for this PBE to exist, the voter would also have to believe that a deviation to *oppY*, yielding the off-path outcome (*oppY, oppX*), was from case 16 with 100 percent certainty; that in case 12, candidate 1 would *never* deviate. While unusual, this very specific set of beliefs would support the strategies in table B.3 as a PBE.

Modeling Decisions Using Quantal Response Equilibrium

The logit QRE, which is used in this study, is a theoretical extension of the logit models commonly used to empirically estimate discrete choice in individual decision-making, and has been used in analysis of both experimental and non-experimental data (e.g., McKelvey and Palfrey 1995; Signorino 1999). In the logit QRE, all players' quantal response functions are logit functions of the expected utilities that are implied by the mixed strategies. Using logit quantal response functions yields the following voter strategy equation, where $\sigma_{R_\ell R_{-\ell}}$ is the probability of voting for candidate ℓ given the campaigns R_ℓ and $R_{-\ell}$ of candidates ℓ and $-\ell$, respectively, and $EU(\ell)$ is the expected utility from voting for candidate ℓ.

$$\textbf{(1)} \qquad \sigma_{R_\ell R_{-\ell}} = \frac{e^{\lambda EU(\ell)}}{e^{\lambda EU(\ell)} + e^{\lambda EU(-\ell)}}$$

$\sigma_{R_\ell R_{-\ell}}$ is a 5×5 matrix with one row and column for each of the five possible campaign choices. The parameter λ measures the relative closeness to the equilibrium. When $\lambda = 0$, voters will choose randomly between the candidates, voting for each 50 percent of the time regardless of the expected utilities. As $\lambda \to \infty$, strategies converge to the Nash equilibrium, which means that players choose the response with the highest expected utility 100 percent of the time. Because λ values are highly sensitive to the payoff structure, they only are meaningful in context; thus we cannot determine the extent of player mistakes solely from the magnitude of any single λ value.

The candidate strategy equations are dependent on the candidates' types θ_ℓ and $\theta_{-\ell}$, and are shown in the equation below, which assumes that candidate strategies are symmetric:

$$\textbf{(2)} \qquad \rho_{\theta_\ell \theta_{-\ell}}^{R_i} = \frac{e^{\lambda EU(R_i)}}{\displaystyle\sum_{j=1}^{5} e^{\lambda EU(R_j)}} \;.$$

$\rho_{\theta_\ell \theta_{-\ell}}^{R_i}$ is a 4 x 4 x 5 matrix. The candidates' expected utility for each campaign option is $EU(R_i) = 100 * \sum_{j=1}^{5} \sigma_{R_i R_j} \rho_{\theta_\ell \theta_{-\ell}}^{R_j}$, where $\rho_{\theta_\ell \theta_{-\ell}}^{R_j}$ is, due to symmetry, candidate ℓ's probability of choosing campaign j when the types are reversed. The QRE will be the fixed point solution for these choice probability functions.

We use distinct choice probability functions for naïve and sophisticated voters, each assuming that voter tries to maximize payoffs with or without Bayesian updating, respectively. The parameter χ is the probability that the voter is naïve, and thus uses the naïve probability function; candidates must take this into account directly, but it still affects voters indirectly, as regardless of type they must adjust to the candidates' adjustments.

We also include voter risk aversion in the QRE to improve the fit of the model by better capturing the fact that voters will face a lottery if the campaigns do not yield full information about the candidates' traits. This allows us to consider the extent to which voters are biased toward positive campaigning simply because voting for a positive campaigner provides a "sure thing" payoff. All other things equal, a risk-averse voter is more likely to choose a guaranteed payoff over an uncertain payoff with a higher expected value.

Risk aversion is measured by the Arrow-Pratt coefficient of contrast relative risk aversion (q) that transforms a given payoff π into $\pi^{1-q}/1-q$.[1] Setting the risk parameter $q = 0$ leaves π unchanged and thus is equivalent to risk neutrality. While candidates' payoffs are structured so that they do not face an analogous lottery, their campaign decisions will be influenced by voters' risk aversion. For instance, as a naïve voter's risk aversion increases, she becomes more likely to favor a Y campaigner over an $oppX$ campaigner.

To determine the Cursed/QRE equilibrium, we estimated the parameters χ (probability of naïve voting), λ (subject error) and q (risk aversion) using Matlab software to calculate a fixed point for the QRE equations shown above. These best-fitting values for the empirical data were calculated via maximum likelihood estimation. Table 5.6 in chapter 5 shows the results from this estimation.

Notes

Chapter One

1. Joseph Cummins, in his engaging book *Anything for a Vote* (2007), chronicles the long history of negativity in American presidential campaigns with interesting tidbits on every election.

2. Pew Research Center, February 19, 2004. Percentages are from the 785 Form 1 respondents.

3. Poll conducted by Fox Broadcasting Company, February 25, 2000.

4. From the advertisement "Campaign: Negative," retrieved from the Stanford University Political Communications Lab website: http://pcl.stanford.edu.

5. 145 Cong. Rec. S10, 105–6 (daily edition, September 29, 1997) (statement of Senator McCain).

6. 145 Cong. Rec. S10, 123 (daily edition, September 29, 1997) (statement of Senator Durbin).

7. "Rombo," Youtube video, posted by "RickSantorum," February 12, 2012, http://www.youtube.com/watch?v=OtOcrS6axnE.

8. From *Meet the Press*, NBC, May 20, 2012.

9. A notable exception is Rich (2012), whose article "Nuke 'Em" described negative ads as essential to political arguments. "Any president," he writes, "should go negative early, often, and without apology if the goal is victory."

10. From *Meet the Press*, NBC, May 27, 2012.

11. Note that Lau's (1985; Lau and Pierce 2010) "figure ground hypothesis" would suggest that for negativity to be memorable and more likely to be incorporated into evaluations it must stick out in some way, that is, be unusual. Given the rise in negative advertising, it may be hard to argue that negative advertising is in fact an unusual event in modern campaigns. If so, then voters may become more immune to it and a purported strategic reason for its use—that it breaks through—might not be a valid assumption. While Lau and Pierce (2010) find only limited support for declining negativity effects, the possibility remains.

12. Portrait of America poll, August 4, 2000, retrieved via the Polling the Nations database.

13. Among political pundits, the analogue to Geer's book is Mark (2006), which argues that negative campaigning is useful for voters and that voter backlash is limited to those instances where candidates' negativity is egregious.

14. We do, of course, understand that much of the money that has flooded American politics is used to fund negative advertising by both candidates and outside groups. But having said that, no one really has made any effort to disentangle whether voter cynicism is driven by negativity *per se*, or rather by the feeling citizens have that politicians in Washington are too partisan and too focused on drawing lines in the sand than on compromising to govern. In the aftermath of the 2011 debt ceiling crisis and the intensive debate over the national debt, public opinion polling suggested that voters wanted a middle ground, and were disgusted by the failure of politicians to find one. This is not, however, the same as saying voters are specifically damaged by negative advertising.

15. "Three of a Kind, One and the Same: Sarah Steelman," Youtube video, posted by "ClaireMcCaskill2012," July 19, 2012, http://www.youtube.com/watch?v=JwPWqg_z4EQ.

16. "Three of a Kind, One and the Same: John Brunner," Youtube video, posted by "ClaireMcCaskill2012," July 19, 2012, http://www.youtube.com/watch?v=tgadPOH5FHw.

17. "Three of a Kind, One and the Same: Todd Akin," Youtube video, posted by "ClaireMcCaskill2012," July 19, 2012, http://www.youtube.com/watch?v=ec4t_3vaBMc.

18. KTVI, *JACO Report,* August 19, 2012, http://fox2now.com/2012/08/19/the-jaco-report-august-19-2012/. KTVI is a St. Louis–based FOX network affiliate.

19. "Real Words—Women," Youtube video, posted by "ClaireMcCaskill 2012," October 28, 2012, http://www.youtube.com/watch?v=Ag0iHDkXNrg.

20. Wesleyan Media Project, November 2, 2012, "Presidential Ad War Tops 1M Airings," http://mediaproject.wesleyan.edu/.

21. Opensecrets.org, "2012 Presidential Race," http://www.opensecrets.org/pres12/index.php, accessed December 16, 2013.

22. Indiana Debate Commission, "2012 U.S. Senate Fall Debate," October 23, 2012, retrieved from http://indianadebatecommission.com/.

23. "The Romney-Mourdock Ticket," Youtube video, posted by "americanbridge21st," October 23, 2012, http://www.youtube.com/watch?v=zdnnETAyGmM.

24. From realclearpolitics.com.

25. Scott Brown, with support from many independent voters, had won the Massachusetts seat in a special election after the death of Ted Kennedy. Brown defeated Democrat Martha Coakley, whose positive ad we included in our study described later.

26. "Who Knows," Youtube video, posted by "scottbrownma," September 24, 2012, http://www.youtube.com/watch?v=doxWBRNrDfw.

27. It is worth noting here that Warren's ad was a clear issues-based attack, something about which we will show in subsequent chapters voters have no real qualms. Brown's initial response was a meta-attack, attacking Warren for being negative. Voters, at least in our studies, say they do not find such attacks useful at all. Finally, the claims about Warren's supposed use of her heritage are clear personal attacks, which are seen less favorably than issue-based challenges, though not universally condemned in our studies.

28. Andrew E. Smith and Chad Novak, "Boston Globe Poll #35," boston.com, October 29, 2012, http://cache.boston.com/multimedia/2012/10/29poll/report.pdf.

29. Suffolk University Poll, October 25–28, 2012, retrieved via realclearpolitics .com, http://www.realclearpolitics.com/docs/2012/Suffolk_MA_1030.pdf.

30. Public Policy Polling, "Democrats Set to Win Massachusetts, Connecticut Senate Races," November 2, 2012, http://www.publicpolicypolling.com/pdf/2011 /PPP_Release_MACT_1102.pdf.

31. Another type of formal models focuses on voter uncertainty and/or voter turnout. Notable models include Hinich and Munger (1989), in which candidates use negative campaigning to increase the variance of their opponent's policy, and positive campaigning to decrease the variance of their own policy. In their model, negative campaigning cannot be used to clarify information. Skaperdas and Grofman (1995) focus on voter turnout and conversion; they assume that positive campaigning gains voters, while negative campaigning cannot gain votes but rather moves supporters of both candidates into the undecided pool.

32. But as Geer (2006) points out, negative ads are usually carefully documented with citations to various sources for their claims. While we are not suggesting that such citations guarantee the accuracy of the ad, this does suggest that negativity is not necessarily the same as untruth. In fact, Jamieson, Waldman, and Sherr (2000) show that presidential ads mentioning an opponent are on average *more* truthful than self-advocacy ads. The need to convince voters by documenting claims in attack ads seems to increase their actual credibility.

33. Here we owe a debt to Callander and Wilkie (2007), who developed a formal model that explicitly accounts for variations in and effects of candidates' deception. They model a campaign in which candidates have an internal characteristic that determines their propensity to lie.

34. The opponent's ad was unrelentingly negative, reading in part, "David Redlawsk is lying to you about Chickie Haines [the challenger]. Here's why. Redlawsk took $52,000 from a developer who is suing [the town] to build 2,400 new apartments. . . . It's a fact. The Democrats' apartments will cost you higher property taxes and will lower the value of your homes. Keep the Democrats' apartments out. . . . Vote NO on Redlawsk." The ad was accompanied by images of money changing hands, high-rise public housing projects, and a large black-and-white

headshot of Redlawsk with "Redlawsk is lying" superimposed. For his part, Red-lawsk's negative ad started, "Something smells . . . and this time it isn't a farm. It's shady deals between . . . Republicans and greedy developers." The ad goes on to accuse his challenger, Haines, of taking campaign funding from developers and approving developments, noting that the FBI is investigating local officials. Red-lawsk's ad included both positive and negative images: a family, Redlawsk walking in open space, back-room deals, and a file cabinet labeled "FBI."

Chapter Two

1. Krupnikov (2012) supports this argument in finding that undecided voters exposed to negativity were more likely to select a preferred candidate; presumably the negativity helped to differentiate the candidates.

2. Quotes are taken from Amira's (2012) article in *New York Magazine*, titled "Every Presidential Campaign Is the Meanest, Nastiest, Dirtiest Ever," which has multiple quotes from each election year.

3. Ibid.

4. Pew Research Center, November 7–10, 1996, retrieved from ipoll.com.

5. Pew Research Center, November 6–10, 1998, retrieved from ipoll.com.

6. Gallup.com, Presidential Job Approval Center, http://www.gallup.com/poll /124922/Presidential-Approval-Center.aspx.

7. National Security PAC, 1988, "Willie Horton," retrieved from http://www .livingroomcandidate.org.

8. The same study found that much of this was driven by what we call the talk-ing head media, which takes sides. Liberal talk-show portrayals of Mitt Romney were 89 percent negative, and conservative talk-show portrayals of Barack Obama were 93 percent negative. These 2012 character narratives continued through the last weeks of the race, but with some adjustments. In those final weeks, the Pew Research Center found Obama received both more coverage than Romney in sto-ries where he was a significant presence (i.e., where more than 25 percent of the story was about him) and more positive coverage than he had received in pre-vious weeks and months. In fact, even though the overall narratives for Obama and Romney were still quite negative, the tone for Obama was markedly more positive than for Romney in the last week before the election, with 29 percent of stories with tone holding a positive tone, as opposed to the 16 percent of stories holding a positive for Romney. Pew (2012b) reported that "Romney may have suf-fered in the final days from the press focusing less on him relative to his opponent. After receiving roughly identical levels of coverage for most of October, in the last week of campaigning Obama was a significant presence in eight out of 10 cam-paign stories compared with six in 10 for Romney—one of the biggest disparities in any week after Labor Day."

9. "Windsurfing," 2004, retrieved from http://www.thelivingroomcandidate.org.

10. We should note that Sigelman and Kugler (2003) find that voters can strongly disagree in their perceptions about the tone of a given campaign.

11. "Romney Narrows VP Choices; Condi Emerges as Frontrunner," July 12, 2012, http://www.drudgereport.com/flashcm.htm.

12. A compilation of praise for Gingrich from pundits across many mainstream media sources can be found in the newsmax.com post from December 11, 2011, "Newt Praised after Key Iowa Debate." http://www.newsmax.com/InsideCover /Republican-Debate-Des-Moines/2011/12/11/id/420552.

13. Quotes from this debate are taken from McCormick and Jensen (2012).

14. Results are posted on Pulitzer.org, http://www.pulitzer.org/citation/2009 -National-Reporting.

15. The Message Machine can be found at: http://www.politifact.com/truth -o-meter/partnerships/message-machine/.

16. *Meet the Press*, NBC, January 8, 2012.

17. Another example is the Obama claim that Romney said, "I like to fire people," which Obama advertising and surrogates (and earlier, Republican primary opponents) regularly touted as an example of how Romney felt about working people, painting him as an uncaring plutocrat. Romney, of course, did say this, but it was in the context of a larger statement advocating consumer choice of health insurance providers, and it was clear he was not talking about ordinary workers. This did not deter CBS News from running a story (Madison and Boxer 2012) titled "Mitt Romney: 'I Like Being Able to Fire People' for Bad Service," which in addition to the somewhat misleading headline, offers no editorial opinion about whether Romney's words should be taken as in-context. We have more to say about out-of-context deception in chapter 6.

18. From a blog post on Chrysler.com, "Message from Sergio Marchionne Regarding Jeep Production," October 30, 2013, accessed December 2013 at http://blog .chryslergroupllc.com/entry/1950/message_from_sergio_marchionne_regarding _jeep_production.

19. However, we should note that one of Romney's campaign consultants resubmitted the Chrysler ad to the *Washington Post* in January 2013, asking for a reconsideration of the verdict (Kessler 2013).

20. "Proving the Incompetence of Politifact," blog posting on dailykos.net from user "mikepridmore," August 7, 2012, http://www.dailykos.com/story/2012/08/07 /1117721/-Just-how-incompetent-is-Politifact.

21. See Cooper (2012) in the *New York Times*, which lays out the fact-checkers' claim. An article in the *Atlantic* about Ryan's speech and the "post-truth" era includes links to a litany of articles that say, outright, that Ryan was lying. For more on fact-checking, a good outline of the post-truth argument comes from a pair of articles by James Fallows (2012a, 2012b) writing for the *Atlantic*.

22. Gallup.com, "Majority in US Continues to Distrust the Media, Perceive

Bias," September 22, 2011. http://www.gallup.com/poll/149624/majority-continue-distrust-media-perceive-bias.aspx.

23. Gallup.com, "US Distrust in Media Hits New High," September 21, 2012. http://www.gallup.com/poll/157589/distrust-media-hits-new-high.aspx.

24. Pew Research Center, "Further Decline in Credibility Ratings for Most News Organizations," August 16, 2012. http://www.people-press.org/2012/08/16/further-decline-in-credibility-ratings-for-most-news-organizations/.

25. Pew Research Center, "Press Widely Criticized, But Trusted More than Other Information Sources," September 22, 2011. http://www.people-press.org/2011/09/22/press-widely-criticized-but-trusted-more-than-other-institutions/.

26. Ibid.

Chapter Three

1. See Mutz (2011) for a comprehensive discussion of survey experiments and their value in improving external validity while maintaining internal validity in population-based studies.

2. Kahn and Kenney (1999) were among the first to suggest that different topics of negative advertising might cause different responses from voters. They in particular differentiate between "mudslinging"—defined as "negative attacks in a harsh and strident tone and about topics with little relationship to the affairs . . . of a nation"—which is found to depress voter turnout, and more legitimate types of negativity, which appear to play a role in actually increasing turnout.

3. We conducted randomization checks for all three studies to show that the assignment of different versions of the questions to random subsets of respondents was successful. With just one exception (gender in study 2, which we discuss later in this chapter) our randomly assigned groups do not differ significantly on gender, age, race, income, or party identification.

4. Marcus, Neuman, and MacKuen (2000) operationalize anxiety as a combination of anger and fear and in factor analyses of negative emotions the two generally load on the same factor. Fear has been shown to have a critical role in mediating the effect of candidates' appearance on voting decisions, especially in a low-information environment (Mattes et al. 2010; Spezio et al. 2008). Furthermore, some well-known negative advertisements, such as Lyndon Johnson's infamous "Daisy" ad, clearly attempt to evoke fear. However, anger is more appropriate to claims against negativity, since by and large pundits argue that voters are angered by negative ads, rather than afraid of them. Moreover, it may be in the best interest of negative advertisements to specifically invoke anger, which has been shown to increase attention (Moons and Mackie 2007) and significantly affect information processing and attitude formation (Keltner, Ellsworth, and Edwards 1993; Lerner, Goldberg, and Tetlock 1998).

5. We would not argue from this that Democrats are generally more concerned about negativity than are Republicans, though Ansolabehere and Iyengar (1995a) do make this claim. If anything, perceptions of who is more negative that arise out of the facts of a particular campaign will interact with questions asking support or opposition to "negative" campaigning in ways unique to each campaign. But our point here is simply that when "negative" is in the question it triggers this effect, but fails to do so when it is not.

6. For "lack of experience," $\chi^2 = 13.6$ ($p < .001$); "prior record in office," $\chi^2 = 22.6$ ($p < .001$); "position on issues," $\chi^2 = 46.6$ ($p < .001$). For "family," the difference is small but statistically significant, $\chi^2 = 5.2$ ($p < .02$).

7. The one randomization failure in our experiments occurs here. While 53 percent of respondents in the explicit negative condition were male, only 43 percent were male in the self-definition condition. We investigated the differences between men and women on expressing anger to ensure that this does not interfere with our findings. On a scale of 1 to 4, combining treatments, and averaging across the four issues, men expressed slightly less anger than did women (a mean of 2.32 for men, 2.37 for women), but this was not statistically significant (t-test $p = 0.16$) In comparison, mean anger across the four topics was 2.17 in the self-defined treatment and 2.50 in the explicit negative condition. This difference is significant at $p < 0.001$.

Comparing men and women within the experimental conditions show the following anger response across topics: Explicit negative (male) = 2.45; explicit negative (female) = 2.55; self-defined (male) = 2.15; self-defined (female) = 2.17. The difference between male and female anger is significant in the explicit negative condition (men are less angry, $p = 0.04$), but not in the self-defined treatment. Since women were more likely to express anger, and since there were fewer women in the explicit negative condition (where people were angrier), if anything the randomization failure lessened the overall anger difference across treatments. Just as with the partisan differences we noted in study 1, the lack of difference in the self-defined treatment here suggests that it is the specific keying of the idea of "negativity" in the questions that generates differential anger responses, rather than the actual activity of going negative. Taking gender into account, we find that the difference in anger across treatments is significant both for men and women at $p < 0.001$.

8. For details, visit the CCES home page at http://projects.iq.harvard.edu/cces.

9. According to the article, one of Nelson's ads stated about his opponent, "Representative Ron Kind pays for sex," and showed a picture of Kind with "XXX" stamped across his face. Nelson lost the election, receiving only 35 percent of the vote.

10. "Clean money" laws, by which candidates voluntarily accept public funding under the condition that they limit spending and limit private campaign contributions, have been passed in Arizona, Maine, Vermont, Massachusetts, New

Mexico, and North Carolina. See http://www.caclean.org/problem/ for more information.

11. Gallup.com provides a history of their trust in government polling starting
from 1992. In only one poll (taken in October 2001) was this not the case.

Chapter Four

1. We will generally refer to ads by the last name of the candidate endorsing
the ad, regardless of whether the ads were technically sponsored by "independent"
groups. In our studies, we make it clear that the candidates themselves are the ones
running the ads. There is some evidence that voter backlash decreases when the
ads are run by independent organizations as opposed to the candidates' campaigns
(Brooks and Murov 2012), though it requires that the voter consider the independent group to actually be independent.

2. This aired against Democrat Rick Mullin's opponent, Republican Rick Bertrand,
in an Iowa state senate election that Bertrand won. Bertrand, an owner of several
local businesses, argued that the claims in the ads were false and had hurt his business reputation, thus causing him economic harm. A jury agreed, awarding $231,000
in total damages, though the Iowa Supreme Court later reversed the decision.

3. See Rosenthal 2013.

4. The ads most reported as seen were, as expected, [Dole] 9%, [Hagan] 6%, and
[Conway] 4%.

5. The study can be accessed at http://dpte.polisci.uiowa.edu/dpte/action
/player/launch/466/?test=1&&pass=passphrase. Click "Submit" and then "Launch
Player." This will load the full study 4 in test mode so no data are recorded. The
system requires Flash so will not run on devices without Flash functionality.

6. At some point a completion code was apparently shared in MTurk "back-
channels" and we had about twenty people claim completion using that code. Because they had not actually completed the task, there was no data collected, and
nothing to remove from our dataset. These Mturk workers were banned by us and,
with a few exceptions that slipped through, not paid.

7. We classified nine states as battleground states (CO, FL, IA, NV, NH, NC,
OH, VA, WI).

8. Of course, as we discussed in chapter 2, some have argued the real problem
with negative ads is that they depress turnout, most notably Ansolabehere and Iyengar (1995a). Not all scholars agree, and since we cannot actually measure turnout in our studies, we leave this question to others, see, for example, Brooks 2006,
Lau et al. 1999, and Lau, Sigelman, and Rovner 2007.

9. CNN Political Ticker, "Dole's 'Godless' Ad Causes Stir," October 29, 2008.
Posted by Alexander Mooney, available at http://politicalticker.blogs.cnn.com/2008
/10/29/doles-godless-ad-causes-stir/.

10. Ibid.

Chapter Five

Note: This chapter is based in part on Mattes, "What Happens When a Candidate Doesn't Bark? 'Cursed' Voters and Their Impact on Campaign Discourse," *Journal of Politics* 74, no. 2 (2012): 369–82.

1. Whether voters could infer McCain was losing is not clear, though we doubt that voters are trying to make (or have any reason to make) such an inference, since inference is not needed—one could easily gather that information from political polling. In any case, the existing literature (e.g., Sigelman and Buell 2003; Sigelman and Shiraev 2002; Theilmann and Wilhite 1998) provides mixed results about whether the closeness of the race impacts the tone of the campaign.

2. By "positive" and "negative" traits, we mean positions on issues that are either viewed favorably or unfavorably by the voter. We assume that the candidates are biased, and thus are unlikely to reveal their own negative traits or the opponents' positive traits. There are also formal models in which third-party media outlets instead choose which information to publish. Puglisi (2004) allows for candidates to "spin" the information by making one dimension more salient. Duggan and Martinelli (2010) show how balanced media coverage may be worse for voter welfare than slanted coverage.

3. Taken from Gallup's compilation of congressional job approval ratings, available at http://www.gallup.com/poll/1600/Congress-Public.aspx.

4. An alternative theory is that negative campaigning is used for "inoculation" (Pfau and Kenski 1990) against an opponent's attacks. Assuming such information is verifiable, this view is compatible with this model in that it assumes that negative campaigns effectively transmit information to voters.

5. In Polborn and Yi (2006), candidates' traits are drawn from a continuous distribution on both dimensions, but candidates are allowed only two campaign choices—positive campaigning on one dimension or negative campaigning on the other.

6. In the case with $E_\mu U_\nu(\ell) = E_\mu U_\nu(-\ell)$, then the voter is indifferent between all voting strategies.

7. Later in the chapter we include the possibility of voter error, where the probability of voter error increases as the utility difference between candidates decreases. In that case, choosing the option R_ℓ that maximizes $d_\ell(R_\ell)$ is a strictly dominant strategy.

8. For more information about the CIT Social Science Experimental Laboratory, see http://www.ssel.caltech.edu/info/. The computer program used was an extension to the open source Multistage game software. See http://multistage.ssel.caltech.edu for more information on this program.

9. The treatments were ordered as follows: session 1 (9 subjects, 50% treatment, 30%, 70%); session 2 (15 subjects, 70, 50, 30), session 3 (15 subjects, 30, 50, 70), session 4 (9 subjects, 50, 70, 30). There were no significant order effects. Session

4 subjects ran only ten rounds at 50%, then twenty-five consecutive rounds in the other two treatments. As a result, there were 335 elections overall (670 candidate choices, 335 voter choices) in both the 30% and 70% treatments, and 290 (480 candidate choices, 290 voter choices) in the 50% treatment.

10. Eighty percent of these were made by candidates negative on both dimensions $(-,-)$ and 45 percent were in the specific case $(-,-)$ vs. $(+,+)$, where the $(-,-)$ candidate's only options were "I choose not to make a statement" or revealing some kind of unfavorable information. Incidentally, after choosing to reveal unfavorable information, candidates won only 2 percent of the elections (versus 5 percent when revealing nothing), suggesting refusing to campaign was the better option.

11. In this equilibrium, in the (off-path) case where a candidate reveals damaging information about himself or good information about the opponent, the sophisticated voter believes that candidate is $(-,-)$ and facing a $(+,+)$ opponent.

12. We note one exception in the discussion surrounding table B.3 in appendix B, which requires an unusual and rather inconsistent set of off-path voter beliefs.

13. By using QRE we are making an assumption of bounded rationality, though we are not testing the psychological cause of this behavior. One possibility is that the mistakes are caused by satisficing—looking for information that is "good enough"—which is more likely to go wrong as the differences among choices become smaller.

14. The best-fitting χ values with each treatment considered separately were: $\chi = 0.73$ in the 30% treatment, $\chi = 0.75$ in the 50% treatment, and $\chi = 0.70$ in the 70% treatment. Chi-squared tests on whether the latter two were different from a constrained estimate of $\chi = 0.73$ yielded p-values of 0.49 (50% treatment) and 0.10 (70% treatment).

15. In their experiment, which used a single ideological dimension, they found that people would place a candidate on a 0–100 scale as more liberal (conservative) if that candidate attacked an opponent as too conservative (liberal). Subjects also placed the attacked candidate in the direction specified by the attack. In contrast, our experiment assumes that candidates are campaigning about two specific topics, and we clearly define the subjects' payoffs. In their experiment the effect on voter utility is less clear, but could be partially inferred by using the subject's ideological self-placement.

Chapter Six

1. Or, at least, someone conjectures that this has occurred. For example, during the Democratic primaries in 2007–8, it was alleged that Hillary Clinton's campaign had "scandalous information" on Barack Obama but had "decided not to use it" (FOX News 2007). The candidates temporarily sparred over it, and the topic was also brought up during one of the Democratic debates.

2. For all analyses in this and the following sections we have removed respondents who refused to answer the question or answered "Don't know" to make the results clearer. Including a "Don't know" category has no substantive effect on our results.

Chapter Seven

1. Due to a coding error in our Z-tree program that we did not catch and resolve until after four sessions had been completed, in those sessions whenever the campaign topics were Competence and Religion, the two negative messages were both shown to the voter as "My opponent does not believe in God." The candidates were not aware of this unless they had mistakenly been caught lying, which happened thirty-three times in total (on average 0.69 times per subject). Because of this we exclude from our analysis *all* rounds from the first four studies in which the two topics were competence and religion, so 416 rounds in total.

2. Now, as we noted in chapter 5, one of the difficulties with this kind of Perfect Bayesian Equilibrium analysis is the wide range of beliefs we can assign to voters for off-path messages. We could require that voters think every off-path campaign is a lie, and thus vote for the candidate choosing X. To support a single-message equilibrium, we would just need the voter to believe that the expected payoff from the not-X campaigner is less than or equal to that from the X campaigner.

3. Assuming the candidate using Y is telling the truth, the voter would receive 40 points for the candidate being positive on Y, and would believe there is a 70 percent chance the same candidate is positive on X (which is worth 60 points), thus the calculation.

4. Of course, PBE does not actually require that the voter hold such a belief, so this leaves open many other PBEs with an all-X strategy.

5. Of these cases, 43 percent gave the voter a choice between a candidate campaigning with X and a candidate campaigning with Y. The next most frequent decisions were X vs. *oppX* (18%), X vs. *oppY* (18%), and Y vs. *oppX* (14%). The Y vs. *oppY* (1%, 14 overall) was too rare to meaningfully separate out by treatment; voters overall were equally likely to choose the Y and the *oppY* campaigner.

6. See Dover 2012.

7. See Cordes and Crawford 2012.

8. Video taken from MSNBC show *Morning Joe*, October 4, 2012, available at http://www.nbcnews.com/id/3036789/ns/msnbc-morning_joe/vp/49285798/.

Appendix B

1. We follow Holt and Laury (2002) in assuming the natural logarithm is used when q = 1. The (1 − q) is necessary for increasing utility when q > 1.

References

Adams, James, and Samuel Merrill, III. 2008. "Candidate and Party Strategies in Two-stage Elections Beginning with a Primary." *American Journal of Political Science* 52 (2): 344–59.

Adams-Webber, J. R. 1979. *Personal Construct Theory: Concepts and Applications.* New York: Wiley.

Alvarez, R. Michael. 1998. *Information and Elections.* Ann Arbor: University of Michigan Press.

Amira, Dan. 2012. "Every Presidential Campaign Is the Meanest, Nastiest, Dirtiest Ever." *New York Magazine,* August 22. Available at http://nymag.com/daily /intelligencer/2012/08/most-negative-campaign-ever.html.

Ansolabehere, Stephen, and Shanto Iyengar. 1995a. "Can the Press Monitor Campaign Advertising? An Experimental Study." *Harvard International Journal of Press/Politics* 1 (1): 72–86.

———. 1995b. *Going Negative: How Political Advertisements Shrink and Polarize the Electorate.* New York: Free Press.

Ansolabehere, Stephen, Shanto Iyengar, Adam Simon, and Nicholas Valentino. 1994. "Does Attack Advertising Immobilize the Electorate?" *American Political Science Review* 88 (4): 829–38.

Ansolabehere, Stephen, and James M. Snyder. 2000. "Valence Politics and Equilibrium in Spatial Election Models." *Public Choice* 103:327–36.

Applebome, Peter. 1988. (No Headline). *New York Times Magazine,* October 30. Available at http://www.nytimes.com/1988/10/30/magazine/no-headline-708788 .html.

Aragones, Enriqueta, and Thomas R. Palfrey. 2002. "Mixed Equilibrium in a Downsian Model with a Favored Candidate." *Journal of Economic Theory* 103:131–61.

———. 2004. "The Effect of Candidate Quality on Electoral Equilibrium: An Experimental Study." *American Political Science Review* 98 (1): 77–90.

Austen-Smith, David, and Jeffrey S. Banks. 1996. "Information Aggregation, Rationality, and the Condorcet Jury Theorem." *American Political Science Review* 90:34–45.

Avlon, John. 2012. "Romney Ramps Up Attack Ads Against Gingrich to Unprecedented Levels." *Daily Beast*, January 31. Available at http://www.thedailybeast.com/articles/2012/01/31/romney-ramps-up-attack-ads-against-gingrich-to-unprecedented-levels.html.

Bailey, Eric, and Robert W. Stewart. 1992. "Dornan Outdoes Himself as Presidential Point Man." *Los Angeles Times*, October 18. Available at http://articles.latimes.com/1992-10-18/news/mn-1122_1_bob-dornan.

Balz, Dan 2012. "The Take: President Obama, Mitt Romney Running a Most Poisonous Campaign." *Washington Post*, August 15. Available at http://www.washingtonpost.com/politics/a-most-poisonous-campaign/2012/08/15/16715a08-e6e7-11e1-8f62-58260e3940a0_story.html.

Bartels, Larry M. 1993. "Messages Received: The Political Impact of Media Exposure." *American Political Science Review* 87:267–85.

Battaglini, Marco, Rebecca Morton, and Thomas. R. Palfrey. 2010. "The Swing Voter's Curse in the Laboratory." *Review of Economic Studies* 77:61–89.

Begala, Paul. 2012. "Why We Need More Negative Political Ads." *Newsweek*, March 19. Available at http://www.newsweek.com/paul-begala-why-we-need-more-negative-political-ads-63753.

Benjafield, John. 1985. "A Review of Recent Research on the Golden Section." *Empirical Studies of the Arts* 3:117–34.

Bennet, James. 2012. "We're Not Going to Let Our Campaign Be Dictated by Fact-Checkers." *The Atlantic*, August 28. http://www.theatlantic.com/politics/archive/2012/08/were-not-going-to-let-our-campaign-be-dictated-by-fact-checkers/261674/.

Berinsky, Adam J. 1999. "The Two Faces of Public Opinion." *American Journal of Political Science* 43 (4): 1209–30.

———. 2002. "Political Context and the Survey Response: The Dynamics of Racial Policy Options." *Journal of Politics* 64 (2): 567–84.

Berinsky, Adam J., Gregory Huber, and Gabriel Lenz. 2012. "Using Mechanical Turk as a Subject Recruitment Tool for Experimental Research." *Political Analysis* 20 (3): 351–68.

Bierman, Noah. 2012. "Brown, Warren Fight via Negative TV Ads." *Boston Globe*, September 15. Available at http://www.bostonglobe.com/metro/2012/09/14/brown-warren-fight-via-negative-advertisements-senate-campaign-heats/ui7SK4Et9gBnBLY3DfyBFJ/story.htm

Bingham, Amy, Devin Dwyer, and Emily Friedman. 2012. "Hilary Rosen Apologizes for Attacking Ann Romney as a Stay-At-Home Mom." *ABC News*, April 12. Available at http://abcnews.go.com/Politics/OTUS/hilary-rosen-apologizes-ann-romney-jab/story?id=16124396.

Bishop, George F., Alfred J. Tuchfarber, and Robert W. Oldendick. 1978. "Change in the Structure of American Political Attitudes: The Nagging Question of Question Wording." *American Journal of Political Science* 22 (2): 250–69.

Blake, Aaron. 2012. "CNN, Fox Jump the Gun on Supreme Court Health Care Decision." *Washington Post* (blog), June 28. Available at http://www.washington post.com/blogs/the-fix/post/networks-jump-the-gun-mistakenly-report-that -supreme-court-struck-down-mandate/2012/06/28/gJQAmsa98V_blog.html.

Blow, Charles M. 2012. "The G.O.P. Fact Vacuum." *New York Times*, August 31. Available at http://www.nytimes.com/2012/09/01/opinion/blow-the-gop-fact -vacuum.html.

Boydstun, Amber E. 2013. *Making the News: Politics, the Media, and Agenda Setting.* Chicago: University of Chicago Press.

Brader, Ted. 2006. *Campaigning for Hearts and Minds: How Emotional Appeals in Political Ads Work.* Chicago: University of Chicago Press.

Brooks, Deborah Jordan. 2006. "The Resilient Voter: Moving Toward Closure in the Debate over Negative Campaigning and Turnout." *Journal of Politics* 68 (3): 684–96.

Brooks, Deborah Jordan, and John G. Geer. 2007. "Beyond Negativity: The Effects of Incivility on the Electorate." *American Journal of Political Science* 51 (1): 1–16.

Brooks, Deborah Jordan, and Michael Murov. 2012. "Assessing Accountability in a Post–Citizens United Era: The Effects of Attack Ad Sponsorship by Unknown Independent Groups." *American Politics Research* 40 (3): 383–418.

Buchanan, Bruce. 2000. "Regime Support and Campaign Reform." In *Campaign Reform: Insights and Evidence*, ed. Larry M. Bartels and Lynn Vavreck, 173–200. Ann Arbor: University of Michigan Press.

Buhrmester, Michael D., Tracy Kwang, and Samuel D. Gosling. 2011. "Amazon's Mechanical Turk: A New Source of Inexpensive, Yet High-Quality, Data?" *Perspectives on Psychological Science* 6 (1): 3–5.

Caccioppo, John T., and Wendi L. Gardner. 1999. "Emotion." *Annual Reviews of Psychology* 50:191–214.

Callander, Steven, and Simon Wilkie. 2007. "Lies, Damned Lies, and Political Campaigns." *Games and Economic Behavior* 60:262–86.

Campbell, Angus, Philip. E. Converse, Warren. E. Miller, and Donald. E. Stokes. 1960. *The American Voter.* New York: Wiley.

Capella, Joseph, and Kathleen Hall Jamieson. 1997. *The Spiral of Cynicism: The Press and the Public Good.* New York: Oxford University Press.

Carraro, Luciana, and Luigi Castelli. 2010. "The Implicit and Explicit Effects of Negative Political Campaigns: Is the Source Really Blamed?" *Political Psychology* 31 (4): 617–45.

Carrillo, Juan D., and Thomas R. Palfrey. 2009. "The Compromise Game: Two-sided Adverse Selection in the Laboratory." *American Economic Journal: Microeconomics* 1:151–81.

Chang, Linchiat, and Jon A. Krosnick. 2009. "National Surveys via RDD Telephone Interviewing Versus the Internet Comparing Sample Representativeness and Response Quality." *Public Opinion Quarterly* 73 (4): 641–78.

Cicero, Quintus Tullius. 2012. *How to Win an Election: An Ancient Guide for Modern Politicians.* Translated by Philip Freeman. Princeton, NJ: Princeton University Press.

CNN. 2012. "Truth Squad: Did Gingrich, Romney Invest in Fannie and Freddie?" CNN, January 27. Available at http://www.cnn.com/2012/01/27/politics/truth -squad-investments.

Coate, Stephen. 2004. "Political Competition with Campaign Contributions and Informative Advertising." *Journal of the European Economic Association* 2 (5): 772–804.

Cobb, Michael D., and James H. Kuklinski. 1997. "Changing Minds: Political Arguments and Political Persuasion." *American Journal of Political Science* 41 (1): 88–121.

Collier, Kenneth E., Richard D. McKelvey, Peter C. Ordeshook, and Kenneth C. Williams. 1987. "Retrospective Voting: An Experimental Study." *Public Choice* 53:101–30.

Cooper, Michael. 2012. "Campaigns Play Loose With Truth in a Fact-Check Age." *New York Times*, September 1. Available at http://www.nytimes.com/2012/09/01 /us/politics/fact-checkers-howl-but-both-sides-cling-to-false-ads.html.

Cordes, Nancy, and Jan Crawford. 2012. "Obama Retools, Romney Builds on Momentum Post-debate." *CBS News*, October 4. Available at http://www.cbsnews .com/8301-18563_162-57526507/obama-retools-romney-builds-on -momentum-post-debate/.

Cummins, Joseph. 2007. *Anything for a Vote: Dirty Tricks, Cheap Shots, and October Surprises.* Philadelphia: Quirk Books.

Davis, Michael L., and Michael Ferrantino. 1996. "Towards a Positive Theory of Political Rhetoric: Why Do Politicians Lie?" *Public Choice* 88:1–13.

DellaVigna, Stefano, and Ethan Kaplan. 2007. "The Fox News Effect: Media Bias and Voting." *Quarterly Journal of Economics* 122 (3): 1187–1234.

Dickson, Eric S., Catherine Hafer, and Dimitri Landa. 2008. "Cognition and Strategy: A Deliberation Experiment." *Journal of Politics* 70 (4): 974–89.

Diermeier, Daniel, and Rebecca Morton. 2005. "Experiments in Majoritarian Bargaining." In *Social Choice and Strategic Decisions*, ed. David Austen-Smith and John Duggan, 201–6. Berlin: Springer.

Dionne, E. J. 1991. *Why Americans Hate Politics.* New York: Simon & Schuster.

Dover, Elicia. 2012. "Gingrich: 'You Cannot Debate Somebody Who Is Dishonest.'" *ABC News* (blog), January 28. Available at http://abcnews.go.com/blogs /politics/2012/01/gingrich-you-cannot-debate-somebody-who-is-dishonest/.

Doyle, Arthur Conan. 1894. "The Adventure of Silver Blaze." In *The Memoirs of Sherlock Holmes.* New York: Harper and Brothers.

Druckman, James N., and Michael Parkin. 2005. "The Impact of Media Bias: How Editorial Slant Affects Voters." *Journal of Politics* 67:1030–49.

Duggan, John, and Cesar Martinelli. 2010. "A Spatial Theory of Media Slant and Voter Choice." Unpublished manuscript. Available at http://ciep.itam.mx /~martinel/lastrevised.pdf.

Durrant, Gabriele B., Robert M. Groves, Laura Staetsky, and Fiona Steele. 2010. "Effects of Interviewer Attitudes and Behaviors on Refusal in Household Surveys." *Public Opinion Quarterly* 74:1–36.

Eyster, Erik, and Matthew Rabin. 2005. "Cursed Equilibrium." *Econometrica* 73 (5): 1623–72.

Fallows, James. 2012a. "Paul Ryan and the Post-Truth Convention Speech." *The Atlantic*, August 30. Available at http://www.theatlantic.com/politics/archive /2012/08/paul-ryan-and-the-post-truth-convention-speech/261775/.

———. 2012b. "Truth, Lies, Politics, and the Press, in Three Acts." *The Atlantic*, August 18. Available at http://www.theatlantic.com/politics/archive/2012/08/truth -lies-politics-and-the-press-in-three-acts/261297/.

Feddersen, Timothy J., and Wolfgang Pesendorfer. 1996. "The Swing Voter's Curse." *American Economic Review* 86 (3): 408–24.

Files, John. 2006. "A Playboy Party at the Super Bowl, a Wink, and an Invitation." *New York Times*, October 26. Available at http://www.nytimes.com/2006/10/26 /us/26adbox.html.

Finkel, Steven E., and John G. Geer. 1998. "A Spot Check: Casting Doubt on the Demobilizing Effect of Attack Advertising." *American Journal of Political Science* 42 (2): 573–95.

Fiorina, Morris P., and Ken A. Shepsle. 1989. "Is Negative Voting an Artifact?" *American Journal of Political Science* 33:423–39.

Fischbacher, Urs. 2007. "z-Tree: Zurich Toolbox for Ready-made Economic Experiments." *Experimental Economics* 10 (2): 171–78.

Fiske, Susan T. 1980. "Attention and Weight in Person Perception: The Impact of Negative and Extreme Behavior." *Journal of Personality and Social Psychology* 38:889–906.

FOX News. 2007. "Novak Stands by Obama Dirt Story, Compares Clinton Campaign Tactics to Nixon." *FOX News*, November 19. Available at www.foxnews .com/story/2007/11/19/novak-stands-by-obama-dirt-story-compares-clinton -campaign-tactics-to-nixon.

Fowler, Erika Franklin, and Travis Ridout. 2013. "Negative, Angry, and Ubiquitous: Political Advertising in 2012." *The Forum* 10 (4): 51–61.

Fréchette, Guillaume R., John H. Kagel, and Massimo Morelli. 2005. "Gamson's Law Versus Non-cooperative Bargaining Theory." *Games and Economic Behavior* 51 (2): 365–90.

Freedman, Paul, and Ken Goldstein. 1999. "Measuring Media Exposure and the Effects of Negative Campaign Ads." *American Journal of Political Science* 43 (4): 1189–1208.

Freedman, Paul, William Wood, and Dale Lawton. 1999. "Feature: Do's and Don'ts of Negative Ads: What Voters Say." *Campaigns and Elections* 20:20–25.

Fridkin, Kim L., and Patrick J. Kenney. 2004. "Do Negative Messages Work? The Impact of Negativity on Citizens' Evaluations of Candidates." *American Politics Research* 32 (5): 570–605.

———. 2008. "The Dimensions of Negative Messages." *American Politics Research* 36 (5): 694–723.

———. 2011. "Variability in Citizens' Reactions to Different types of Negative Campaigns." *American Journal of Political Science* 55 (2): 307–25.

Friedman, Emily. 2011. "Mitt Romney SuperPAC Highlights Gingrich's 'Baggage.'" *ABC News* (blog), December 8. Available at http://abcnews.go.com/blogs/politics/2011/12/mitt-romney-superpac-highlights-gingrichs-baggage/.

Fuess, Claude M. 1940. *Calvin Coolidge: The Man from Vermont.* Boston: Little, Brown.

Geer, John G. 2006. *In Defense of Negativity: Attack Ads in Presidential Campaigns.* Chicago: University of Chicago Press.

———. 2012a. "The News Media and the Rise of Negativity in Presidential Campaigns." *PS: Political Science and Politics* 45:422–27.

———. 2012b. "The Public Sees Merit in Negative Ads." *Yougov* (blog), May 21. Available at http://today.yougov.com/news/2012/05/21/public-sees-merit-negative-ads/.

Geer, John G., and Keena Lipsitz. 2013. "Comparing How Citizens and Scholars Perceive Negativity in Political Advertising." Presented at the annual meeting of the American Political Science Association, Chicago, August 2013.

Geer, John G. and Lynn Vavreck. 2014. "Negativity, Information, and Candidate Position-Taking." *Political Communication* 31 (2): 218–36.

Giroux, Greg. 2012. "Obama, Romney Bash Each Other with 90% Negative Ads." *Bloomberg,* July 15. Available at http://www.bloomberg.com/news/2012-07-16/obama-romney-bash-each-other-with-90-negative-ads.html.

Greenstein, Nicole. 2012. "Negative Ads: A Shift in Tone for the 2012 Campaign." *Time,* July 17. Available at http://swampland.time.com/2012/07/17/negative-ads-a-shift-in-tone-for-the-2012-campaign.

Groseclose, Tim J. 2001. "Model of Candidate Location When One Candidate Has a Valence Advantage." *American Political Science Review* 45(4): 862–86.

Grunwald, Michael. 2006. "The Year of Playing Dirtier." *Washington Post,* October 27. Available at http://www.washingtonpost.com/wp-dyn/content/article/2006/10/26/AR2006102601811.html.

Haberman, Maggie. 2012. "CMAG: Obama Swamped Romney on Number of Unique Ads." *Politico,* November 9. Available at http://www.politico.com/blogs/burns-haberman/2012/11/cmag-obama-swamped-romney-on-number-of-unique-ads-149130.html.

Haddock, Geoffrey, and Mark P. Zanna. 1997. "Impact of Negative Advertising on Evaluations of Political Candidates: The 1993 Canadian Federal Election." *Basic and Applied Social Psychology* 19:204–23.

Halloran, Liz. 2008. "McCain Wages Negative TV Ad Campaign against Obama." *US News*, October 8. Available at http://www.usnews.com/news/campaign-2008/articles/2008/10/08/mccain-wages-negative-tv-ad-campaign-against-obama.

Hamilton, David L., and Mark P. Zanna. 1972. "Differential Weighting of Favorable and Unfavorable Attributes in Impressions of Personality." *Journal of Experimental Results in Personality* 6:204–12.

Harrington, Joseph E., Jr., and Gregory D. Hess. 1996. "A Spatial Theory of Positive and Negative Campaigning." *Games and Economic Behavior* 17:209–29.

Heerwig, Jennifer A., and Brian J. McCabe. 2009. "Education and Social Desirability Bias: The Case of a Black Presidential Candidate." *Social Science Quarterly* 90:674–86.

Hinich, Melvin J., and Michael C. Munger. 1989. "Political Investment, Voter Perceptions, and Candidate Strategy: An Equilibrium Spatial Analysis." In *Models of Strategic Choice in Politics*, ed. Peter. C. Ordeshook, 49–68. Ann Arbor: University of Michigan Press.

Holan, Angie Drobnic. 2012. "Lie of the Year: the Romney Campaign's Ad on Jeeps Made in China." *Politifact*, December 12. Available at http://www.politifact.com/truth-o-meter/article/2012/dec/12/lie-year-2012-Romney-Jeeps-China/.

Holbrook, Allyson L., and Jon A. Krosnick. 2010. "Social Desirability Bias in Voter Turnout Reports: Tests Using the Item Count Technique." *Public Opinion Quarterly* 74 (1): 37–67.

Holbrook, Allyson L., Jon A. Krosnick, Penny S. Visser, Wendi L. Gardner, and John T. Cacioppo. 2001. "Attitudes toward Presidential Candidates and Political Parties: Initial Optimism, Inertial First Impressions, and a Focus on Flaws." *American Journal of Political Science* 45 (4): 930–50.

Holt, Charles A., and Susan K. Laury. 2002. "Risk Aversion and Incentive Effects." *American Economic Review* 92 (5): 1644–55.

Hook, Janet. 2004. "The Race for the White House: Campaigns Accentuate the Negative." *Los Angeles Times*, October 17, A1.

Horrigan, Marie. 2006. "Midterm Meanness: Negative Ads Rule the 2006 Elections." *New York Times*, October 15. Available at http://www.nytimes.com/cq/2006/10/15/cq_1632.html.

Horton, John J., David G. Rand, and Richard J. Zeckhauser. 2010. "The Online Laboratory: Conducting Experiments in a Real Labor Market." Unpublished manuscript. Available at http://ssrn.com/abstract=1591202.

Houston, David A., Kelly Doan, and David Roskos-Ewoldsen. 1999. "Negative Political Advertising and Choice Conflict." *Journal of Experimental Psychology: Applied* 5 (1): 3–16.

Huber, Gregory A., Seth J. Hill, and Gabriel S. Lenz. 2012. "Sources of Bias in Retrospective Decision Making: Experimental Evidence on Voters' Limitations in Controlling Incumbents." *American Political Science Review* 106 (4): 720–41.

Hughes, Dana. 2012. "Drudge Report Lists Condi Rice as Top Romney VP Candidate." *ABC News* (blog), July 12. Available at http://abcnews.go.com/blogs /politics/2012/07/drudge-report-lists-condi-rice-as-top-romney-vp-candidate/.

Husted, Thomas A., Lawrence W. Kenny, and Rebecca B. Morton. 1995. "Constituent Errors in Assessing Their Senators." *Public Choice* 83:251–71.

Iyengar, Shanto. 2011. *Media Politics: A Citizen's Guide.* 2nd ed. New York: W. W. Norton.

Jackson, Robert A., and Thomas M. Carsey. 2007. "US Senate Campaigns, Negative Advertising, and Voter Mobilization in the 1998 Midterm Election." *Electoral Studies* 26 (1): 180–95.

Jamieson, Kathleen Hall. 1992. *Dirty Politics: Deception, Distraction, and Democracy.* New York: Oxford University Press.

———. 2000. *Everything You Think You Know about Politics . . . And Why You're Wrong.* New York: Basic Books.

Jamieson, Kathleen Hall, and Joseph N. Cappella. 1997. "Setting the Record Straight: Do Ad Watches Help or Hurt?" *Journal of Press/Politics* 2:13–22.

Jamieson, Kathleen Hall, Michael G. Hagen, Dan Orr, Lesley Sillaman, Suzanne Morse, and Kim Kirn. 2000. "What Did the Leading Candidates Say, and Did It Matter?" *Annals of the American Academy of Political and Social Sciences* 572:12–16.

Jamieson, Kathleen Hall, Paul Waldman, and Susan Sherr. 2000. "Eliminate the Negative? Categories of Analysis for Political Advertising." In *Crowded Airwaves: Campaign Advertising in Elections*, ed. James A. Thurber, Candice J. Nelson, and David A. Dulio, 44–64. Washington, DC: Brookings Institution Press.

Kahn, Kim F., and Patrick J. Kenney. 1999. "Do Negative Campaigns Mobilize or Suppress Turnout? Clarifying the Relationship between Negativity and Participation." *American Political Science Review* 93 (4): 877–89.

———. 2002. "The Slant of the News: How Editorial Endorsements Influence Campaign Coverage and Citizens' Views of Candidates." *American Political Science Review* 96:381–94.

Kaid, Lynda Lee, and Anne Johnston. 2001. *Video Style in Presidential Campaigns: Style and Content of Televised Political Advertising.* Westport CT: Praeger.

Kane, Emily W., and Laura J. Macaulay. 1993. "Interviewer Gender and Gender Attitudes." *Public Opinion Quarterly* 57 (1): 1–28

Kann, Peter. 1996. "A Political Tourist in New Hampshire." *Wall Street Journal,* February 21.

Kaplan, Rebecca. 2012. "Santorum Says, 'I Don't Care What the Unemployment Rate's Going to Be.'" *CBS News*, March 19. Available at http://www.cbsnews .com/news/santorum-says-i-dont-care-what-the-unemployment-rates-going -to-be/.

Karl, Jonathan. 2012. "The Statistic of the Campaign: Romney's Single Positive Ad in Florida." *ABC News* (blog), January 31. Available at http://abcnews.go.com

/blogs/politics/2012/01/the-statistic-of-the-campaign-romneys-single-positive
-ad-in-florida/.

Karp, Jeffrey A., and David Brockington. 2005. "Social Desirability and Response
Validity: A Comparative Analysis of Over-Reporting Voter Turnout in Five
Countries." *Journal of Politics* 67 (3): 825–40.

Kartik, Navin, and R. Preston McAfee. 2006. "Signaling Character in Electoral
Competition." *American Economic Review* 97 (3): 852–70.

Keltner, Dacher, Phoebe C. Ellsworth, and Kari Edwards. 1993. "Beyond Simple
Pessimism: Effects of Sadness and Anger on Social Perception." *Journal of Personality and Social Psychology* 64:740–52.

Kernell, Samuel. 1977. "Presidential Popularity and Negative Voting: An Alternative Explanation of the Midterm Congressional Decline of the President's
Party." *American Political Science Review* 71 (1): 44–66.

Kessler, Glenn. 2013. "Reaffirmed: 4 Pinocchios for a Misleading Mitt Romney Ad
on Chrysler and China." *Washington Post* (blog), January 25. Available at http://
www.washingtonpost.com/blogs/fact-checker/post/reaffirmed-4-pinocchios
-for-a-misleading-mitt-romney-ad-on-chrysler-and-china/2013/01/24
/095964a8-667d-11e2-9e1b-07db1d2ccd5b_blog.html.

Kolhatkar, Sheelah. 2012. "Brown vs. Warren: It's Getting Ugly in Massachusetts." *Bloomberg Businessweek*, September 7. Available at http://www
.businessweek.com/articles/2012-09-27/brown-vs-dot-warren-its-getting
-ugly-in-massachusetts.

Krupnikov, Yanna. 2012. "Negative Advertising and Voter Choice: The Role of Ads
in Candidate Selection." *Political Communication* 29 (4): 387–413.

Kuklinski, James H., Michael D. Cobb, and Martin Gilens. 1997. "Racial Attitudes
and the 'New South.'" *Journal of Politics* 59 (2): 323–49.

Lau, Richard R. 1982. "Negativity in Political Perception." *Political Behavior* 4 (4):
353–78.

———. 1985. "Two Explanations for Negativity Effects in Political Behavior."
American Journal of Political Science 29:119–38.

Lau, Richard R., and Douglas Pierce. 2010. "Negativity Effects in Political Perceptions: A Test of the Figure-Ground Hypothesis." Paper presented at the
68th annual meeting of the Midwest Political Science Association, Chicago,
April 22–25.

Lau Richard R., and Gerald M. Pomper. 2004. *Negative Campaigning: An Analysis
of U.S. Senate Elections.* New York: Rowman & Littlefield.

Lau, Richard R., and David P. Redlawsk. 2006. *How Voters Decide: Information
Processing in Election Campaigns.* New York: Cambridge University Press.

Lau, Richard R., Lee Sigelman, Caroline Heldman, and Paul Babbitt. 1999. "The
Effects of Negative Political Advertisements: A Meta-analytic Assessment."
American Political Science Review 93 (4): 851–75.

Lau, Richard R., Lee Sigelman, and Ivy Brown Rovner. 2007. "The Effects of

Negative Political Campaigns: A Meta-Analytic Reassessment." *Journal of Politics* 69 (4): 1176–1209.

Leach, James. 2008. "Negative Political Ads Hurt the United States." *US News*, October 6. Available at http://www.usnews.com/opinion/articles/2008/10/06/james-leach-negative-political-ads-hurt-the-united-states.

Lerner, Jennifer S., Julie H. Goldberg, and Philip E. Tetlock. 1998. "Sober Second Thought: Effects of Accountability, Anger, and Authoritarianism on Attributions of Responsibility." *Personality and Social Psychology Bulletin* 24 (6): 563–74.

Lichter, S. Robert, and Richard E. Noyes. 2000. "There They Go Again: Media Coverage of Campaign '96." In *Political Parties, Campaigns, and Elections*, ed. Robert DiClerico, 95–108. Upper Saddle River, NJ: Prentice-Hall.

Liptak, Kevin. 2012. "Florida Primary 'The Most Negative Campaign Ever,' Says Media Group." *CNN* (blog), January 31. Available at http://politicalticker.blogs.cnn.com/2012/01/31/florida-primary-the-most-negative-campaign-ever-says-media-group/.

Londregan, John, and Thomas Romer. 1993. "Polarization, Incumbency, and the Personal Vote." In *Political Economy: Institutions, Competition, and Representation: Proceedings of the Seventh International Symposium in Economic Theory and Econometrics*, ed. William A. Barnett, Melvin Hinich, and Norman Schofield, 355–77. New York: Cambridge University Press.

Maccoby, Eleanor E., and Nathan Maccoby. 1954. "The Interview: A Tool of Social Science." In *Handbook of Social Psychology*, ed. Gardner Lindzey, 449–87. Cambridge, MA: Addison-Wesley.

Madison, Lucy, and Sarah B. Boxer. 2012. "Mitt Romney: 'I Like Being Able to Fire People' for Bad Service." *CBS News*, January 9. http://www.cbsnews.com/news/mitt-romney-i-like-being-able-to-fire-people-for-bad-service/

Maisel, L. Sandy. 2012. "The Negative Consequences of Uncivil Political Discourse." *PS: Political Science and Politics* 45:405–11.

Maisel, L. Sandy, Darrell M. West, and Brett M. Clifton. 2007. *Evaluating Campaign Quality*. New York: Cambridge University Press.

Marcus, George E., W. Russell Neuman, and Michael MacKuen. 2000. *Affective Intelligence and Political Judgment*. Chicago: University of Chicago Press.

Mark, David. 2006. *Going Dirty: The Art of Negative Campaigning*. Lanham, MD: Rowman and Littlefield.

Marquardt, Alexander. 2008. "Obama Says Palin's Family Off Limits." *CNN*, September 1. Available at http://www.cnn.com/2008/POLITICS/09/01/obama.palin.

Martinelli, César. 2001. "Elections with Privately Informed Parties and Voters." *Public Choice* 108:147–67.

Mattes, Kyle. 2007. "Attack Politics: Who Goes Negative and Why?" Unpublished manuscript. Available at http://mh-hss-p1.caltech.edu/SSPapers/wp1256.pdf.

———. 2012. "What Happens When a Candidate Doesn't Bark? Cursed Voters and Their Effect on Campaign Discourse." *Journal of Politics* 74 (2): 369–82.

Mattes, Kyle, Michael Spezio, Hackjin Kim, Alexander Todorov, Ralph Adolphs, and R. Michael Alvarez. 2010. "Predicting Election Outcomes from Positive and Negative Trait Assessments of Candidate Images." *Political Psychology* 31 (1): 41–58.

Mayer, William G. 1996. "In Defense of Negative Campaigning." *Political Science Quarterly* 111 (3): 437–55.

McCormick, John, and Kristin Jensen. 2012. "Gingrich Confronts Personal and Professional Questions in Debate." *Bloomberg*, January 19. Available at http://www.bloomberg.com/news/2012–01–20/gingrich-knocks-media-for-open-marriage-questions-at-republican-debate.html.

McKelvey, Richard D., and Thomas R. Palfrey. 1995. "Quantal Response Equilibria for Normal Form Games." *Games and Economic Behavior* 10 (1): 6–38.

Min, Young. 2002. "Intertwining of Campaign News and Advertising: The Content and Electoral Effects of Newspaper Ad Watches." *Journalism and Mass Communication* 79:927–44.

———. 2004. "News Coverage of Negative Political Campaigns: An Experiment of Negative Campaign Effects on Turnout and Candidate Preference." *Harvard International Journal of Press/Politics* 9 (4): 95–111.

Moons, Wesley G., and Diane M. Mackie. 2007. "Thinking Straight While Seeing Red: The Influence of Anger on Information Processing." *Personality and Social Psychology Bulletin* 33 (5): 706–20.

Morris, Dick. 2008. "Negative Campaigning Is Good for America." *US News*, October 6. Available at http://www.usnews.com/opinion/articles/2008/10/06/dick-morris-negative-campaigning-is-good-for-america.

Mutz, Diana C. 2011. *Population-based Survey Experiments*. Princeton, NJ: Princeton University Press.

Mutz, Diana C., and Byron Reeves. 2005. "The New Videomalaise: Effects of Televised Incivility on Political Trust." *American Political Science Review* 99 (1):1–15.

Nie, Norman, Sidney Verba, and John R. Petrocik. 1976. *The Changing American Voter*. Cambridge, MA: Harvard University Press.

Niven, David. 2006. "A Field Experiment on the Effects of Negative Campaign Mail on Voter Turnout in a Municipal Election." *Political Research Quarterly* 59 (2): 203–10.

Nyhan, Brendan. 2010. "Why the 'Death Panel' Myth Wouldn't Die: Misinformation in the Health Care Reform Debate." *The Forum* 8 (1). DOI: 10.2202/1540-8884.1354.

O'Connor, Patrick, and Sara Murray. 2012. "Rice's Name Is Floated as Potential VP Choice." *Wall Street Journal.* July 13. Available at http://online.wsj.com/article/SB10001424052702303740704577523631390995126.html.

Ortony, Andrew, Gerald L. Clore, and Allan Collins. 1988. *The Cognitive Structure of Emotions.* New York: Cambridge University Press.

Patterson, Thomas. 2002. *The Vanishing Voter: Public Involvement in an Age of Uncertainty.* New York: Knopf.

Pew Research Center. 2012a. "The Master Narratives in Campaign 2012." *Pew Research Journalism Project*, August 23. Available at http://www.journalism.org /2012/08/23/2012-campaign-character-narratives/.

———. 2012b. "The Final Days of the Media Campaign 2012." *Pew Research Journalism Project*, November 19. Available at http://www.journalism.org/2012/11 /19/final-days-media-campaign-2012/.

Pfau, Michael, and Henry Kenski. 1990. *Attack Politics: Strategy and Defense.* Ann Arbor: University of Michigan Press.

Phillips, Todd. 2012. "How Negative Campaigning Is Crippling America." *Huffington Post*, May 31. Available at http://www.huffingtonpost.com/todd-phillips /negative-political-campaigning_b_1554744.html.

Picket, Kerry. 2012. "PICKET: Santorum to Romney on Earmarks: 'You Don't Know What You're Talking About.'" *Washington Times*, February 22. Available at http://www.washingtontimes.com/blog/watercooler/2012/feb/22/picket -santorum-and-romney-face-over-earmarks-cnn-/.

Pinkleton, Bruce. 1997. "The Effects of Negative Comparative Political Advertising on Candidate Evaluations and Advertising Evaluations: An Exploration." *Journal of Advertising* 26 (1): 19–29.

Polborn, Mattias K., and David T. Yi. 2006. "Informative Positive and Negative Campaigning." *Quarterly Journal of Political Science* 1 (4): 351–71.

Poole, Keith T., and Howard Rosenthal. 1985. "A Spatial Model for Legislative Roll Call Analysis." *American Journal of Political Science* 29 (2): 357–84.

Popkin, Samuel L. 1991. *The Reasoning Voter: Communication and Persuasion in Presidential Campaigns.* Chicago: University of Chicago Press.

Pratto, Felicia, and Oliver P. John. 1991. "Automatic Vigilance: The Attention-grabbing Power of Negative Social Information. *Journal of Personality and Social Psychology* 61 (3): 380–91.

Puglisi, Riccardo. 2004. "The Spin Doctor Meets the Rational Voter: Electoral Competition with Agenda-Setting Effects." Unpublished manuscript. Available at SSRN: http://ssrn.com/abstract=581881.

Rasinski, Kenneth A. 1989. "The Effect of Question Wording on Public Support for Government Spending." *Public Opinion Quarterly* 53 (3): 388–94.

Redlawsk, David P. 2002. "Hot Cognition or Cool Consideration: Testing the Effects of Motivated Reasoning on Political Decision Making." *Journal of Politics* 64:1021–44.

Redlawsk, David P., Andrew J. W. Civettini, and Karen M. Emmerson. 2010. "The Affective Tipping Point: Do Motivated Reasoners Ever 'Get It'?" *Political Psychology* 31 (4): 563–93.

Redlawsk, David P., and Richard R. Lau. 2013. "Dynamic Process Tracing Environment (DPTE) Version 3.0 Documentation." Available at http://dpte.polisci.uiowa.edu/dpte/assets/docs/DPTE_Help_Manual.pdf.

Redlawsk, David P., Caroline J. Tolbert, and William Franko. 2010. "Voters, Emotions, and Race in 2008: Obama as the First Black President." *Political Research Quarterly* 63 (4): 875–89.

Rich, Frank. 2012. "Frank Rich: Nuke 'Em." *New York Magazine*, June 17. Available at http://nymag.com/news/frank-rich/negative-campaigning-2012-6/.

Ridout, Travis N. and Glen R. Smith. 2008. "Free Advertising: How the Media Amplify Campaign Messages." *Political Research Quarterly* 61 (4): 598–608.

Rose, Jonathan. 2012. "Are Negative Ads Positive? Political Advertising and the Permanent Campaign." In *How Canadians Communicate IV: Media and Politics*, ed. David Taras and Christopher Waddell, 149–68. Edmonton, AB: Alberta University Press.

Rosenthal, Andrew. 2013. "The Wrong Way to Attack Mitch McConnell." *New York Times* (blog), February 26. Available at http://takingnote.blogs.nytimes.com/2013/02/26/the-wrong-way-to-attack-mitch-mcconnell/.

Schoenberg, Shira. 2012. "Scott Brown-Elizabeth Warren 'People's Pledge' Could Become a National Model." *The Republican*, November 16. Available at http://www.masslive.com/politics/index.ssf/2012/11/scott_brown-elizabeth_warren_peoples_pledge_could_become_national_model.html.

Scher, Richard K. 1997. *The Modern Political Campaign: Mudslinging, Bombast, and the Vitality of American Politics*. Armonk, NY: M. E. Sharpe.

Shear, Michael D. 2012a. "The Caucus: A Trial Balloon Loses Some Air." *New York Times*, July 14. Available at http://query.nytimes.com/gst/fullpage.html?res=9D01E4D9143FF937A25754C0A9649D8B63.

———. 2012b. "The 2012 Cycle: Attack, Feign Outrage, Repeat." *New York Times* (blog), August 9. Available at http://thecaucus.blogs.nytimes.com/2012/08/09/the-2012-cycle-attack-feign-outrage-repeat/.

Sides, John, Keena Lipsitz, and Matthew Grossmann. 2010. "Do Voters Perceive Negative Campaigns as Informative Campaigns?" *American Politics Research* 38 (3): 502–30.

Sigelman, Lee, and Emmett H. Buell. 2003. "You Take the High Road and I'll Take the Low Road? The Interplay of Attack Strategies and Tactics in Presidential Campaigns." *Journal of Politics* 65 (2): 518–31.

Sigelman, Lee, and Mark Kugler. 2003. "Why Is Research on the Effects of Negative Campaigning So Inconclusive? Understanding Citizens' Perceptions of Negativity." *Journal of Politics* 65 (1): 142–60.

Sigelman, Lee, and Eric Shiraev. 2002. "The Rational Attacker in Russia? Negative Campaigning in Russian Presidential Elections." *Journal of Politics* 64 (1): 45–62.

Signorino, Curtis S. 1999. "Strategic Interaction and the Statistical Analysis of International Conflict." *American Political Science Review* 93 (2): 279–97.

Simon, Herbert A. 1955. "A Behavioral Model of Rational Choice." *Quarterly Journal of Economics* 69 (1): 99–118.

Simon, Richard. 2006. "Iowa Candidates Accentuate Positive, Eliminate Negative." *Los Angeles Times*, November 14.

Skaperdas, Stergios, and Bernard Grofman. 1995. "Modeling Negative Campaigning." *American Political Science Review* 89 (1): 49–61.

Slack, Donald. 2012. "RIP Positive Ads in 2012." *Politico*, November 4. Available at http://www.politico.com/news/stories/1112/83262.html.

Smith, Ben 2012. "Romney Camp Bets on Welfare Attack." *Buzzfeed*, August 28. Available at http://www.buzzfeed.com/bensmith/romney-camp-bets-welfare-attack.

Sniderman, Paul M., Gretchen C. Crosby, and William G. Howell. 2000. "The Politics of Race." In *Racialized Politics: The Debate about Racism in America*, ed. David O. Sears, Jim Sidanius, and Lawrence Bobo, 236–79. Chicago: University of Chicago Press.

Spezio, Michael L., Antonio Rangel, R. Michael Alvarez, John P. O'Doherty, Kyle Mattes, Alexander Todorov, Hackjin Kim, and Ralph Adolphs. 2008. "A Neural Basis for the Effect of Candidate Appearance on Election Outcomes." *Social Cognitive and Affective Neuroscience* 3 (4): 344–52.

Stevens, Daniel, Barbara Allen, John Sullivan and Eric Lawrence. 2013. "Fair's Fair? Principles, Partisanship, and Perceptions of the Fairness of Campaign Rhetoric." *British Journal of Political Science*. doi:10.1017/S0007123413000045.

Stevens, Daniel, John Sullivan, Barbara Allen, and Dean Alger. 2008. "What's Good for the Goose Is Bad for the Gander: Negative Political Advertising, Partisanship, and Turnout." *Journal of Politics* 70 (2): 527–41.

Stokes, Donald. 1992. "Valence Politics." In *Electoral Politics*, ed. Dennis Kavanagh, 141–64. Oxford: Clarendon Press.

Streb, Matthew J. 2008. *Rethinking American Electoral Democracy*. New York: Routledge.

Streb, Matthew J., Barbara Burrell, Brian Frederick, and Michael A. Genovese. 2008. "Social Desirability Effects and Support for a Female American President." *Public Opinion Quarterly* 72 (1): 76–89.

Swint, Kerwin C. 2006. *Mudslingers: The Top 25 Negative Campaigns of All Time*. London: Praeger.

Taber, Charles S., and Milton Lodge. 2006. "Motivated Skepticism in the Evaluation of Political Beliefs." *American Journal of Political Science* 50 (3): 755–69.

Theilmann, John, and Allen Wilhite. 1998. "Campaign Tactics and the Decision to Attack." *Journal of Politics* 60 (4): 1050–62.

Walls, Seth Colter. 2008 "Dole Ad Fabricates Audio of Opponent Yelling 'There Is No God.'" *Huffington Post*, October 29. Available at http://www.huffingtonpost.com/2008/10/29/dole-ad-fabricates-audio_n_138874.html.

Ward, Jon. 2011. "Newt Gingrich Threat to Mitt Romney Rises after Iowa Debate." *Huffington Post*, December 11. Available at http://www.huffingtonpost.com /2011/12/11/newt-gingrich-mitt-romney-iowa-debate_n_1141568.html.

Watt, Nicholas. 2001. "Archbishops Call for End to Negative Campaigning." *Guardian Unlimited*, May 25.

Wattenberg, Martin P., and Craig Leonard Brians. 1999. "Negative Campaign Advertising: Demobilizer or Mobilizer?" *American Political Science Review* 93 (4): 891–99.

Wayne, Stephen J. 2007. *Is This Any Way to Run a Democratic Election? Debating American Electoral Politics.* 3rd ed. Washington, DC: CQ Press.

Weissman, Stephen R., and Ruth A. Hassan. 2005. "Public Opinion Polling Concerning Public Financing of Federal Elections, 1972–2000." Washington DC: Campaign Finance Institute. Available at http://www.cfinst.org/president/pdf /PublicFunding_Surveys.pdf.

Wemple, Erik. 2012. "Colorado Shootings: ABC News's Bogus Report." *Washington Post*, July 20. Available at http://www.washingtonpost.com/blogs/erik -wemple/post/abc-news-invites-bias-claims-with-bogus-aurora-report/2012 /07/20/gJQAJJWCyW_blog.html.

West, Darrell M. 1993. *Air Wars: Television Advertising in Election Campaigns, 1952–1992.* Washington, D.C.: CQ Press.

———. 2008. "Commentary: 2008 Campaign Attack Ads Hit an All-time Low." *CNN*, September 15. Available at http://www.cnn.com/2008/POLITICS/09/15 /west.negative/index.html.

Zagaroli, Lisa. 2008. "Critics Slam Dole Ad as Hagan Fights Back." *Charlotte Observer*, October 31. Available at http://www.charlotteobserver.com/2008/10/31 /290258/critics-slam-dole-ad-as-hagan.html.

Index

The letters *t* or *f* after a page number indicate a table or figure.

Lightning Source UK Ltd.
Milton Keynes UK
UKHW010649050221
378300UK00001B/72